Get the eBook FREE!
(PDF, ePub, Kindle, and liveBook all included)

We believe that once you buy a book from us, you should be able to read it in any format we have available. To get electronic versions of this book at no additional cost to you, purchase and then register this book at the Manning website.

Go to https://www.manning.com/freebook and follow the instructions to complete your pBook registration.

That's it!
Thanks from Manning!

Vue.js in Action

ERIK HANCHETT
WITH BEN LISTWON

MANNING
SHELTER ISLAND

Manning Publications Co.
20 Baldwin Road
PO Box 761
Shelter Island, NY 11964

Development editor:	Toni Arritola
Technical development editor:	Doug Warren
Review editor:	Ivan Martinović
Project manager:	Lori Weidert
Copy editor:	Katie Petito
Proofreader:	Elizabeth Martin
Technical proofreader:	Jay Kelkar
Typesetter and cover designer:	Marija Tudor

ISBN 9781617294624
Printed in the United States of America
1 2 3 4 5 6 7 8 9 10 – DP – 23 22 21 20 19 18

contents

foreword

Frontend web development has become astoundingly complex. If you've never used a modern JavaScript framework, building your first app that only displays "Hello" can take a whole week! That might sound ridiculous—and I would agree, it *is*. The problem is that most frameworks assume knowledge of the terminal, advanced JavaScript, tools such as the Node Package Manager (NPM), Babel, Webpack, and often more.

Vue, refreshingly, doesn't assume. We call it the "progressive" JavaScript framework because it scales *down* as well as up. If your app is simple, you can use Vue the same way you use jQuery: by dropping in a `<script>` tag. But as your skills and needs grow more advanced, Vue grows with you to make you more powerful and productive.

Something else typically stands out. Vue is built not only by computer scientists, but also by designers, educators, and others from more people-focused trades. As a result, our documentation, guides, and devtools are world-class. The experience of *using* Vue is as important to us as its performance, reliability, and versatility.

Erik has carried that people-focused spirit into this book. First, it's remarkably visual. The many detailed illustrations and annotated screenshots firmly ground his examples in the workflow of real developers. As a result, you actually learn how to use the browser and Vue's devtools to confirm what you're learning—and more importantly, troubleshoot when something goes wrong.

For those without a strong background in frontend development, JavaScript, or even programming, Erik also carefully explains the foundational concepts for understanding what Vue is doing and why. That, combined with his project-centered approach to introducing new features, means the book is ideal for relatively new developers looking to expand their skills with Vue as their first modern, frontend framework.

—CHRIS FRITZ, Vue core team member and docs curator

preface

In early 2017, I was approached with an opportunity to write this book after Benjamin Listwon had to bow out for personal reasons. I had recently finished my MBA from the University of Nevada, Reno, and it had been a full year since I published my last book, the *Ember.js Cookbook* (Pact Publishing, 2016). I'd begun my YouTube channel, *Program with Erik*, and I was spending most of my time trying to figure out how best to record programming tutorials for my small but growing audience. Around this time, I started a screencast series on Vue.js and got positive feedback from my viewers. This made me want to explore Vue.js more.

I began by listening to Evan You, the creator of Vue.js, and his roadmap for the framework. I then watched countless YouTube tutorials and videos from other creators. I dropped into online forums and Facebook groups to see what people were talking about. Everywhere I went, people were excited about Vue.js and the possibilities for the framework. This made me want to explore the possibility of writing this book.

After much consideration, and a talk with my wife, I decided to go for it. Luckily, Benjamin had laid out a great foundation for me to build on, so I could hit the ground running. For the next 10 months, I spent countless nights and weekends researching, testing, and writing.

I wish I could tell you that writing this book was easy, or that I didn't run into any problems. Let's say it didn't go exactly as planned. I had personal setbacks, missed deadlines, suffered writer's block, and if that wasn't enough, I ended up having to do major revisions after Vue.js did an update.

With all that said, I'm very proud of this book. With every setback, I was motivated to work twice as hard. I was determined to get this book finished with the highest possible quality that I could muster. I hope that comes through when you're reading it.

Thank you, reader, so much for buying this book. I really hope it helps you in your journey in learning Vue.js. Please let me know if it did. You can tweet me at @ErikCH, email me at erik@programwitherik.com or join my mailing list at https://goo.gl /UmemSS! Thanks again!

acknowledgments

First and foremost, I'd like to thank my wife, Susan, because without her help, this book would have never been completed. I'd like to thank my son, Wyatt, and my daughter, Vivian. They're why I work so hard. I'd like to thank all the reviewers, the Vue.js in Action forum members, and anyone else who helped give feedback on this book. Your help has made this book immensely better than I could have ever done alone. Also, thank you, Chris Fritz, for writing an amazing foreword. Last, I'd like to give my warmest heartfelt gratitude to the Vue.js community, Evan You, and everyone who makes Vue.js such a great framework.

—ERIK HANCHETT

Above all, I'd like to give my most sincere thanks to my wife, Kiffen, for her support and encouragement, not only for my participation in this endeavor, but in every aspect of our lives. To our son, Leo, the star at the center of our family's universe, I'd like to thank you for your bottomless smiles, hugs, and cheer. For all their encouragement, understanding and support, I'd like to wholeheartedly thank the editorial team at Manning. To Erik, without whom this book would not have come to life, my genuine thanks and appreciation; I wish you all the best. Finally, to Evan You and all the many folks who have contributed to Vue.js, thanks for bringing together a great bit of software, and an even greater community. It's truly my honor to be a small part of that community.

—BENJAMIN LISTWON

We would both like to thank our technical proofreader, Jay Kelkar, as well as all the reviewers who provided feedback along the way, including Alex Miller, Alexey Galiullin, Chris Coppenbarger, Clive Harber, Darko Bozhinovski, Ferit Topcu, Harro Lissenberg, Jan Pieter Herweijer, Jesper Petersen, Laura Steadman, Marko Letic, Paulo Nuin, Philippe Charriere, Rohit Sharma, Ronald Borman, Ryan Harvey, Ryan Huber, Sander Zegveld, Ubaldo Pescatore, and Vittorio Marino.

about this book

Before you dive into learning how to make Vue.js applications, let's talk about a few things you should know first.

In this book we'll look at everything you need to know to become proficient in Vue.js. The goal of the book is to get you the knowledge you need so you can jump into any Vue.js application without hesitation.

While doing research for this book, I heard repeatedly that the official Vue.js guides were the best resource for learning Vue.js. While the official guides are great, and I highly recommend you check them out as additional references while you learn Vue.js, they don't cover everything, and they're not perfect. As I wrote the book, I took it upon myself to go beyond what the official guides covered. I made the examples more understandable and relatable, so you could more easily adapt the concepts to your own projects. Where I thought a topic was beyond the scope of the book, or not important enough, I added a reference where you can learn more about it inside the official guides.

This book can be used in a couple of different ways. You can read it from front to back. In that instance, you'll get the full breadth of what Vue.js has to offer. Or you can use this book as a reference manual to look up whatever concept you need more information on. Either way is acceptable and fine.

Later in the book we'll transition to creating Vue.js apps using a build system. Don't worry, I've included instructions on how to get started with a Vue.js build tool called Vue-CLI in appendix A. One of the most important benefits of Vue-CLI is that it helps us create more complex Vue.js applications without having to worry about building or transpiling our code.

Throughout the book we'll create a Vue.js pet store application. Certain chapters use the pet store example more than others. I did this on purpose, so you could easily learn a concept without having to learn how it works with the pet store app. But people who prefer to learn with a real application still have that option.

Audience

This book is for anyone who's interested in learning Vue.js and has JavaScript, HTML, and CSS experience. I don't expect you to have much knowledge on this but knowing the basics, such as arrays, variables, loops, and HTML tags will help. As for CSS, we'll use Bootstrap 3, a CSS library. However, you don't need to know anything about Bootstrap to follow along with the examples. It's only there to help with styling.

Early in the book, I introduce the example code using ECMAScript 2015, otherwise known as ES6. It would be a good idea to look it over before you start this book. For the most part, I use only a few ES6 features, such as arrow functions and ES6 imports. I'll warn you in the book when we make this transition.

Roadmap

The book is broken into three parts, each building upon the previous one. Part 1 is keyed toward getting to know Vue.js. In chapters 1 and 2 we'll create our first Vue.js application. We'll look at what a Vue.js instance is and how it relates to our application.

In part 2, chapters 3–9, we'll look more closely at the View and ViewModel. In this section we dive into several of the meatiest parts of Vue.js. Part 1 is more of an appetizer to Vue.js, while part 2 is the main course. You'll learn the intricacies of how to create a Vue.js application. We'll begin by learning the reactive model, and we'll create a pet store application that we'll use throughout the rest of the book.

We'll add in forms and inputs and how to bind information using Vue.js's powerful directives, then look at conditionals, looping, and forms.

Chapters 6 and 7 are extremely important. We'll learn how to break a Vue.js app into several logical parts using components, and we'll have a first look at the build tools you'll need to create Vue.js apps.

Chapter 7 also covers routing. In earlier chapters, we use simple conditionals to navigate our application. With the addition of routing, we can properly move around our application and pass information between routes.

Chapter 8 introduces you to the powerful animations and transitions you can perform using Vue.js. These features are baked into the language and are nice features you should check out.

In chapter 9 we'll learn how to use mixins and custom directives to easily extend Vue without repeating ourselves.

Part 3 is all about modeling data, consuming APIs, and testing. In chapters 10 and 11, we begin with a deep dive into Vue's state management system called Vuex. We'll then look at how we can start communicating to a backend server, and we'll learn more about Nuxt.js, a server-side rendered framework.

Chapter 12 is dedicated to testing. In any professional environment, you'll need to know testing, and we'll look at the essentials you must know.

Book Forum

Purchase of *Vue.js in Action* includes free access to a private web forum run by Manning Publications where you can make comments about the book, ask technical questions, and receive help from the author and from other users. To access the forum, go to https://forums.manning.com/forums/vue-js-in-action. You can also learn more about Manning's forums and the rules of conduct at https://forums.manning.com/forums/about.

Manning's commitment to our readers is to provide a venue where a meaningful dialogue between individual readers and between readers and the author can take place. It is not a commitment to any specific amount of participation on the part of the author, whose contribution to the forum remains voluntary (and unpaid). We suggest you try asking the author some challenging questions lest his interest stray! The forum and the archives of previous discussions will be accessible from the publisher's website as long as the book is in print.

Source code

This book contains many examples of source code, both in numbered listings and in-line with normal text. In both cases, source code is formatted in a `fixed-width font like this` to separate it from ordinary text. Sometimes **boldface** is used to highlight code that has changed from previous steps in the chapter, such as when a new feature is added to an existing line of code.

In many cases, the original source code has been reformatted; we've added line breaks and reworked indentation to accommodate the available page space in the book. In rare cases, even this was not enough, and listings include line-continuation markers (➥). Additionally, comments in the source code have often been removed from the listings when the code is described in the text. Code annotations accompany many of the listings, highlighting important concepts.

The source code for this book is available to download from the publisher's website (www.manning.com/books/vue-js-in-action) and from my personal GitHub repository (https://github.com/ErikCH/VuejsInActionCode). You can also find more instructions on downloading the code and setting up your programming environment in appendix A.

While going through the book, you'll notice I often split the source code into separate files. I've included both the completed file and the separated files in each chapter with the source code, so you can follow along. If you find a bug in the code, feel free to send over a pull request to my GitHub. I'll maintain the repo, and I'll leave a comment in the readme with any updates.

Software requirements

To make things easy, all the code in this book will work on any modern browser. I've tested it personally on Firefox 58, Chrome 65, and Microsoft Edge 15. I wouldn't recommend trying to run any of my apps on older browsers, because you'll certainly run into problems. Vue.js itself doesn't support IE8 and below. It must have a ECMA-Script 5 compliant browser.

In several of the earlier chapters, I use a few ES6 features. You'll need to have a modern web browser to run those examples.

The pet store app we'll create throughout the book will work on a mobile browser. However, the pet store application isn't optimized for mobile, so I recommend you run the examples on a desktop computer.

You don't have to worry about your operating system. If the web browser runs, you should be fine. There are really no other requirements.

Online resources

As I mentioned earlier, the Vue.js official guides are great to use as references while you're working the examples in the book. You can find the guides at https://vuejs .org/v2/guide/. They're continually being updated.

There's a curated list of awesome things related to Vue.js on the GitHub page https://github.com/vuejs/awesome-vue. Here, you can find links to Vue.js podcasts, additional Vue.js resources, third-party libraries, and even companies that use Vue.js. I highly recommend checking it out.

The Vue.js community is huge and is continuously growing. One of the best places to talk to other Vue.js developers is the official Vue.js forum at https://forum.vuejs .org/. Here you can discuss or get help on anything Vue.

If you're looking for more video tutorials, my channel, http://erik.video on You-Tube, covers a ton of information on Vue.js and JavaScript in general. Check it out!

More info?

In this 300-page book I cover a large amount of material. Please, don't hesitate to reach out to me, the author, if you're getting stuck, or you need help. If I can't help you, I'll at least point you in the right direction. Don't be shy. You'll find those of us in the Vue.js community are approachable to beginners.

Also, as you go through the book, try to take several of the concepts you learn and implement them yourself. One of the best ways of learning is doing. For example, instead of following along with the pet store app, try to create your own ecommerce site. Use the book as guide rails to make sure you don't get stuck.

One last thing: have fun. Be creative and make something cool. Make sure to hit me up on twitter @ErikCH if you do!

about the author

 ERIK HANCHETT is a web developer with more than 10 years of development experience. He's the author of the *Ember.js Cookbook* (Packt Publishing, 2016), a YouTuber at http://erik.video, and a blogger at http://programwitherik.com. He runs a mailing list where he gives out tips and tricks for JavaScript developers at https://goo.gl /UmemSS. When he's not working or writing code, he spends time with his children, Wyatt and Vivian, and his wife, Susan.

about the cover illustration

The figure on the cover of *Vue.js in Action* is captioned "Habit of a Young Market Woman of Octha in Russia in 1765." The illustration is taken from Thomas Jefferys' *A Collection of the Dresses of Different Nations, Ancient and Modern* (four volumes), London, published between 1757 and 1772. The title page states that these are hand-colored copperplate engravings, heightened with gum arabic.

Thomas Jefferys (1719–1771) was called "Geographer to King George III." He was an English cartographer who was the leading map supplier of his day. He engraved and printed maps for government and other official bodies and produced a wide range of commercial maps and atlases, especially of North America. His work as a map maker sparked an interest in local dress customs of the lands he surveyed and mapped, which are brilliantly displayed in this collection. Fascination with faraway lands and travel for pleasure were relatively new phenomena in the late 18th century, and collections such as this one were popular, introducing both the tourist as well as the armchair traveler to the inhabitants of other countries.

The diversity of the drawings in Jefferys' volumes speaks vividly of the uniqueness and individuality of the world's nations some 200 years ago. Dress codes have changed since then, and the diversity by region and country, so rich at the time, has faded away. It's now often hard to tell the inhabitants of one continent from another. Perhaps, trying to view it optimistically, we've traded a cultural and visual diversity for a more varied personal life—or a more varied and interesting intellectual and technical life.

At a time when it's difficult to tell one computer book from another, Manning celebrates the inventiveness and initiative of the computer business with book covers based on the rich diversity of regional life of two centuries ago, brought back to life by Jeffreys' pictures.

Part 1

Getting to know Vue.js

Before we can learn all the cool things Vue has to offer, we need to get to know it first. In these first two chapters, we'll look at the philosophy behind Vue.js, the MVVM pattern, and how it relates to other frameworks.

Once we understand where Vue is coming from, we'll look deeper at the Vue instance. The root Vue instance is the heart of the application, and we'll explore how it's structured. Later, we'll look at how we can bind data in our application to Vue.

These chapters will give you a great start in Vue.js. You'll learn how to create a simple app and how Vue works.

Introducing Vue.js

This chapter covers

- Exploring the MVC and MVVM design patterns
- Defining a reactive application
- Describing the Vue lifecycle
- Evaluating the design of Vue.js

Interactive websites have been around for a long time. During the beginning of the Web 2.0 days in the mid-2000s, a much larger focus was put on interactivity and engaging users. Companies such as Twitter, Facebook, and YouTube were all created during this time. The rise of social media and user-generated content was changing the web for the better.

Developers had to keep up with these changes to allow more interactivity for the end user and early on, libraries and frameworks started making interactive websites easier to build. In 2006, jQuery was released by John Resig, greatly simplifying the client-side scripting of HTML. As time progressed, client-side frameworks and libraries were created.

At first these frameworks and libraries were big, monolithic, and opinionated. Now, we've seen a shift to smaller, lighter-weight libraries that can be easily added to any project. This is where Vue.js comes in.

Vue.js is a library that enables us to add that interactive behavior and functionality to any context where JavaScript can run. Vue can be used on individual webpages for simple tasks or it can provide the foundation for an entire enterprise application.

> **TIP** The terms Vue and Vue.js are used somewhat interchangeably around the web. Throughout the book, I use the more colloquial Vue for the most part, reserving Vue.js for when I'm referring specifically to the code or the library.

From the interface that visitors interact with to the database that provides our application with its data, we'll explore how Vue and its supporting libraries enable us to build complete, sophisticated web applications.

Along the way, we'll examine how each chapter's code fits into the bigger picture, what industry best practices are applicable, and how you can incorporate what we're working on into your own projects, both existing and new.

This book is primarily written for web developers who have a moderate degree of JavaScript familiarity and a healthy understanding of HTML and CSS. That said, owing much to the versatility of its application programming interface (API), Vue is a library that grows with you as a developer as it grows with your project. Anyone who wants to build a prototype or an app for a personal side project should find this book a reliable guide on that journey.

1.1   On the shoulders of giants

Before we write any code for our first application, or even dig into Vue at a high level, it's important to understand a little bit of software history. It's difficult to truly appreciate what Vue does for us without knowledge of the problems and challenges that web applications have faced in the past and what advantages Vue brings to the table.

1.1.1   The Model–View–Controller pattern

A testament to its utility, the client-side Model–View–Controller (MVC) pattern provides the architectural blueprint used by many modern web application development frameworks. (If you're familiar with MVC, feel free to skip ahead.)

It's worth mentioning before we continue that the original MVC design pattern has changed throughout the years. Sometimes known as Classic MVC, it involved a separate set of rules on how the view, controller, and model interacted. For the sake of simplicity, we'll discuss a simplified version of the client-side MVC pattern. This pattern is a more modern interpretation for the web.

As you can see in figure 1.1, the pattern is used to separate the application's concerns. The view is responsible for displaying information to the user. This represents the graphical user interface (GUI). The controller is in the middle. It helps transform events from the view to the model and data from the model to the view. Finally, the model holds business logic and could contain a kind of datastore.

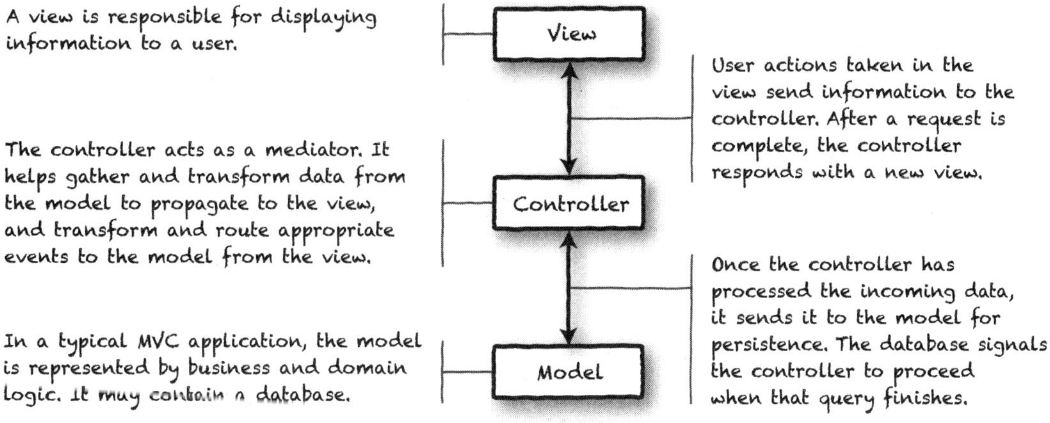

A view is responsible for displaying information to a user.

The controller acts as a mediator. It helps gather and transform data from the model to propagate to the view, and transform and route appropriate events to the model from the view.

In a typical MVC application, the model is represented by business and domain logic. It may contain a database.

User actions taken in the view send information to the controller. After a request is complete, the controller responds with a new view.

Once the controller has processed the incoming data, it sends it to the model for persistence. The database signals the controller to proceed when that query finishes.

Figure 1 1   The roles of the model, view, and controller as described by the MVC pattern.

INFO   If you're interested in learning more about the MVC pattern, start with Martin Fowler's page on the evolution of MVC at https://martinfowler.com/eaaDev/uiArchs.html.

Many web framework authors have used a variation of this MVC pattern because of its solid, time-tested architecture. If you want to know more about how modern web frameworks are designed and architected, check out *SPA Design and Architecture* by Emmitt A. Scott Jr. (Manning, 2015).

In modern software development, the MVC pattern is often used as a part of a single application and provides a great mechanism for separating the roles of application code. For websites using the MVC pattern, every request initiates a flow of information from the client to the server, then the database, and all the way back again. That process is time-consuming, resource-intensive, and doesn't provide a responsive user experience.

Over the years, developers have increased the interactivity of web-based applications by using asynchronous web requests and client-side MVC so that requests sent to the server are non-blocking and execution continues without a reply. But as web applications begin to function more like their desktop counterparts, waiting for any client/server interaction can make an application feel sluggish or broken. That's where our next pattern comes to the rescue.

A word about business logic

You'll find a good degree of flexibility in the client-side MVC pattern when considering where business logic should be implemented. In figure 1.1 we consolidated the business logic in the model for simplicity's sake, but it may also exist in other tiers of the

(continued)

application, including the controller. The MVC pattern has changed since it was introduced by Trygve Reenskaug in 1979 for Smalltalk-76.

Consider the validation of a ZIP Code provided by a user:

- The view might contain JavaScript that validates a ZIP Code as it's entered or prior to submission.
- The model might validate the ZIP Code when it creates an address object to hold the incoming data.
- Database constraints on the ZIP Code field may mean that the model is also enforcing business logic, although this could be considered bad practice.

It can be difficult to define what constitutes actual business logic, and in many cases, all the previous constraints may come into play within a single request.

As we build our application in this book, we'll examine how and where we're organizing our business logic, as well as how Vue and its supporting libraries can help keep functionality from bleeding across boundaries.

1.1.2 The Model–View–ViewModel pattern

When JavaScript frameworks began to support asynchronous programming techniques, web applications were no longer required to make requests for complete web pages. Websites and applications could respond faster with partial updates to the view, but doing so required a degree of duplicated effort. Presentation logic often mirrored business logic.

A refinement of MVC, the primary difference in the Model–View–ViewModel (MVVM) pattern is the introduction of the *view-model*, and its data bindings (collectively, the *binder*). MVVM provides a blueprint for us to build client-side applications with more responsive user interaction and feedback, while avoiding costly duplication of code and effort across the overall architecture. It's also easier to unit test. With that said, MVVM may be overkill for simple UIs, so take that into consideration.

For web applications, the design of MVVM allows us to write software that responds immediately to user interaction and allows users to move freely from one task to the next. As you can see from figure 1.2, the view-model also wears different hats. This consolidation of responsibility has a single, profound implication for our application's views: when data changes in the view-model, any view bound to it is automatically updated. The data binder exposes data and helps guarantee that when data changes, it's reflected in the view.

INFO You can find more information on the MVVM pattern on Martin Fowler's page on the Presentation model at https://martinfowler.com/eaaDev/PresentationModel.html.

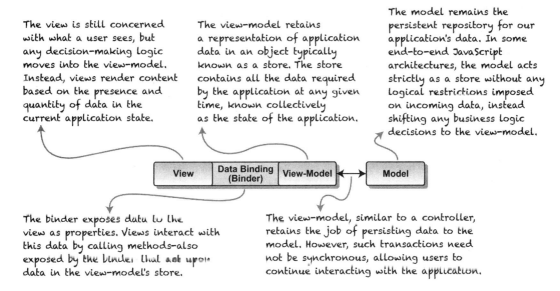

The view is still concerned with what a user sees, but any decision-making logic moves into the view-model. Instead, views render content based on the presence and quantity of data in the current application state.

The view-model retains a representation of application data in an object typically known as a store. The store contains all the data required by the application at any given time, known collectively as the state of the application.

The model remains the persistent repository for our application's data. In some end-to-end JavaScript architectures, the model acts strictly as a store without any logical restrictions imposed on incoming data, instead shifting any business logic decisions to the view-model.

The binder exposes data to the view as properties. Views interact with this data by calling methods—also exposed by the binder that act upon data in the view-model's store.

The view-model, similar to a controller, retains the job of persisting data to the model. However, such transactions need not be synchronous, allowing users to continue interacting with the application.

Figure 1.2 The components of the Model–View–ViewModel pattern.

1.1.3 What's a reactive application?

The reactive programming paradigm isn't necessarily a new idea. Its adoption by web applications is relatively new and owes much to the availability of JavaScript frameworks such as Vue, React, and Angular.

Many great resources on reactive theory are available on the web, but our needs are perhaps a bit more focused. For a web application to be thought of as reactive, it should do the following:

- Observe changes in application state
- Propagate change notification throughout the application
- Render views automatically in response to changes in state
- Provide timely feedback for user interactions

Reactive web applications accomplish these goals by employing MVVM design principles using asynchronous techniques to avoid blocking continued interaction and using functional programming idioms where possible.

While the MVVM pattern doesn't imply a reactive application and vice versa, they share a common intention: to provide a more responsive, reliable experience to the users of an application. Superman and Clark Kent may present themselves differently, but they both want to do right by humanity. (No, I won't say which of MVVM and Reactive I think wears the cape and which the glasses.)

INFO If you'd like to learn more about Vue's reactive programming paradigm, check out the *Reactivity in Depth* guide at https://vuejs.org/v2/guide/reactivity.html.

1.1.4   *A JavaScript calculator*

To better understand the notions of data binding and reactivity, we'll start by implementing a calculator in plain, vanilla JavaScript, as shown in this listing.

Listing 1.1   The JavaScript calculator: chapter-01/calculator.html

```html
<!DOCTYPE>
<html>
  <head>
    <title>A JavaScript Calculator</title>
    <style>
     p, input { font-family: monospace; }
     p, { white-space: pre; }
    </style>
  </head>
  <!-- Bind to the init function -->
  <body>
    <div id="myCalc">
       <p>x <input class="calc-x-input" value="0"></p>
       <p>y <input class="calc-y-input" value="0"></p>
       <p>-------------------</p>
         <p>= <span class="calc-result"></span></p>
    </div>
    <script type="text/javascript">
     (function(){

       function Calc(xInput, yInput, output) {
         this.xInput = xInput;
         this.yInput = yInput;
         this.output = output;
       }

       Calc.xName = 'xInput';
       Calc.yName = 'yInput';

       Calc.prototype = {
         render: function (result) {
           this.output.innerText = String(result);
         }
       };

       function CalcValue(calc, x, y) {
         this.calc = calc;
         this.x = x;
         this.y = y;
         this.result = x + y;
       }

       CalcValue.prototype = {
         copyWith: function(name, value) {
           var number = parseFloat(value);

           if (isNaN(number) || !isFinite(number))
             return this;
```

Forms input to collect x and y that bind to the runCalc function

Shows results of x and y

Shows constructor to create calc instance

Shows constructor to create values for a calc instance

```
      if (name === Calc.xName)
        return new CalcValue(this.calc, number, this.y);

      if (name === Calc.yName)
        return new CalcValue(this.calc, this.x, number);

      return this;
    },
    render: function() {
      this.calc.render(this.result);
    }
  };

  function initCalc(elem) {                          Initializes calc
                                                     component
    var calc =
      new Calc(
        elem.querySelector('input.calc-x-input'),
        elem.querySelector('input.calc-y-input'),
        elem.querySelector('span.calc-result')
      );
    var lastValues =
      new CalcValue(
        calc,
        parseFloat(calc.xInput.value),
        parseFloat(calc.yInput.value)
      );


    var handleCalcEvent =                            Shows the
      function handleCalcEvent(e) {                  event handler
        var newValues = lastValues,
          elem = e.target;

        switch(elem) {
          case calc.xInput:
            newValues =
              lastValues.copyWith(
                Calc.xName,
                elem.value
              );
            break;
          case calc.yInput:
            newValues =
              lastValues.copyWith(
                Calc.yName,
                elem.value
              );
            break;
        }

        if(newValues !== lastValues){
          lastValues = newValues;
          lastValues.render();
        }
      };
                                                     Sets the event
                                                     listener on keyup
    elem.addEventListener('keyup', handleCalcEvent, false);
```

```
        return lastValues;
      }

      window.addEventListener(
        'load',
        function() {
          var cv = initCalc(document.getElementById('myCalc'));
          cv.render();
        },
        false
      );

    }());
  </script>
</body>
</html>
```

This is a calculator using ES5 JavaScript (we'll use the more modern version of Java-Script ES6/2015 later in the book). We're using an immediately invoked function expression that kicks off our JavaScript. A constructor is used to hold values and the `handleCalcEvent` event handler fires on any `keyup`.

1.1.5 A Vue calculator

Don't worry too much about the syntax of the Vue example because our goal here isn't to understand everything going on in the code, but to compare the two implementations. That said, if you have a good sense of how the JavaScript example works (as shown in the following listing), much of the Vue code should make sense at least on a theoretical level.

Listing 1.2   The Vue calculator: chapter-01/calculatorvue.html

```
<!DOCTYPE html>
<html>
<head>
  <title>A Vue.js Calculator</title>
  <style>
    p, input { font-family: monospace; }
    p { white-space: pre; }
  </style>
</head>
<body>
  <div id="app">                                    ⟵  Shows the DOM
    <p>x <input v-model="x"></p>                        anchor for our app
    <p>y <input v-model="y"></p>                   ⟵  Shows the form inputs
    <p>-------------------</p>                          for the application
    <p>= <span v-text="result"></span></p>        ⟵  Results will show
  </div>                                                up in this span.

  <script src="https://unpkg.com/vue/dist/vue.js"></script>   ⟵  Lists the script tag that
  <script type="text/javascript">                                adds the Vue.js library
```

```
function isNotNumericValue(value) {
    return isNaN(value) || !isFinite(value);
}

var calc = new Vue({
    el: '#app',
    data: { x: 0, y: 0, lastResult: 0 },
    computed: {
        result: function() {
            let x = parseFloat(this.x);
            if(isNotNumericValue(x))
                return this.lastResult;

            let y = parseFloat(this.y);
            if(isNotNumericValue(y))
                return this.lastResult;

            this.lastResult = x + y;

            return this.lastResult;
        }
    }
});
</script>
</body>
</html>
```

Initializes the application — `var calc = new Vue({`

Connects to the DOM — `el: '#app',`

Shows the variables added to the app — `data: { x: 0, y: 0, lastResult: 0 },`

Calculation is done here using a computed property.

1.1.6 Comparison of JavaScript and Vue

The code for both calculator implementations is, for the most part, different. Each sample shown in figure 1.3 is available in the repository that accompanies this chapter, so you can run each one and compare how they operate.

```
17    <script type="text/javascript">
18    (function(){
19
20        function Calc(xInput, yInput, output) {
21            this.xInput = xInput;
22            this.yInput = yInput;
23            this.output = output;
24        }
25
26        Calc.xName = 'xInput';
27        Calc.yName = 'yInput';
28
29        Calc.prototype = {
30            render: function (result) {
31                this.output.innerText = String(result);
32            }
33        };
34
35        function CalcValue(calc, x, y) {
36            this.calc = calc;
37            this.x = x;
38            this.y = y;
39            this.result = x + y;
40        }
41
```

```
18    <script src="https://unpkg.com/vue/dist/vue.js"></script>
19    <script type="text/javascript">
20    function isNotNumericValue(value) {
21        return isNaN(value) || !isFinite(value);
22    }
23        var calc = new Vue({
24            el: '#app',
25            data: { x: 0, y: 0, lastResult: 0 },
26            computed: {
27                result: function() {
28                    let x = parseFloat(this.x);
29                    if(isNotNumericValue(x))
30                        return this.lastResult;
31
32                    let y = parseFloat(this.y);
33                    if(isNotNumericValue(y))
34                        return this.lastResult;
35
36                    this.lastResult = x + y;
37
38                    return this.lastResult;
39                }
40            }
41        });
42    </script>
```

Figure 1.3 Side-by-side comparison of a reactive calculator written using vanilla JavaScript (on the left) and Vue (on the right).

The key difference between the two applications is how an update to the final calculation is triggered and how the result finds its way back to the page. In our Vue example, a single binding `v-model` takes care of all the updates and calculations on the page. When we instantiate our application with new `Vue({ ... })`, Vue examines our JavaScript code and HTML markup, then creates all the data and event bindings needed for our application to run.

1.1.7   *How does Vue facilitate MVVM and reactivity?*

Vue is sometimes referred to as a *progressive framework*, which broadly means that it can be incorporated into an existing web page for simple tasks or that it can be used entirely as the basis for a large-scale web application.

Regardless of how you choose to incorporate Vue into your project, every Vue application has at least one *Vue instance.* The most basic application will have a single instance that provides bindings between designated markup and data stored in a view-model (see figure 1.4).

Being built entirely out of web technologies, a single Vue instance exists entirely in the web browser. Crucially, this means that we don't depend on server-based page reloads for updated views, executing business logic, or any other task that falls under the domain of the view or view-model. Let's revisit our form submission example with that in mind.

Perhaps the most striking change relative to the client-side MVC architecture is that the browser page needs to rarely, if ever, reload during the user's entire session. Because the view, view-model, and data bindings are all implemented in HTML and JavaScript,

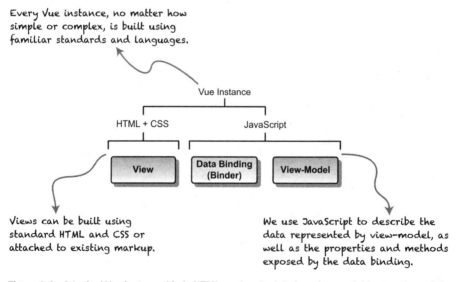

Figure 1.4   **A typical Vue instance binds HTML markup to data in a view-model by creating a data binding between them.**

our application can delegate tasks to the model asynchronously, leaving users free to continue with other tasks. When new data is returned from the model, the bindings established by Vue will trigger whatever updates need to happen in the view.

Arguably, it's Vue's primary role to facilitate user interaction by creating and maintaining the binding between the views we create and the data in our view-model. In this capacity, as we'll see in our first application, Vue provides a solid bedrock for any reactive web application.

1.2 Why Vue.js?

When starting a new project, there are many decisions to make. One of the most important is the framework or library that should be used. If you're an agency or even a solo developer, picking the correct tool for the job is extremely important. Luckily, Vue.js is versatile and can handle many different situations.

What follows are several of the most commonly voiced concerns that you might have when starting a new project as a solo developer or agency, plus a description of how Vue helps to address them, either directly or as part of a larger movement toward reactive web applications.

- *Our team isn't strong at working with web frameworks.* One of the greatest advantages of using Vue for a project is that it doesn't require any specialist knowledge. Every Vue application is built with HTML, CSS, and JavaScript—familiar tools that allow you to be productive right from the get-go. Even teams that have little experience developing any sort of frontend find a comfortable foothold in the MVVM pattern because of their familiarity with MVC in other contexts.

- *We've got existing work we'd like to continue using.* Don't worry, there's no need to scrap your carefully crafted CSS or that cool carousel you built. Whether you're dropping Vue into an existing project with many dependencies, or you're starting a new project and want to leverage other libraries you are already familiar with, Vue won't get in the way. You can continue using tools such as Bootstrap or Bulma as a CSS framework, keep jQuery or Backbone components around, or incorporate your preferred library for making HTTP requests, handling Promises or other extended functionality.

- *We need to prototype quickly and gauge users' reactions.* As we saw in our first Vue application, all we need to do to start building with Vue is include Vue.js in any standalone webpage. No complicated build tools required! Getting a prototype in front of users can happen within a week or two of starting development, allowing you to gather feedback early and iterate often.

- *Our product is used almost exclusively on mobile devices.* The minified and gzipped Vue.js file weighs in at around 24 KB, which is quite compact for a frontend framework. The library is easily delivered over cellular connections. New to Vue 2 is server-side rendering (SSR). Such a strategy means that an application's initial load can be minimal, allowing you to pull in new views and resources only as required. Combining SSR with efficient caching of components reduces bandwidth consumption even further.

- *Our product has unique and custom functionality.* Architected from the ground up with modularity and extensibility in mind, Vue applications use reusable components. Vue also supports extending components through inheritance, incorporating functionality with mix-ins, and extending Vue's functionality with plugins and custom directives.
- *We have a large user base and performance is a concern.* Recently rewritten for reliability, performance, and speed, Vue now uses a virtual DOM. What that means is that Vue first performs operations on a DOM representation that isn't attached to the browser then "copies" those changes to the view we see. As a result, Vue routinely outperforms other frontend libraries. Because generalized tests are often too abstract, I always encourage clients to select several of their typical use cases and a few extreme ones, develop a testing scenario, and measure the results for themselves. You can learn more about the virtual DOM and how it compares to its competitors at https://vuejs.org/v2/guide/comparison.html.
- *We have an existing build, test, and/or deployment process.* In the latter chapters of the book we'll explore these topics in depth, but the takeaway is that Vue is easily integrated into many of the most popular build (Webpack, Browserify, and others) and test (Karma, Jasmine, and so on) frameworks. In many instances, unit tests are directly portable if you've already written them for an existing framework. And if you're starting out but want to use these tools, Vue provides project templates that integrate these tools for you. In the simplest of terms, it's easy to add and adapt Vue to existing projects.
- *What do we do if we need help during or after our engagement?* Two of the immeasurable benefits of Vue are its community and support ecosystem. Vue is well-documented, both in online docs and within the code itself, and the core team is active and responsive. Perhaps even more crucial, the community of developers working with Vue is equally as strong. Resources such as Gitter and the Vue forums are full of helpful folks, and there's a growing list of plugins, integrations, and library extensions that bring popular code to the platform nearly every day.

After asking many of these questions on my own projects, I now recommend Vue on almost all my projects. As you become confident in your mastery of Vue throughout this book, my hope is that you'll feel comfortable advocating for Vue in your next project.

1.3   *Future thoughts*

We've covered much ground in this introductory chapter alone. If you're new to web application development, this may be your first contact with the MVVM architecture or reactive programming, but we've seen that building a reactive application isn't as intimidating as the jargon can make it feel.

Perhaps the biggest takeaway from this chapter isn't about Vue itself, but how reactive applications are easier to work with and easier to write with. It's also nice that we have less boilerplate interface code to write. Not having to script all our user's interactions frees us up to focus on how to model our data and design our interface. Wiring them up is something Vue makes effortless.

If you're like me, then you're already thinking of the gazillion ways you can make our modest application better. This is a good thing, and you should absolutely experiment and play with the code. Here are a few things I think about when I look at the app:

- How would we eliminate the need to repeat text strings in so many places?
- Can we clear the default input when a user focuses on an input? What about restoring it if they leave the field blank?
- Is there a way to avoid hand-coding each input?

In part 2, we'll find answers to all these questions and many more. Vue was designed to grow with us as developers, as much as with our code, so we'll always make sure to look at different strategies, compare their strengths and weaknesses, and learn how to decide which is the best practice for a given situation.

All right, let's see how we can improve on some of what we wrote!

Summary

- A brief history of how models, views, and controllers work, and how they're tied into Vue.js.
- How Vue.js can save you time when creating an application.
- Why you should consider Vue.js for your next project.

The Vue instance

2

This chapter covers

- Creating a Vue instance
- Observing the Vue lifecycle
- Adding data to a Vue instance
- Binding data to markup
- Formatting our output

Over the course of this book we're going to build a complete web application: a webstore with product listings, a checkout process, an administrative interface, and more. The completed webstore may seem like it's a long way off, especially if you're new to web application development, but Vue allows you to start small, build on what you learn, and ship a sophisticated product in one smooth progression.

The key to Vue's consistency at every stage of an application's growth is the Vue instance. A Vue application is a Vue instance, Vue components are all Vue instances, and you can even extend Vue by creating instances with your own custom properties.

It's impossible to touch on all the facets of the Vue instance in a single chapter, so we'll build on the foundation we establish as our application evolves. As we explore new features in chapters to come, we'll often refer to what we learn about the Vue instance and the Vue lifecycle in this chapter.

2.1 Our first application

To begin our journey, we're going to create the foundation of our webstore application, display its name, and create a single product listing. Our focus is on how we create a Vue application and the relationship of the data in our view-model to how it's displayed in the view. Figure 2.1 shows what our application should look like by the end of this chapter.

Figure 2.1   A preview of our humble webstore's beginnings.

> **BTW**   If you tried the simple calculator sample in listing 1.2, technically this will be your second Vue application. You're a seasoned veteran already!

Before we begin, download the vue-devtools plugin for your browser. You can find more information on how to download this plugin in appendix A.

2.1.1   The root Vue instance

At the heart of every Vue application, no matter how big or small, is the *root Vue instance,* Vue instance for short. Creating a root Vue instance is done by invoking the *Vue constructor,* new Vue(). The constructor bootstraps our application by compiling an HTML template for our app, initializing any instance data, and creating the data and event bindings that make our application interactive.

The Vue constructor accepts a single JavaScript object, known as the *options object*, `new Vue({ /* options go here */ })`. It's our job to populate that object with everything the Vue constructor needs to bootstrap our application, but to start off we're focusing on a single option, the `el` option.

The `el` option is used by Vue to specify a DOM element (hence `el`) where Vue will mount our application. Vue will locate the corresponding DOM element in our HTML and use it as the mount point for our application.

This code is the beginning of our webstore application. To make things easier to follow, I've included each code listing in its own file that you can download for this chapter. But to run the application, you'll need to combine each snippet of code from each file into a single index.html file. Yes, the index.html file will get rather large as we progress through the book, and that's normal. In future chapters, we'll discuss ways of splitting our application into separate files.

If you'd like to see the completed application from this chapter, look for the index.html file that's included with the code in the chapter-02 folder. (If you haven't downloaded the code that accompanies this chapter, learn how and where to get it in appendix A.) Let's create our first Vue application.

Listing 2.1   Our first Vue application: chapter-02/first-vue.html

```
<html>
  <head>
    <title>Vue.js Pet Depot</title>                          Lists the CDN
    <script src="https://unpkg.com/vue"></script>            version of Vue.js
    <link rel="stylesheet" type="text/css" href="assets/css/app.css"/>
    <link rel="stylesheet"
  href="https://maxcdn.bootstrapcdn.com/bootstrap/3.3.7/css/
    bootstrap.min.css" crossorigin="anonymous">
                                                       Our internal app.css
  </head>                                              stylesheet as well as the
  <body>                                               Bootstrap stylesheet
    <div id="app"></div>              The element where
                                      Vue will mount our
    <script type="text/javascript">   application
      var webstore = new Vue({
        el: '#app'                    Lists a CSS selector
      });                             used to locate the
    </script>                         DOM mounting point
  </body>
</html>
```

The Vue constructor → `var webstore = new Vue({`

The markup contains a single `div` element with a CSS ID selector, #app. Vue uses that value to locate our `div` and mount the application to it. This selector matches the same syntax used by CSS (such as `#id`, `.class`).

NOTE Throughout this book we'll use Bootstrap 3 for all layout and design. This works great and helps keep the focus on Vue.js. As of the time of writing, Bootstrap 4 was recently released, but because the focus of this book isn't on design, I decided to leave Bootstrap 3 in. These examples will work on

Bootstrap 4; but you may need to swap out several of the classes to the newer Bootstrap 4 classes if you do switch over. Keep that in mind.

If the CSS selector we provide resolves to more than one DOM element, Vue will mount the application to the first element that matches the selector. If we had an HTML document with three `div` elements, and we invoked the Vue constructor as `new Vue({ el: 'div' })`, Vue would mount the application at the first `div` element of the three.

If you need to run multiple Vue instances on a single page, you could mount them to different DOM elements by using unique selectors. This may seem like an odd practice, but if you use Vue to build small components, such as an image carousel or a web-form, it's easy to see how you could have several root Vue instances all running on a single page.

2.1.2 *Making sure our application is running*

Let's head over to Chrome and open the file you created for your first Vue application from listing 2.1, though it won't yet render anything you can see in the main browser window. (After all, there's no visible HTML!)

Once the page loads, open the JavaScript console if it isn't already open, and hopefully you'll see . . . <drum roll> . . . absolutely nothing (or perhaps a note about downloading vue-devtools if you haven't already done so, or a note that you're running Vue in development mode). Figure 2.2 shows what your console might look like.

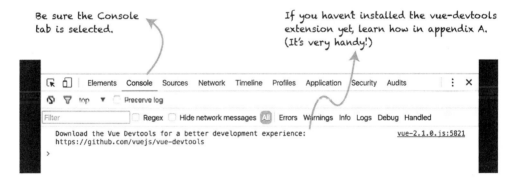

Figure 2.2 The JavaScript console with no errors or warnings.

Vue debugging 101

Even as simple as our application is so far, we can still run into trouble when we load our file in Chrome. Here are two common issues to look out for when things don't go as planned:

- `Uncaught SyntaxError: Unexpected identifier` almost always indicates a typo in the JavaScript code and can usually be traced to a missing

(continued)

comma or curly brace. You can click the filename and line number displayed on the right of the error to jump to the corresponding code. Keep in mind that you may have to hunt a few lines up or down to find the offending typo.

- `[Vue warn]: Property or method "propertyname" is not defined . . .` lets you know something wasn't defined in the options object when the instance was created. Check to see whether the property or method exists in your options object, and if it does, check for typos in its name. Also check to be sure the name is spelled correctly in the binding in your markup.

Tracking down errors the first few times can be frustrating, but after you've resolved a few errors the process will become more natural.

If you run into something you can't figure out, or you find a particularly nasty error, you can check out the Help section of the Vue forum at https://forum.vuejs.org/c/help or ask for help in the Vue Gitter chat at https://gitter.im/vuejs/vue.

After Vue finishes initializing and mounting the application, it returns a reference to the root Vue instance, which we stored in the `webstore` variable. We can use that variable to inspect our application in the JavaScript console. Let's use it now to make sure that our application is alive and well before continuing.

With the console open, enter `webstore` at the prompt. The result is a Vue object that we can inspect further in the console. For now, click the disclosure triangles (▸) to expand the object and look at the properties of our root Vue instance as seen in figure 2.3.

1 Enter `webstore` at the prompt.

2 Expanding the disclosure triangle of the Vue object will allow you to see the properties of our Vue instance.

3 There's our `el` property, bound to the div we specified in listing 2.1.

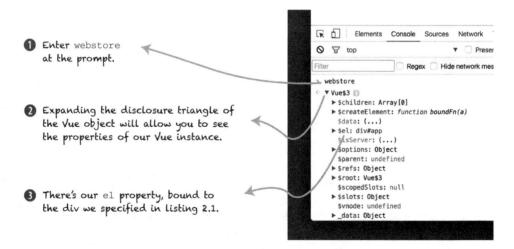

Figure 2.3   Using the webstore variable to display a representation of the Vue instance and explore its properties.

You may have to scroll around a bit, but you should be able to locate the el property we specified as part of our application's options object. In future chapters, we'll use the console to access our instance for debugging, manipulating data, and triggering behaviors in our application while it's running, so we can validate that it behaves as expected. We can also use vue-devtools to peek inside our application while it's running. (Again, if you don't yet have vue-devtools installed, visit appendix A to learn how to install it.) Let's see how it compares with using the JavaScript console. Figure 2.4 shows the different parts of the vue-devtools.

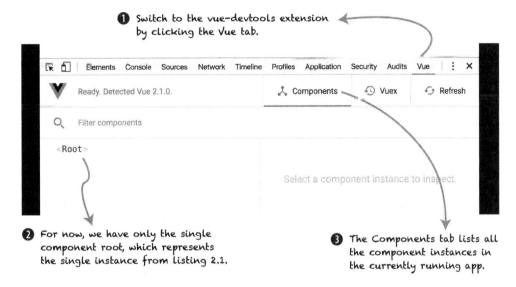

Figure 2.4 The vue-devtools window with nothing selected.

The vue-devtools extension provides big functionality for inspecting a Vue application, its data, and the relationship of its components. As an application grows in complexity, the searchable tree view in vue-devtools shows the relationship of components in a way the JavaScript console cannot. We'll discuss more about Vue components and how they relate to the Vue instance in a later chapter.

We'll frequently use both tools to zero in on problems with our application as we build it. In fact, we can use vue-devtools to discover another way to access our application instance in the JavaScript console as seen in figure 2.5.

When you select an instance in the tree view, as in figure 2.5, vue-devtools assigns a reference to the instance to the $vm0 variable. We can use $vm0 the same way we used our webstore variable. Try using $vm0 in the JavaScript console to see if you can inspect the root Vue instance

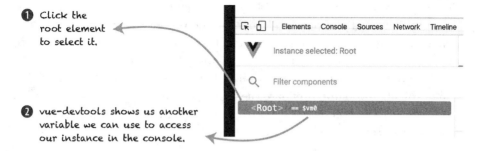

① Click the
root element
to select it.

② vue-devtools shows us another
variable we can use to access
our instance in the console.

**Figure 2.5 The root instance selected in vue-devtools with a variable dynamically assigned
to the instance.**

Why do we need more than one reference?

Having multiple ways to access the same instance may appear redundant, but it's
helpful to have both.

When we assigned our root Vue instance to the global variable `webstore`, we gave
ourselves a way to refer to the application in other JavaScript code on the page. Doing
so allows us to integrate with other libraries, frameworks, or our own code that may
require a reference back to our application.

The Vue instance assigned to the `$vm0` variable reflects the current selection made
in vue-devtools. When an application is made up of hundreds, or even thousands of
instances, it isn't practical to declaratively assign each instance, so having a way to
access specific instances that are created programmatically becomes indispensable
when inspecting and debugging such a complex application.

2.1.3 *Displaying something inside our view*

Until now, our application has been a real snoozefest. Let's liven it up by displaying
data from our application instance in our application's template. Remember, our Vue
instance uses the DOM element we provide as the basis for its template.

We're going to start by adding the name of our webstore. This will show us how to
pass data into the Vue constructor, and how to bind that data to a view. In this listing
let's update the application code from listing 2.1.

Listing 2.2 Adding data and a data binding: chapter-02/data-binding.html

```html
<html>
  <head>
    <title>Vue.js Pet Depot</title>
    <script src="https://unpkg.com/vue"></script>  </head>
  <body>
    <div id="app">
```

```
        <header>
          <h1 v-text="sitename"></h1>
        </header>
      </div>

      <script type="text/javascript">
        var webstore = new Vue({
          el: '#app', // <=== Don't forget this comma!
          data: {
            sitename: 'Vue.js Pet Depot'
          }
        });
      </script>
    </body>
</html>
```

Shows data binding for the sitename property → `<h1 v-text="sitename"></h1>`

A header element is added to the div.

Shows the sitename property we bind to in the header → `sitename: 'Vue.js Pet Depot'`

Adds a data object to the Vue options

We've added a data object to the options we pass into our Vue constructor. That data object contains a single property, `sitename`, which contains the name of our webstore.

Our site's name needs a home, so we've also added a header element to the markup inside of the application's root `div` element. On the heading element `<h1>`, we use a data binding element directive, `v-text="sitename"`.

A `v-text` directive prints a string representation of the property it references. In this case, once our application is up and running we should see a header with the text "Vue.js Pet Depot" displayed inside it.

If you need to display a property value in the middle of a larger string, you can use Mustache syntax—`{{ property-name }}`—to bind to a property. To include the name of our webstore in a sentence, you might write `<p>Welcome to {{ sitename }}</p>`.

> **TIP** Vue only borrows the `{{ ... }}` syntax from Mustache for text interpolations, not from the entire Mustache specification. But if you're curious where it comes from, visit the online manual at https://mustache.github.io/mustache.5.html.

With our data binding in place, let's go see how our new header looks in the browser.

2.1.4 *Inspecting properties in Vue*

When you reload the application in Chrome, you should see the header proudly displaying the value of our `sitename` property as seen in figure 2.6. The visual appearance

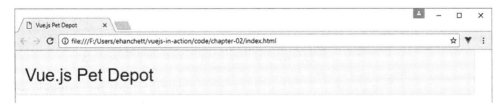

Figure 2.6 Our `sitename` property displayed in the header of our webstore.

of our header is provided by the stylesheet in chapter-02/assets/css/app.css. We'll use our stylesheet and Bootstrap to design our application. If you'd like to tinker with the appearance of the header, open that file and find the styles defined by `header h1`.

Vue automatically creates getter and setter functions for each property of the data object when it initializes our application. That gives us the ability to retrieve the current value of, or set a new value for, any of our instance's properties without writing any additional code. To see these functions in action, let's start by using the getter to print the value of the `sitename` property.

As you can see in figure 2.7, the getter and setter functions for our `sitename` property are exposed at the root level of our application instance. That lets us access the property from the JavaScript console, or from any other JavaScript that interacts with our application.

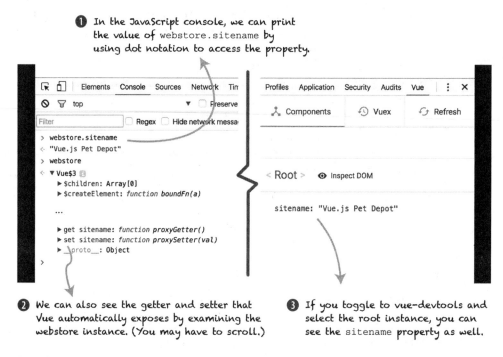

Figure 2.7   Using the console and vue-devtools, we can check on our `sitename` property.

You can also see the property listed in vue-devtools when we select the `<root>` instance. Now let's see what happens in figure 2.8 when we use the setter to set the value of `sitename` in the JavaScript console.

Once we provide a new value for `sitename` and hit Enter, the output in our header element is automatically updated. This is Vue's event loop in action. Let's look at the Vue lifecycle to see how and when changes to our data trigger updates to the view.

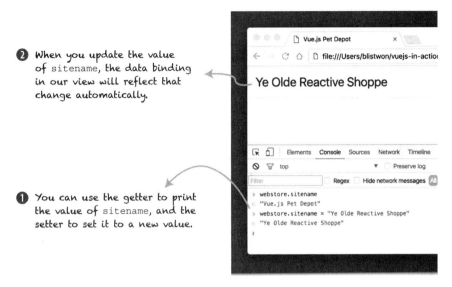

② When you update the value of `sitename`, the data binding in our view will reflect that change automatically.

① You can use the getter to print the value of `sitename`, and the setter to set it to a new value.

Figure 2.8 Using Vue's property getter and setter to print and update the `sitename` property, respectively.

2.2 The Vue lifecycle

When a Vue application is first instantiated, it begins its journey through a sequence of events known collectively as the Vue lifecycle. Although a long-running Vue application will likely spend most of its time cycling within the event loop, much of the heavy lifting of the library itself occurs when an application is first created. Let's take a high-level look at the lifecycle in figure 2.9.

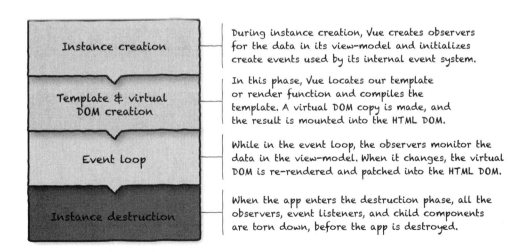

During instance creation, Vue creates observers for the data in its view-model and initializes create events used by its internal event system.

In this phase, Vue locates our template or render function and compiles the template. A virtual DOM copy is made, and the result is mounted into the HTML DOM.

While in the event loop, the observers monitor the data in the view-model. When it changes, the virtual DOM is re-rendered and patched into the HTML DOM.

When the app enters the destruction phase, all the observers, event listeners, and child components are torn down, before the app is destroyed.

Figure 2.9 Diagram of the Vue lifecycle, divided into four phases.

Each phase builds upon the previous phase to create the Vue lifecycle. You may wonder what the virtual DOM is and how the render function works. The *virtual DOM* is a lightweight abstraction that represents the DOM. It mimics the DOM tree that's normally accessed by the browser. Vue can make updates to the virtual DOM much quicker than the browser-specific DOM. The render function is the way Vue can display information to the user. For more information on the Vue instance and lifecycle hooks, please check out the official guides at https://vuejs.org/v2/guide/instance.html.

2.2.1 Adding lifecycle hooks

To see when our application instance passes through the different phases of the lifecycle, we can write callback functions for Vue's lifecycle hooks. Let's update the code in our main application file (index.html) in listing 2.3.

> **INFO** A *hook* is a function that gets "hooked" onto a part of the Vue library's code. Whenever Vue reaches that part of the code during execution, it calls the function you define or continues along if there's nothing to do.

Listing 2.3   Adding lifecycle hooks to our instance: chapter-02/life-cycle-hooks.js

```
var APP_LOG_LIFECYCLE_EVENTS = true;          ◁──┐  Shows a variable used
                                                  │  to enable or disable
var webstore = new Vue({                          │  our callbacks
  el: "#app",
  data: {
    sitename: "Vue.js Pet Depot",
  },
  beforeCreate: function() {
    if (APP_LOG_LIFECYCLE_EVENTS) {
      console.log("beforeCreate");              Logs the beforeCreate event
    }
  },
  created: function() {
    if (APP_LOG_LIFECYCLE_EVENTS) {
      console.log("created");                   Logs the created event
    }
  },
  beforeMount: function() {
    if (APP_LOG_LIFECYCLE_EVENTS) {
      console.log("beforeMount");               Logs the beforeMount event
    }
  },
  mounted:  function() {
    if (APP_LOG_LIFECYCLE_EVENTS) {
      console.log("mounted");                   Logs the mounted event
    }
  },
  beforeUpdate:  function() {
    if (APP_LOG_LIFECYCLE_EVENTS) {
      console.log("beforeUpdate");              Logs the beforeUpdate event
    }
  },
```

```
  updated: function() {
    if (APP_LOG_LIFECYCLE_EVENTS) {
      console.log("updated");          │  Logs the updated event
    }
  },
  beforeDestroy: function() {
    if (APP_LOG_LIFECYCLE_EVENTS) {
      console.log("beforeDestroy ");    │  Logs the beforeDestroy event
    }
  },
  destroyed: function() {
    if (APP_LOG_LIFECYCLE_EVENTS) {
      console.log("destroyed");         │  Logs the destroyed event
    }
  }
});
```

The first thing you'll notice in listing 2.3 is that we've defined a variable, APP_LOG_LIFECYCLE_EVENTS, that we can use to enable or disable logging of lifecycle events. We define our variable outside the Vue instance, so it can be used globally by the root instance or any child components we write later. Also, if we defined it inside our application instance, it wouldn't be available in the beforeCreate callback because it hasn't yet been created!

> **NOTE** APP_LOG_LIFECYCLE_EVENTS uses the uppercase syntax typically reserved for constant definition because, when we start using ECMAScript 6 later in the book, we'll use the const feature to create constants. Planning ahead means we won't have to do any find-and-replace to change the name in the rest of our code.

The remainder of the code defines functions that log each lifecycle event as it's encountered. Let's revisit our console exploration of the sitename property to see what happens in the Vue lifecycle.

2.2.2 Exploring the lifecycle code

If you open the console in Chrome and reload the app, you should immediately see the output from several of our callbacks as seen in figure 2.10.

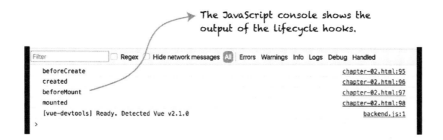

Figure 2.10   Output from some of our lifecycle functions can be seen in the console.

As you might expect, the first four lifecycle hooks get triggered as Vue creates
and mounts our application. To test the
other hooks, we'll need to interact with
the console a bit. First, let's trigger the
update callbacks by setting a new name
for our site. Figure 2.11 displays how
this can be done.

When you change the `sitename`
property, the update cycle kicks off as
the data binding in the application's
header is updated with the new value.
Now let's destroy our application!

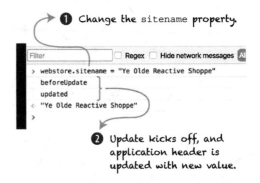

❶ Change the `sitename` **property.**

❷ Update kicks off, and application header is updated with new value.

Figure 2.11   Setting the `sitename` property triggers the update lifecycle callbacks.

(Don't worry, it'll come right back with a reload.) To trigger the last two lifecycle
hooks, we use our instance's `$destroy` method.

> **TIP** Special methods that Vue creates on our instance are available using the
> $ prefix. For more information on Vue's lifecycle instance methods, you can
> visit the API documentation at https://vuejs.org/v2/api/#Instance-Methods-
> Lifecycle.

These last two hooks are typically used for cleanup activities in an application or component. If our application created an instance of a third-party library, we should call
that library's teardown code, or de-allocate any references to it manually, so that we
avoid leaking memory allocated to our application. Figure 2.12 shows how calling the
`$destroy()` instance method will trigger the destroy hooks.

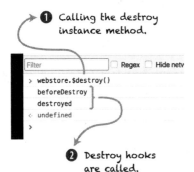

❶ Calling the destroy instance method.

❷ Destroy hooks are called.

Figure 2.12   Calling the destroy instance method triggers the final pair of lifecycle callbacks.

2.2.3   *Keeping the lifecycle code, or not*

The lifecycle hooks provide a great way to see what's going on as an application runs,
but I'm the first to admit that there's repetitive, verbose code required to log messages

to the console. Because they're fairly bulky, I won't include these debugging functions in code listings from here on, but we'll occasionally use lifecycle hooks to explore new behavior or for functional reasons in the application itself.

If you do keep these hooks around, and the console gets too noisy with output, you can disable the logging by setting `APP_LOG_LIFECYCLE_EVENTS` to `false`. Bear in mind that you can disable them completely by changing the value in the index.html, or you can temporarily toggle logging on and off by setting the value at runtime using the JavaScript console.

2.3 Displaying a product

Displaying the name of our webstore is a good start, but there are a few more aspects of displaying data in our markup that we should cover before moving on. Our webstore will display products in one of several ways: in a list, in a grid, as a featured product, and on its own individual product page. As we design and mark up each view, we'll continue to use the same data, but we'll use Vue's functionality to manipulate it differently for each display without altering the underlying values or structure.

2.3.1 Defining product data

For now, we're only going to display a single product, so let's add a sample product to our `data` object.

Listing 2.4 Adding product data to our Vue instance: chapter-02/product-data.js

```
data: {
  sitename: "Vue.js Pet Depot",        An object for our
  product: {                           product data
    id: 1001,
    title: "Cat Food, 25lb bag",
    description: "A 25 pound bag of <em>irresistible</em>,"+    The product's
                 "organic goodness for your cat.",             attributes are
    price: 2000,                                               properties of our
    image: "assets/images/product-fullsize.png"               product object.
  }
},
```

Adding a `product` object to our `data` option is relatively straightforward:

- *The `id` property is used to uniquely identify a product.* This property will increment if we add more products.
- *Although the title and description properties are both strings, the description contains HTML markup.* We'll look at what that means when we get around to displaying each of those values in our product markup.
- *The price property represents the cost of our product as an integer.* This simplifies calculations we'll do later, and this format avoids potentially destructive type casting that occurs when values are stored as floats or strings in a database.

- *The image property provides a path to our product's primary image file.* We're going to iterate on this one quite a bit, so if seeing a hardcoded path here makes you nervous, breathe easy, because we'll explore better options.

With our data in place, let's get our view up to speed.

2.3.2   *Marking up the product view*

Now we can focus on adding the product markup to our HTML. Beneath the header element, we'll add a main element that acts as the primary container for the content of our application. The main element, <main>, is a new addition to HTML5 and is meant to contain the primary content of a webpage or application.

> **INFO**   For more information about the main element (and others), start by visiting www.quackit.com/html_5/tags/html_main_tag.cfm.

The product layout uses two columns so that the product image is displayed to the side of the product information (figure 2.13). Our stylesheet (chapter-02/assets/css/app.css) already has all the column styles defined, so we only need to include the appropriate class names in our markup.

Listing 2.5   Adding product markup: chapter-02/product-markup.html

```
<main>
  <div class="row product">
    <div class="col">
      <figure>
        <img v-bind:src="product.image">    <-- The product's image path is
      </figure>                                  bound to the src of the img
    </div>                                       tag using a v-bind directive.
    <div class="col col-expand">
      <h1 v-text="product.title"></h1>
      <p v-text="product.description"></p>    Other product properties are
      <p v-text="product.price" class="price"></p>    displayed using the v-text directive.
    </div>
  </div>
</main>
```

One thing you'll notice right away is the use of JavaScript dot notation in the data bindings. Because product is an object, we must provide each binding with the entire path to a property. Most of the properties of our product data—title, description and price—are bound using the v-text directives, the same way we bound the sitename property in the header.

The product's image path introduces an *attribute binding*. We use the v-bind directive because element attributes cannot be bound using simple text interpolations. Any valid element attribute can be bound using the v-bind directive, but it's important to note that there are special cases for styles, class names, and other scenarios that we'll come to in future chapters.

NOTE You can use a shorthand for the v-bind directive. Instead of typing out v-bind every time you need to use it, you can remove the v-bind and type :, so instead of using v-bind:src=" ... ", you can type :src=" ... ".

Using expressions in bindings

We don't need to restrict our data bindings to properties of our data. Vue allows us to use any valid JavaScript expression inside any of our bindings. A few examples using the code from listing 2.5 might be:

```
{{ product.title.toUpperCase() }} -> CAT FOOD, 25LB BAG
{{ product.title.substr(4,4) }} -> Food
{{ product.price - (product.price * 0.25)  }} -> 1500
<img :src="product.image.replace('.png', '.jpg')"> -> <img src=" //assets/
images/product-fullsize.png">
```

Though using expressions in this way is convenient, it introduces logic into the view that's almost always better off inside the JavaScript code of the application or component responsible for the view's data. Additionally, expressions like this make it difficult to reason about where an application's data gets manipulated, especially as an application's complexity increases.

In general, using an inline expression is a great way to test something before formalizing that functionality within an application.

The next section and upcoming chapters introduce the best practices for manipulating, filtering, and deriving data from existing values without compromising the integrity of our views or application data. For details on what's considered an expression, please visit https://vuejs.org/v2/guide/syntax.html#Using-JavaScript-Expressions.

Let's flip over to Chrome, reload the page, and confirm that the product information is displayed as designed.

❶ Product description is not being interpreted as HTML.

❷ Price is not formatted.

Figure 2.13   Our product is displayed but has a few issues we need to clean up.

Uh oh, we've got a couple of things to work on:

1. The product description is being output as a string and isn't interpreting the HTML embedded in the description's value.

2. The product's price is displayed as a string representation of the integer `2000`, and not as a well-formatted dollar figure.

Let's solve that first issue first. What we need is an *HTML directive*, so let's update the product markup using the `v-html` binding to output the product's description as intended.

Listing 2.6   Adding product markup: chapter-02/product-markup-cont.html

```
<main>
  <div class="row product">
    <div class="col">
      <figure>
        <img v-bind:src="product.image">
      </figure>
    </div>
    <div class="col col-expand">
      <h1 v-text="product.title"></h1>
      <p v-html="product.description"></p>        ◄─┐ Uses an HTML directive to
      <p v-text="product.price" class="price"></p>  │ output the product description
    </div>                                            as HTML, not plain text
  </div>
</main>
```

Reloading the app in Chrome should now render the value of our product description as HTML and the emphasis tag should italicize the word "irresistible," as shown in figure 2.14.

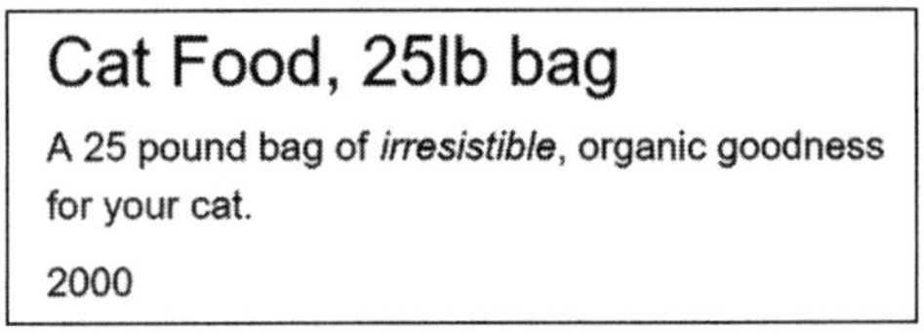

The `v-html` binding will render the bound property as raw HTML. This can be handy but should be used

> # Cat Food, 25lb bag
> A 25 pound bag of *irresistible*, organic goodness for your cat.
>
> 2000

Figure 2.14   Using the `v-html` binding allows us to display the description as raw HTML.

sparingly and only when the value is one you can trust. Now we need to fix the display of that pesky price value.

Cross-site scripting attacks

When we write code that inserts HTML directly into a view, we open our applications up to cross-site scripting (XSS) attacks.

At a high level, if a bad actor visits our site and saves malicious JavaScript in our database by using a form we haven't sanitized, we're vulnerable when we output that code to our HTML.

In general, best practice dictates that we should, at a minimum, follow basic principles regarding HTML and content:

- Only output trusted content when using HTML interpolations.
- Never output user-sourced content when using HTML interpolations, no matter how well-scrutinized the content is.
- If absolutely required, try to implement the feature using a component with its own template, rather than allow HTML elements in text inputs.

For a comprehensive, clear overview of XSS, start with this article at https://excess-xss.com/, and for a deeper understanding of attacks and sample code for each exploit, consult this OWASP wiki at www.owasp.org/index.php/Cross-site_Scripting _(XSS).

2.4 Applying output filters

The last thing left to do is to display our product's price in a familiar format, not as a raw integer. Output filters let us apply formatting to a value before it's displayed in our markup. The general format of an output filter is {{ property | filter }}. In our case, we want to format the product's price to look like $20.00, rather than 2000.

2.4.1 Write the filter function

Output filters are functions that receive a value, perform a formatting task, and return the formatted value for output. When used as part of a text interpolation, the value passed to the filter is the property we're binding to.

All our output filters reside in the `filters` object of the options we pass to our Vue instance, so that's where we'll add our price formatter in the following listing.

Listing 2.7 Adding the formatPrice filter: chapter-02/format-price.js

```
var webstore = new Vue({
  el: '#app',
  data: { ... },                     The filters option contains
  filters: {                         output filters.
    formatPrice: function(price) {              formatPrice takes an integer
      if (!parseInt(price)) { return ""; }      and formats a price value.
      if (price > 99999) {                      If we can't get an integer,
        var priceString = (price / 100).toFixed(2);   return immediately.
        var priceArray = priceString.split("").reverse();
        var index = 3;
        while (priceArray.length > index + 3) {
          priceArray.splice(index+3, 0, ",");       Adds commas every
          index += 4;                               three places
        }
        return "$" + priceArray.reverse().join("");
      } else {
```

Formats values $1,000 and up → (points to `if (price > 99999) {`)

Converts the value to a decimal → (points to `var priceString = (price / 100).toFixed(2);`)

Returns the formatted value → (points to `return "$" + priceArray.reverse().join("");`)

```
            return "$" + (price / 100).toFixed(2);      ◁──┐  If less than $1,000, returns
        }                                                   │  a formatted decimal value
      }
    }
  }
});
```

The `formatPrice` function takes an integer and returns a string formatted to look like a U.S. dollar value. Generically, it will return a value similar to $12,345.67. Depending on the size of the integer provided, the function branches as follows:

1 If the input is greater than 99,999 (the equivalent of $999.99), the output will require commas every three digits to the left of the decimal, so we need to process it accordingly.

2 Otherwise, the input can be converted using `.toFixed`, and returned because no commas are required.

NOTE You can find probably a gazillion ways to format a dollar figure that are more efficient, terse, or whatever quality you're searching for. Here, I've tried to favor clarity over expediency. For an idea of how complex the issue is, and how many solutions there are, dive into this post at http://mng.bz/qusZ.

2.4.2 *Adding the filter to our markup and testing different values*

To use our shiny new filter function, we need to add it to the binding for our product's price. We also need to update our price binding to use the Mustache-style binding to apply the filter, as shown next. Filters cannot be used with the `v-text` binding syntax.

Listing 2.8   Adding product markup: chapter-02/v-text-binding.html

```
<main>
  <div class="row product">
    <div class="col">
      <figure>
        <img v-bind:src="product.image">
      </figure>
    </div>
    <div class="col col-expand">
      <h1>{{ product.title }}</h1>
      <p v-html="product.description"></p>
      <p class="price">
        {{ product.price | formatPrice }}      Uses our new output filter to format
        </p>                                    the value of a product's price
    </div>
  </div>
</main>
```

Remember, bindings with filters have the generic form `{{ property | filter }}`, so we've updated our price binding accordingly, `{{ product.price | formatPrice }}`.

Cat Food, 25lb bag

A 25 pound bag of *irresistible*, organic goodness
for your cat.

$20.00

**Figure 2.15   Our price formatter adds a dollar
sign and the appropriate punctuation to the
display of our price property's value.**

Flip back over to Chrome, refresh, and voilà, we've got a formatted price as seen in
figure 2.15.

We can see how our filter is applied to different product price values in real time if
we tinker with our data in the console. To try different values, open the console and
set the value of `product.price` with a statement such as `webstore.product`
`.price = 150000000`,

Figure 2.16 shows what will occur after the product price is updated. Be sure to try
out small (< 100) and large (> 10000000) values to be sure each is formatted correctly.

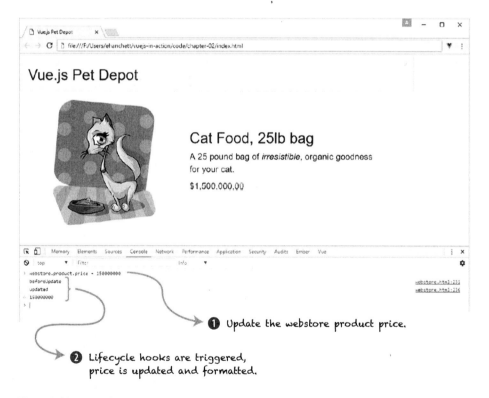

**Figure 2.16   Updating the product price triggers our lifecycle events (if you still have them
enabled), as well as an update to the price, which is now run through our filter function.**

Exercise

Use your knowledge from this chapter to answer this question:

> In section 2.4 we created a filter for the price. Can you think of any other filters that might be helpful?

See the solution in appendix B.

Summary

- Vue gives you the ability to add interactivity to your applications.
- At any time, we can hook into the Vue lifecycle to help perform certain functions.
- Vue.js offers powerful filters to help display information in a certain way.

Part 2

The View and ViewModel

The meat of this book lies in the View and ViewModel section. These chapters look deeper into Vue and all the elements and pieces that make up a Vue application. We'll start out simple and add interactivity to our application. We'll then move onto forms and inputs, conditionals, and looping.

Several of the most important concepts are in chapters 6 and 7, where we look at components in depth. These are truly the building blocks of our application. This is the first chapter where we'll see single-file components—a powerful tool in your Vue.js toolbelt.

The last two chapters will look at transitions, animations, and how to extend Vue. This will make our applications more efficient and look a little prettier.

Adding interactivity

This chapter covers

- Deriving new output from data with computed properties
- Adding event bindings to the DOM
- Observing data during the update portion of the Vue lifecycle
- Responding to user interaction
- Conditionally rendering markup

Believe it or not, now that we've got our first product all wired up, we're ready to add interaction to our webstore.

Adding interactivity to an application means binding to DOM events, responding to them in application code, and providing feedback to users about what happened because of their actions. Vue creates and manages all the event and data bindings for us, but there are decisions we need to make about how to manipulate data within our application, as well as how to meet user expectations in our interface.

We'll begin exploring user interaction by letting customers add our single product to a shopping cart, but along the way we'll also look at how our work fits into the overall picture of a Vue application.

To get a feel for where we're headed in this chapter, figure 3.1 shows how the application will look when all our work is done.

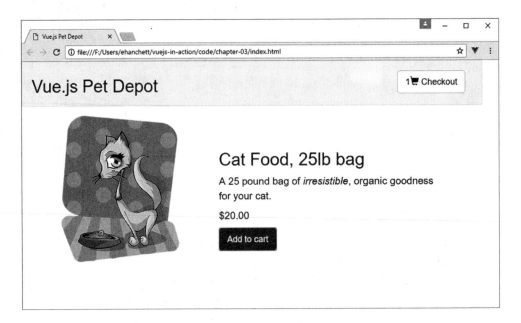

Figure 3.1　Our product listing with new elements: a shopping cart and an Add to cart button.

3.1　*Shopping cart data starts with adding an array*

Before we can build any of our super-cool shopping cart functionality, we'll need a container to hold all those items in our application instance. Fortunately, all we need at this stage is a simple array, onto which we'll push our products.

I've broken up the code into small snippets, similar to the way we did it in the last chapter. You'll need to add these to your index.html file that you created last chapter to continue the application. You can always download the code for this chapter if needed.

Listing 3.1　All we need is an array: chapter-03/add-array.js

```
data: {
  sitename: "Vue.js Pet Depot",
  product: {
    id: 1001,
```
Shows our existing product data, for reference

```
    title: "Cat Food, 25lb bag",
    description: "A 25 pound bag of <em>irresistible</em>,
                  organic goodness for your cat.",
    price: 2000,
    image: "assets/images/product-fullsize.png",
  },
  cart: []
},
...
```

Shows our existing product data, for reference

Shows an array for holding cart items

That gives us our shopping cart . . . done. In all seriousness, though, we'll get good mileage out of this simple array, but eventually we'll create a cart component that will manage its contents internally.

> **REMEMBER** You need to add a comma after product in listing 3.1 before you add the cart array. Forgetting to add one will throw an error in the console and is a common gotcha. (An error I'm well acquainted with!)

3.2 Binding to DOM events

To add interaction to our application, we need to bind elements of the DOM to functions we define in our Vue instance. We can bind an element to any standard DOM event—click, mouseup, keyup, and so on—by using an *event binding*. Vue takes care of all the wiring under the hood, so we can stay focused on how our application reacts to an event when it occurs.

3.2.1 Event binding basics

Event bindings use the v-on directive to bind a snippet of JavaScript, or a function, to a DOM element, as shown in figure 3.2. The bound code or function gets executed when the specified DOM event is triggered.

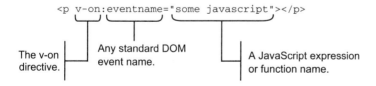

Figure 3.2   The syntax of an event binding.

Here are two common patterns for an event binding's JavaScript:

1 *Using a function name, we can bind an event to a function we define in our instance.* If we had a binding such as v-on:click="clickHappened", a click on our element would call the function clickHappened.

2   *We can write inline JavaScript that acts on an exposed property.* In this case, the binding might look like `v-on:keyup="charactersRemaining -= 1"`, which would decrease the `charactersRemaining` property by one.

Each strategy has its place in an application, but first we're going to look at using a function to handle an event.

> **NOTE**   An easier shorthand way to write the `v-on` directive exists. Instead of using `v-on`, you can replace it with the @ symbol. For example, if you want to use `v-on:click="..."` you could replace that with `@click="..."` instead. We'll use this shorthand later in the book.

3.2.2   Bind an event to the Add to cart button

For a customer to add products to their shopping cart, they need a button. We'll instruct Vue to bind that button's click event to a function that handles pushing a product onto the `cart` array.

Before we add the button to our markup, we should write our function. To do so, we need to add a `methods` object to our application's options. After the `filters` object, add this code. (Don't forget a comma after the `filters` object!)

Listing 3.2   The `addToCart` method: chapter-03/add-to-cart.js

```
methods: {
  addToCart: function() {                         Defines the       The methods
    this.cart.push( this.product.id );            addToCart         object contains
  }                                               function          our new function.
}
```

For now, adding a product to the cart means pushing the product's `id` property from the product data onto the `cart` array. Keep in mind, you'll need to add the `this` keyword to access all data properties.

Pushing the id, not the object

It may seem simpler to push the entire product object onto our `cart` array in the code from listing 3.2—`this.cart.push( this.product );`—but if we did, things would get a bit awkward. JavaScript is neither a pure pass-by-reference language, nor a pure pass-by-copy language, so it takes a bit of practice to know when one or the other will occur.

Pushing the product onto the `cart` array would push a reference to the product object defined in our data, not a copy. If the product definition in our data changes, perhaps when we retrieve new product data from the server, it might be replaced in the cart or the reference may become `undefined`.

By pushing the product `id` onto the `cart` array instead, we push a copy of the value of our product's `id`, not a reference. If the product definition changes, the value(s) in the `cart` array remain unaltered.

Technically speaking, JavaScript is a call-by-sharing language. You can find a brief explanation of call-by-sharing, and how it compares to other strategies, on Wikipedia at https://en.wikipedia.org/wiki/Evaluation_strategy#Call_by_sharing.

Now we've got a function that will add products to our cart so we can go ahead and add button markup. Right after the price markup in our product `div`, add the button from this listing.

Listing 3.3　A button to add products to the cart: chapter-03/button-product.js

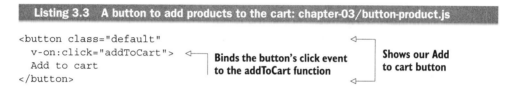

```
<button class="default"
  v-on:click="addToCart">
  Add to cart
</button>
```

Binds the button's click event to the addToCart function

Shows our Add to cart button

Now, when a visitor clicks this button, the `addToCart` function is called. Time to give it a whirl.

Head over to Chrome, ensure that the console is open, and switch to the Vue tab because we'll want to peek at the data that's added to our shopping cart. The `cart` array should be empty, so if you don't see `Array[0]` as shown in figure 3.3, go ahead and reload the page.

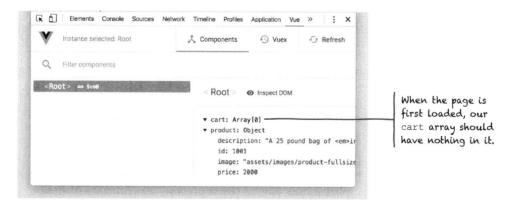

When the page is first loaded, our `cart` array should have nothing in it.

Figure 3.3　An empty array is what we should see before any products are added. If it's not empty, go ahead and reload the page.

Now, click the Add to cart button a few times. Open the vue-devtools pane and click `<Root>`. You should see the product's `id` getting pushed onto the array with each click as seen in figure 3.4.

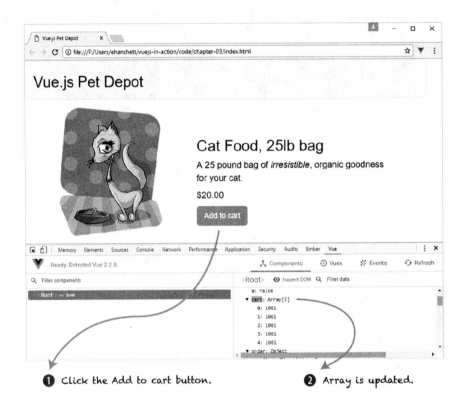

① Click the Add to cart button. ② Array is updated.

Figure 3.4   The array fills up as you add items to the cart.

Seeing how many items are in the shopping cart using vue-devtools or the console may be okay for developers, but customers will need feedback in the view itself. Time to add an item counter.

3.3   *Adding a cart item button and count*

To display the number of items a customer has in the shopping cart, we'll use a *computed property*. Computed properties can be bound to the DOM like any other property defined by our instance, but they typically provide functionality to derive new information from the current state of an application. In addition, we'll add a cart item button that will display our checkout cart.

Before we add an item count to our shopping cart, let's take a more general look at computed properties and how they work.

3.3.1 When to use a computed property

It might help to think of the properties in the data object as representing data we'd store in a database and computed properties as dynamic values that are used primarily within the context of our view. This may be an overly broad characterization, but it serves as a good first rule of thumb.

Let's consider a common example of a computed property that displays a user's full name, as shown in listing 3.4. It makes sense to store someone's first and last names as separate entities in a database, but it would be redundant and error prone to also store their full name. If the need to display a user's full name arose, combining the first and last name from existing data is a perfect use case for a computed property.

Listing 3.4   Computing a user's full name: chapter-03/computed.js

```
computed: {
  fullName: function() {
    return [this.firstName, this.lastName].join(' ');
  }
}
```
fullName returns the value of a user's first and last name, joined by a single space.

The result returned by the fullName function is conceptually equivalent to having a fullName property in our data object, which means we can easily bind to it in our markup (see figure 3.5).

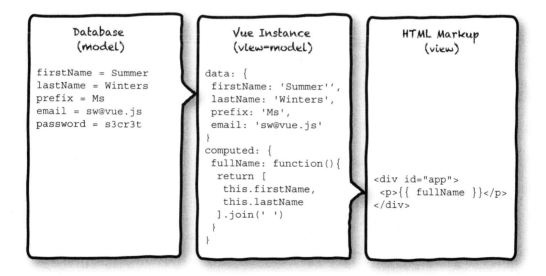

Figure 3.5   Combining the user's first and last name from a dataset into a full name for display.

One additional benefit of using computed properties is that we can change the internals of our function to use different or additional data from our application. In figure 3.5, for example, we could use the `prefix` property to add more formality to a user's full name.

Using computed properties in this way, we can combine, or otherwise manipulate, any instance data without requiring changes to the backend or the database.

3.3.2   *Examining update events with computed properties*

Because computed properties are typically calculated using instance data, their return value is updated automatically when the underlying data changes. Any view markup bound to the computed property will therefore update to reflect the new value as well.

This behavior is at the heart of the update cycle within the greater Vue instance lifecycle. To get a feel for how the update cycle behaves, let's work through another example of when a computed property is a perfect fit for the job. Consider the task of computing the area of a rectangle, based on its length and width.

Listing 3.5   Computing the area of a rectangle: chapter-03/computed-rect.js

```
new Vue({
  data: {
    length: 5,          Shows a data object that contains
    width: 3            length and width properties
  },
  computed: {
    area: function() {            Shows a computed property
      return this.length * this.width;   that exposes area the same
    }                                     as a data property
  }
});
```

The computed property `area` will have an initial value of 15. Any subsequent change to `length` or `width` reactively triggers a series of updates to the application:

1 When the value of `length` or `width` is changed . . .
2 . . . the computed property `area` is recalculated . . .
3 . . . then any markup bound to these properties is updated.

Figure 3.6 shows the update cycle of the application.

We can see the lifecycle in action by using *watch functions* to observe when the data in an instance changes, and the `beforeUpdate` lifecycle hook, which should be executed only after the data changes.

> **INFO**   A watch function works the same way as a lifecycle hook but is triggered when the data it's "watching" is updated. We can even create a watch function to observe a computed property.

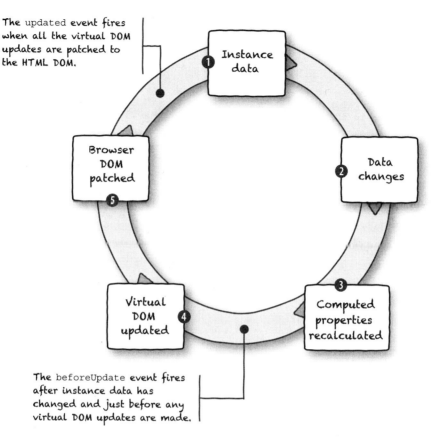

The updated event fires when all the virtual DOM updates are patched to the HTML DOM.

1 Instance data

2 Data changes

3 Computed properties recalculated

4 Virtual DOM updated

5 Browser DOM patched

The beforeUpdate event fires after instance data has changed and just before any virtual DOM updates are made.

Figure 3.6 Changes in an instance's data trigger a cascade of activity within the update cycle of an application.

Listing 3.6 puts our area calculation in the context of a complete application. The application also contains three watch functions that log messages to the console whenever length, width, or area change, and one function to log when the update cycle begins. These functions must be specified in the watch option of the Vue instance for them to work.

TIP You can find the code for this listing in the samples that accompany this chapter in the file chapter-03/area.html. It's entirely self-contained, so you can open it directly in Chrome.

Listing 3.6 Computed properties and update event logging: chapter-03/area.html

```
<html>
<head>
```

```
    <title>Calculating Area - Vue.js in Action</title>
    <script src="https://unpkg.com/vue/dist/vue.js"
      type="text/javascript"></script>
  </head>
<body>
  <div id="app">
    <p>
      Area is equal to: {{ area }}
    </p>
    <p>
      <button v-on:click="length += 1">Add length</button>
      <button v-on:click="width += 1">Add width</button>
    </p>
  </div>
  <script type="text/javascript">
    var app = new Vue({
      el: '#app',
      data: {
        length: 5,
        width: 3
      },
      computed: {
        area: function() {
          return this.width * this.length;
        }
      },
      watch: {
        length: function(newVal, oldVal) {
          console.log('The old value of length was: '
                      + oldVal +
                      '\nThe new value of length is: '
                      + newVal);
        },
        width: function(newVal, oldVal) {
          console.log('The old value of width was: '
                      + oldVal +
                      '\nThe new value of width is: '
                      + newVal);
        },
        area: function(newVal, oldVal) {
          console.log('The old value of area was: '
                      + oldVal +
                      '\nThe new value of area is: '
                      + newVal);
        }
      },
      beforeUpdate: function() {
        console.log('All those data changes happened '
                    + 'before the output gets updated.');
      }
    });
  </script>
</body>
</html>
```

Lists the data binding that displays the value of area

Shows the buttons that increase the value of length or width by 1, respectively

Shows the original values for length and width

Gives the area computed property

Shows the function that logs when length changes

Shows the function that logs when width changes

Shows the function that logs when area changes

Lists the beforeUpdate lifecycle hook function

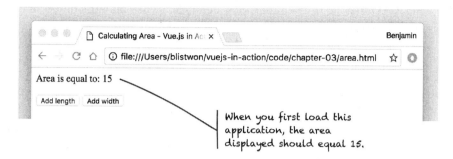

Figure 3.7   The initial state of our area calculating application.

When you load this file in Chrome, you'll see an initial value for area is 15 as seen in figure 3.7. Be sure the JavaScript console is open, then try clicking the buttons to trigger the update cycle. The console should log messages about the application's data when the Add length button and Add width button are clicked (see figure 3.8).

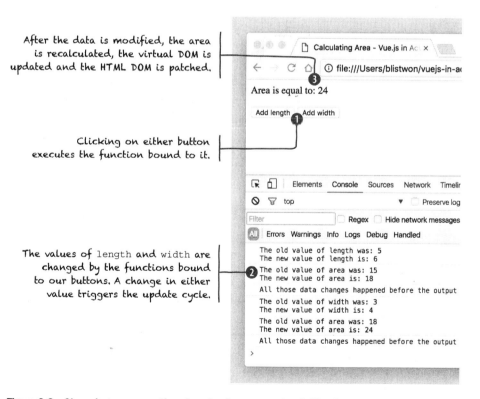

Figure 3.8   Observing our properties changing in response to clicking buttons.

Now that we've seen how the application behaves, we can map the data and functions from listing 3.6 onto our diagram of the update cycle in figure 3.9.

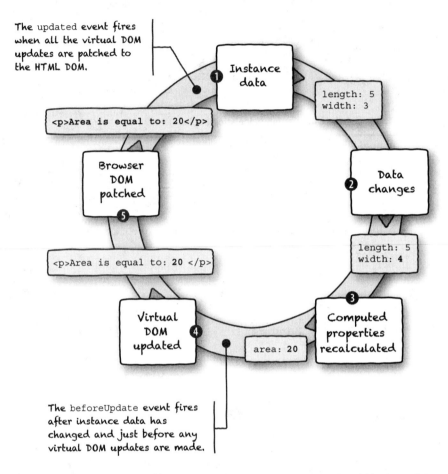

The updated **event fires when all the virtual DOM updates are patched to the HTML DOM.**

Instance data

length: 5
width: 3

<p>Area is equal to: 20</p>

Browser
DOM
patched

Data
changes

length: 5
width: 4

<p>Area is equal to: 20 </p>

Virtual
DOM
updated

area: 20

Computed
properties
recalculated

The beforeUpdate **event fires after instance data has changed and just before any virtual DOM updates are made.**

Figure 3.9   Changes in an instance's data trigger a cascade of activity within the update cycle of an application.

One last thing to note, if you remove the {{ area }} binding from the sample code, and reload the page in your browser, you'll see a difference in the console output when you click either button (see figure 3.10).

With no outlet for the computed property, there's nothing to update, and therefore no reason to enter the update cycle. The beforeUpdate function won't be executed and the corresponding message won't be logged to the console.

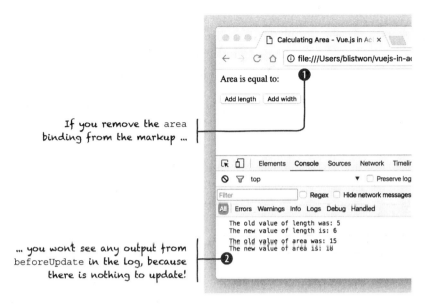

If you remove the area
binding from the markup ...

... you won't see any output from
beforeUpdate in the log, because
there is nothing to update!

Figure 3.10   No update message displays if nothing gets updated.

3.3.3   Displaying a cart item count and testing

Now that we have a good understanding of computed properties, let's look at our shopping cart example again. Let's add a computed property to our Vue instance that will display the number of items in the shopping cart, as shown in the following listing. Don't forget to add a computed object to the options object, so our function will have a place to live.

Listing 3.7   The cartItemCount's computed property: chapter-03/cart-item-count.js

```
computed: {
  cartItemCount: function() {
    return this.cart.length || '';
  }
},
```

Adds a computed object

Returns a count of items in the cart array

This is a straightforward use of a computed property. We use an existing JavaScript property—length—of an array to retrieve our count, because it's really not necessary to add our own counting mechanism for the shopping cart.

This is also a good example of why it's inappropriate to store this kind of data as a property of the data object. Because the value of cartItemCount is the result of user interaction, and not something that came from a database, we wouldn't expect to see it in our data object.

It's worth noting that there are times when such an item count might be in the data object. For example, if a user was looking at a "previous orders" page, there might be an item count associated with each order. This is consistent with our thinking so far, because that data would come from the database after an order had been processed and persisted.

Function in place, we're ready to add a little bit of HTML to our application's header so that we have a shopping cart and a place to display the item count. Update the markup in the header as shown here.

Listing 3.8   Adding the cart indicator: chapter-03/cart-indicator.html

```
<header>
  <div class="navbar navbar-default">
    <h1>{{ sitename }}</h1>
  </div>
  <div class="nav navbar-nav navbar-right cart">          ⟵┐ Aligns our cart
    <span                                                       to the right
class="glyphicon glyphicon-shopping-cart">              ┐ Shows the data binding that
{{ cartItemCount }}</span>                              ⟵┘ displays the computed property
  </div>
</header>
```

We add a new `div` element to the header so we have a place for our cart, and we use the `cartItemCount` binding to display the value of our computed property. The binding is surrounded by a `span` element, which is used as a style hook to add a cart icon next to our counter. It's time to test things out.

After reloading the webstore application in Chrome, clicking Add to cart should cause the indicator to increase with each click. You can double-check that the count is correct by examining the `cart` array in the console once again (see figure 3.11).

Figure 3.11 Observing change in our application's header and inspecting the cart in the console.

3.4 Adding user affordance to our button

People bring a wide variety of experience and expectation with them when they arrive at a website or use a web application. One of the most fundamental, and deeply ingrained, is that when an interactive element behaves differently than expected, a product can feel broken or disorienting. The idea behind *user affordance* is to provide visual (or other) cues and feedback to a user that keeps our application consistent with their expectations.

> **INFO** For more information on user affordance and its importance in the experience of digital products, start at the Interaction Design Foundation at http://mng.bz/Xv96.

We now have a button that lets a customer endlessly add a product to their shopping cart. There may be many reasons to limit the number of items a customer can purchase: limited available product, restrictions on per-customer purchases, quantity discounts, and so on. If there's a limited quantity, then the Add to cart button should become unavailable at some point or otherwise indicate that the action is no longer possible.

To accomplish this task, we need to track our available inventory, compare it against how many instances of a product are in the shopping cart, and act to keep customers from adding more products than there are available. Let's start with tracking the inventory.

3.4.1 Keeping an eye on inventory

To keep a customer from buying too many of a given product, we'll need to add a new property to our product object, as shown in the following listing. The `available-Inventory` property will represent how many individual units of a product our store has available.

Listing 3.9 Adding `availableInventory` to our product:
chapter-03/available-inventory.js

```
data: {
  sitename: "Vue.js Pet Depot",
  product: {
    id: 1001
    title: "Cat Food, 25lb bag",
    description: "A 25 pound bag of <em>irresistible</em>,
                organic goodness for your cat.",
    price: 2000,
    image: "assets/images/product-fullsize.png",
    availableInventory: 5                          ⟵⟍ Adds the availableInventory property
  }                                                   ⎁ after our other product data
  cart: []
}
```

It's still necessary to double-check product availability when a purchase is being finalized—in case another customer has purchased one or more of the same product in the middle of a transaction—but we can implement a simple solution in our application to greatly reduce the chance a user will be disappointed later by hiding, or disabling, the Add to cart button.

> **WARNING**   Never rely on values from the client when it comes to transactions, financial or otherwise. The backend of your application should always interpret the incoming data as expressing the user's intent, not reality.

3.4.2 *Working with computed properties and inventory*

We don't want to mutate the `availableInventory` value, because that represents a fixed value that should be updated only by a process that manages actual inventory (something we'll come back to much later in the book). But we do want to restrict the amount of product a customer can add to their shopping cart based on the value of `availableInventory`.

To do this, we need a way to keep track of the number of items in a customer's shopping cart relative to the fixed amount of product available. We'll use a computed property to perform this calculation in real-time, as a customer adds items to their shopping cart.

**Listing 3.10   A computed property for remaining inventory:
                 chapter-03/computed-remaining.js**

```
computed: {
  cartItemCount: function() {                    Uses the
    return this.cart.length || '';            canAddToCart        Compares availableInventory
  },                                       computed property      to the number of items
  canAddToCart: function() {                       ◁              already in the cart
    return this.product.availableInventory > this.cartItemCount;        ◁
  }
}
```

Because our code can consume computed properties in the same way as properties of our instance data, we get a chance to leverage one computed property, `cartItem-Count`, within another. Our new computed property checks to see whether the available inventory is greater than the number of items already in the shopping cart. If not, that means the customer has added the maximum number of products to their cart, and we'll have to act to keep them from adding more.

"Truthiness" in JavaScript

As you may already be aware, evaluating the truth value of an expression in JavaScript can be a bit tricky. Here's a quick example you can try in a console for yourself.

When using the non-strict equality operator `==`, the integer value `1` compared to the string value `"1"` evaluates to `true`. This occurs because JavaScript, attempting to be "helpful," does a type conversion before the comparison is evaluated. Using the strict equality operator `===` produces the expected `false` result.

In our `canAddToCart` function, we use the greater than operator `>` to compare two integer values. If we had any doubt about where those values came from, or if they were in fact integers, we could force the conversion using the `parseInt` method or otherwise ensuring the values are integers.

Much has been written about JavaScript's type conversions and equality operators, but perhaps the most illuminating reference is this series of diagrams on the topic at https://dorey.github.io/JavaScript-Equality-Table/. Be sure to compare (hah!) the `==` and `===` tabs.

3.4.3 *v-show directive basics*

Now that we have a mechanism to determine whether a customer can take the Add to cart action, let's make the interface respond accordingly. The `v-show` directive renders markup if, and only if, the specified condition evaluates to `true`. Adding it to our existing button results in the button being hidden from the DOM if our `canAddToCart` property returns `false`, shown here.

Listing 3.11   Button with `v-show` directive: chapter-03/button-v-show.html

```
<button class="default"
    v-on:click="addToCart"
    v-show="canAddToCart"
    >Add to cart</button>
```

The v-show directive is bound to our **canAddToCart computed property.**

If you reload the application in Chrome and try adding six products to your shopping cart, the button should disappear on the fifth click, because that's the value of `availableInventory` as seen in figure 3.12.

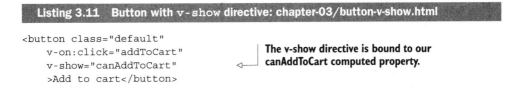

1 Five items in shopping cart.

5🛒 Checkout

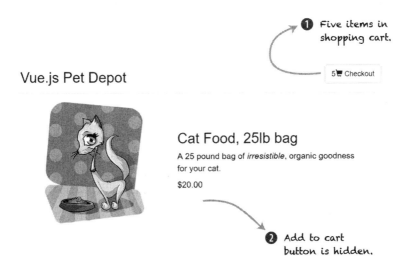

Vue.js Pet Depot

Cat Food, 25lb bag

A 25 pound bag of *irresistible*, organic goodness for your cat.

$20.00

2 Add to cart button is hidden.

Figure 3.12   The Add to cart button is hidden when we exhaust the available inventory.

The v-show directive works a bit differently than other directives we've encountered so far. When the expression evaluates to false, Vue sets the element's display CSS property to none as an inline style. This effectively hides the element (and its contents) from view, though it's still present in the DOM. If the result of the expression later changes to true, the inline style is removed and the element is once again shown to the user.

> **NOTE** One side effect of this behavior is that any inline declaration of display you had will be overwritten. But have no fear, Vue will restore the original value when it removes its own display:none. Still, it's best to avoid inline styles wherever possible in favor of class definitions in your stylesheet.

One other thing to keep in mind is that the v-show directive is most effective when bound to a single element, rather than several adjacent elements. Here's an example.

Listing 3.12 Wrapping content for v-show: chapter-03/wrap-content.html

```
// Avoid this
<p v-show="showMe">Some text</p>          Avoid using the v-show directive
<p v-show="showMe">Some more text</p>     on adjacent elements.
<p v-show="showMe">Even more text</p>

// Prefer this
<div v-show="showMe">
  <p>Some text</p>                        Instead, wrap adjacent
  <p>Some more text</p>                    elements, and use a single
  <p>Even more text</p>                    v-show directive.
</div>
```

To be clear, it's okay to use v-show throughout your application wherever you need to. Whenever possible it's best to aggregate multiple elements that will respond reactively to data, both for better performance and to reduce the chance of forgetting to keep all your elements up-to-date if you make a change. Removing the Add to cart button when inventory is exhausted certainly works, but it's a bit drastic. Let's try another way.

3.4.4 *Using v-if and v-else to display a disabled button*

Removing the Add to cart button certainly keeps a customer from adding too many product instances to the cart, but it's a bit heavy-handed. It might be more informative to the user to render the button disabled, because that doesn't disrupt the continuity of the interface as much and it preserves the layout flow.

The v-if and v-else directives are used to display one of two choices based on the truth value of the provided expression. We'll use canAddToCart as a condition to evaluate, the way we did in the previous example.

In figure 3.13 you can see how the v-if directive works. If the canAddToCart is true the button appears, if not, the button doesn't appear.

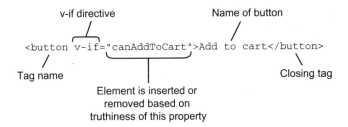

Figure 3.13 Diagram explaining how the v-if directive conditional works.

In this listing we can see how this works with our v-if and v-else directives.

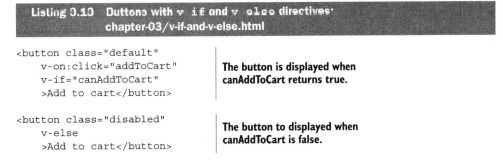

When using v-if and v-else together, we need two elements in our markup, one for when the condition is true and one for when it's false. Additionally, the two elements need to be listed one directly after the other in the markup for Vue to bind to them correctly.

In listing 3.13 we use two different button elements:

- If canAddToCart returns true, we render our familiar button, with the addToCart event binding, and the default CSS class.
- If canAddToCart returns false, we render a button with no event binding so that it becomes unclickable and with a disabled CSS class so that its appearance changes accordingly.

This time, when you try out the application in Chrome, the button should switch the active button (figure 3.14) to the disabled button once you've added five products to the shopping cart.

With the v-if and v-else directives, Vue.js removes the element from the DOM (the false condition) and removes it from the other (the true condition). All of this is accomplished as part of a single, simultaneous update to the DOM. Try it out by fiddling with the value of availableInventory in the console and keeping an eye on the display property of these elements.

Figure 3.14 Using `v-if` and `v-else` means we can render a disabled button, rather than making it disappear entirely when the inventory is exhausted.

As with the `v-show` directive, it's important to have a single containing element to attach `v-if` and `v-else` to, especially with the added criterion that the `v-else` markup must remain adjacent to the `v-if` markup, as shown here.

Listing 3.14 Single container elements for `v-if` and `v-else`
chapter-03/single-container.html

```
// This won't work
<p v-if="showMe">The if text</p>       This won't work; v-if and v-else are broken
<p>Some text related to the if text</p>  up by the second paragraph element.
<p v-else>The else text</p>

// Nor will this
<div>
  <p v-if="showMe">The if text</p>     This won't work; v-if and
</div>                                  v-else are not adjacent in
<div>                                   the markup.
  <p v-else>The else text</p>
</div>

// Instead, consider grouping
<div v-if="showMe">
  <p>The if text</p>
  <p>Some text related to the if text</p>  This will work; wrap related
</div>                                       content in an element, then bind
<div v-else>                                 v-if and v-else to that element.
  <p>The else text</p>
</div>
```

Keeping all the DOM elements for a given condition within an outer element—used as a grouping container—is the goal here. Later, we'll explore different strategies that use templates or components to isolate the markup for conditionals, greatly simplifying the amount of markup needed in the main application itself.

3.4.5 Adding the cart item button as a toggle

Let's add a button for the checkout page. We'll begin by adding a new method and property to our application.

Listing 3.15   Adding the cart button: chapter-03/cart-button.js

```
data: {
  showProduct: true,        ◁──┐ This property tracks whether
  ...                          │ to show product page.
},
methods: {
  ...
  showCheckout() {                                           ◁── The showCheckout method
      this.showProduct = this.showProduct ? false : true;    ◁──────── is triggered after clicking
  },                                                                   the cart button.
}
```

The showCheckout method is triggered after clicking the cart button.

Shows the ternary operation that toggles between true and false

The new `showProduct` property will toggle the display of the checkout page. Let's look at that in more detail. The `showCheckout` method toggles the `showProduct` property by using something called a ternary operation in JavaScript. The *ternary operator* is a shortcut for the `if` statement and takes three parameters. The first parameter is the condition, in this case, `this.showProduct`. If it resolves to true, it then returns the first expression, `false`. Otherwise it returns the last expression, `true`. The ternary conditional operator is a useful tool to have in your back pocket when you need to create a quick conditional statement.

You may have noticed that the method definition was missing the `function()` declaration after `showCheckout()`. ES6, also known as ES2015, allows for a shorter syntax for method definitions. We'll use this syntax for our method definitions throughout the rest of the book.

We now need to add the button to our view and bind it to a click event.

Listing 3.16   Adding the cart button: chapter-03/add-cart-button.html

```
<div class="nav navbar-nav navbar-right cart">
    <button type="button"
        class="btn btn-default btn-lg"
        v-on:click="showCheckout">            ◁──┐ A click event added to
      <span                                      │ button triggers the
class="glyphicon glyphicon-shopping-cart">       │ showCheckout method.
{{ cartItemCount}}</span>
    </span>
      Checkout
    </button>
  </div>
```

When the button is clicked, the `showCheckout` method will fire, causing the `show-Product` method to toggle, or flip, between states. The checkout button is important because we need somewhere to put our checkout information. We'll look at this more in the next section.

3.4.6 *Using v-if to display a checkout page*

Our application is limited. It only shows one product on one page. To make it more complete we need another page that displays checkout information. We can do this many different ways. In chapter 7, we'll learn about components which give us a way to easily break down our application into smaller reusable pieces. This could be one way of adding a checkout page.

Another way is to wrap our view in a v-if directive and bind it to the showProduct property we created earlier. We'll need to add the v-if directive to the top of index file after the main and div elements, as shown in this listing.

> **Listing 3.17   Using v-if to display a checkout page: chapter-03/v-if-checkout.html**

```
<main>
  <div class="row product">
    <div v-if="showProduct">                    ◁──┐  v-if directive that will display
...                                                  if showProduct is true.
    </div>                            ◁──┐
    <div v-else>                          │ Shows the product listing for
                                          │ the view, including the picture
    </div>                                  of the product and description
  </div> <!--end of row-->                    ◁──┐ This is where the
</main> <!--end of main-->                        checkout page will go.
```

Earlier in the chapter, we created a checkout button. When this button is pressed, the showProduct property will toggle, from true to false, or false to true. This will trigger the v-if directive in listing 3.17. Either the product information that we've been creating in this chapter will show, or a blank screen will display with only the top navigation at the top (figure 3.15).

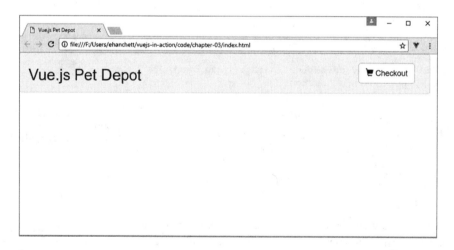

Figure 3.15   View of webstore after checkout button is pressed. Pressing the checkout button again shows the product page.

For now, don't worry about the blank page that we see in figure 3.15. This will be taken care of in the next chapter when we look into different types of input bindings.

3.4.7 Comparing v-show with v-if/v-else

Both techniques—v-show and v-if/v-else—have advantages and disadvantages, for a user and for us as developers. As we know, the v-show directive hides or shows an element using CSS, while the v-if/v-else directive removes the content from the DOM. With that said, understanding when to use one or the other depends mostly on what we're trying to achieve, so perhaps the best way to compare them is to think about a few use cases for each.

The v-show directive is best suited to scenarios where there's no "else" case. That is, when you have markup to show if a condition is true and no alternative content to show when it's false. Here are several possible use cases where v-show is the right choice.

- A message banner for things that are temporal, such as an announcement of a sale or a change in the Terms & Conditions.
- A signup advertisement, or other inducement, when a visitor isn't logged in.
- Paging elements for lists that run across multiple pages, which would be superfluous if there were only one page.

The v-if and v-else directives are the right choice when one of two chunks of markup should be rendered, but *at least* one of them should always be showing. If there's no fallback (else) case, then v-show is more appropriate. Here are several scenarios where v-if and v-else should be used:

- Showing a Log in link for logged out users, versus a Log out link for those who are logged in
- Rendering conditional sections of a form, such as country-specific address fields based on a selection made by a user. For example, a U.S. address form shows a "state" field, where a Canadian address form shows it as a "province."
- Search results listings versus placeholder content when no search has been conducted. (We'll explore an example that adds a third state, using v-else-if, in a later chapter.)

Endless scenarios exist where you'll need to use one conditional or the other. Perhaps the best way to think about which one fits your needs is to consider whether there's a fallback, or default, chunk of content you want to display. Next up, we're going to make our webstore a little more useful to potential customers by offering more than a single bag of cat food.

Exercise

Use your knowledge from this chapter to answer this question:

> Earlier in the chapter we looked at computed properties and methods. What are the differences between them?

See the solution in appendix B.

Summary

- Presenting data that isn't inside the data object using a computed property.
- Conditionally showing parts of our application with a `v-if` and `v-else` directive.
- Adding more functionality to our application with methods.

Forms and inputs

Our application has evolved substantially since chapter 1. We've created items and allowed users to add items to a cart. We now need a way for our customers to check out and enter their information. Let's add input forms to our application so the customer can enter their address and billing information into the app. Then we need to save this information in our app for later use.

To accomplish our goal, we must bind the form data to our model in our application. The v-model directive was made for this use case.

DEFINITION The v-model directive creates a two-way data binding between form or text area inputs and the template. This assures data in our application model will always be in sync with our UI.

Two-way data binding vs. one-way data binding

In practice, two-way data binding (figure 4.1) may, or may not, be the best solution. In certain instances, data will never need to change after it's captured from user input. Other frameworks and libraries such as React and Angular 2 have chosen one-way data bindings by default. Angular 1 started with two-way binding and dropped it for performance management reasons when building Angular 2. One-way data binding occurs when data captured isn't synced from the model to the view when the input changes. Additional logic needs to be added for the values to change in the model or view. Ember.js decided to stick with two-way data binding by default. With the v-model directive, the data is bound two ways. Regardless, we can specify a property as one-way bound in Vue using the v-once directive.

The v-once directive renders an element or component once only. On any additional re-renders, the element or component will be treated as static content and skipped. To learn more about the v-once directive, check out the official API documentation at https://vuejs.org/v2/api/#v-once.

Later in the book we'll discuss component properties and how they can be passed to other components. These properties form a one-way-down binding between the parent property and the child one. This will become useful in the future.

The v-model directive was made to work with all sorts of form inputs, including text boxes, text areas, check boxes, radio buttons, and select drop-down controls. We'll need all these elements to build our new checkout form. Let's look at using the v-model directive and how it works with binding inputs.

4.1   *Using v-model binding*

Model binding in our applications will help us update data on our user inputs with our template. In our application, we've worked primar-

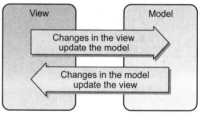

Figure 4.1   **The model updates the view while the view updates the model.**

ily with the Vue data object to display static information. Interaction with the application has been limited to a few button-click events. We need to add a way for users to fill in their shipping information at checkout. To keep track of the form inputs, we'll use the v-model directive and basic input bindings to add more reactivity to the application.

Before we begin, you might be wondering what the differences are between the v-model directive and the v-bind directive that we used in chapter 2. Keep in mind that the v-model directive is used mainly for input and form binding. We'll use the v-model directive in this chapter to bind our text inputs for our checkout page. The v-bind directive is mostly used to bind HTML attributes. We could use v-bind on an src attribute on an <img> tag or bind it to the class attribute on a <div> tag for example. Both are useful, yet they're used in different situations. We'll look at the v-bind directive in more detail later in the chapter.

It's worth mentioning that the v-model directive uses the v-bind directive behind the scenes. Let's say you had <input v-model="something">. The v-model directive is syntactic sugar for <input v-bind:"something" v-on:input="something=$event.target.value">. Regardless, using the v-model directive is much easier to type and understand.

In figure 4.2 we see how the v-model directive is broken down. It is added to the input and creates a two-way data bound object.

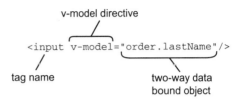

To begin, we'll need to add new HTML to our application. Open the index.html page that you created in the last two chapters and look for the v-else directive (or you can download the supplied index.html file for chapter 3).

Figure 4.2 Up close with the v-model directive

Inside this <div> tag we'll add the HTML code in this chapter. In chapter 7 we'll discuss a better way of breaking up our application into components. For now, we'll use the simple v-if directive as a toggle to display our checkout page.

As with the previous chapters, each code snippet is split into its own file. Please combine this with the index.html to create a completed application.

Listing 4.1   A v-model directive with first and last name inputs: chapter-04/first-last.html

```
<div class="col-md-6">
  <strong>First Name:</strong>
  <input v-model="order.firstName"
    class="form-control"/>
</div>
<div class="col-md-6">
  <strong>Last Name:</strong>
  <input v-model="order.lastName"
    class="form-control"/>   //#A
</div>
<div class="col-md-12 verify">
  <pre>
    First Name:  {{order.firstName}}
    Last Name:   {{order.lastName}}
  </pre>
</div>
```

The firstName and lastName are bound using v-model.

The firstName and lastName properties are displayed in real time as values change in input.

The code creates two text boxes for the first and last name and each text box is bound to a property that's synced in real time. These properties are created in the data object. To make this easier, we'll use an order property to keep these values saved in our Vue instance data object. This will be added to the index.html file.

In the data object, we'll need to add our new order property. We need this order property so we can keep track of the first and last names. Add the following code to the existing index.html data object that we used from the previous chapter.

Listing 4.2   The Vue instance data object `order` property: chapter-04/data-property.js

```
data: {
  sitename: 'Vue.js Pet Depot',
  showProduct: true,
  order: {
    firstName: '',
    lastName: ''
  },
```

The `order` object in this listing is in the data object inside the Vue constructor. We can reference this object throughout our code using the double curly brace Mustache syntax {{}} that we learned about in chapter 2. For example, {{order.firstName}} will be replaced by the `firstName` from the `order` object. Keeping our order information in an object makes it easier to understand where the data is in the future.

It's worth mentioning that we could use an empty `order` object here and not define the properties `firstName` and `lastName` explicitly inside it. Vue.js can implicitly add the properties to the object. For the sake of simplicity, and to keep the code base a little cleaner, we'll add the properties so we can see how everything works.

After typing data into our checkout form, notice that values appear in real time in the box (figure 4.3). This is the beauty of two-way data binding. Values are automatically synced to each other without any other logic needed.

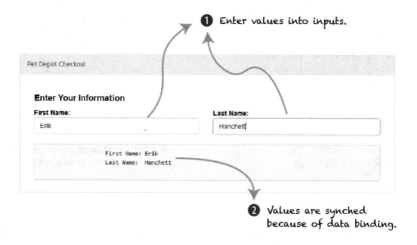

Figure 4.3   Text is updated in real time into the box at the bottom.

We now have the start of our checkout page. Let's add more form inputs to our index.html file so our customer can add in their address information, as shown next. We can add this HTML after the HTML code that we added in listing 4.1.

Listing 4.3 Adding in our other text inputs and select box: chapter-04/text-input.html

```
<div class="form-group">
  <div class="col-md-12"><strong>Address:</strong></div>
  <div class="col-md-12">
    <input v-model="order.address"
      class="form-control" />
  </div>
</div>
<div class="form-group">
  <div class="col-md-12"><strong>City:</strong></div>
  <div class="col-md-12">
    <input v-model="order.city"
      class="form-control" />
  </div>
</div>
<div class="form-group">
  <div class="col-md-2">
  <strong>State:</strong>
    <select v-model="order.state"
      class="form-control">
      <option disabled value="">State</option>
      <option>AL</option>
      <option>AR</option>
      <option>CA</option>
      <option>NV</option>
    </select>
  </div>
</div>
<div class="form-group">
  <div class="col-md-6 col-md-offset-4">
  <strong>Zip / Postal Code:</strong>
    <input v-model="order.zip"
      class="form-control"/>
  </div>
</div>
<div class="col-md-12 verify">
  <pre>
    First Name: {{order.firstName}}
     Last Name: {{order.lastName}}
       Address: {{order.address}}
          City: {{order.city}}
           Zip: {{order.zip}}
         State: {{order.state}}
  </pre>
</div>
```

Annotations on the listing:
- Selects Input with v-model
- Inputs text with v-model
- `<pre>` tag displays data

We added our form fields for the address, city, state, and ZIP Code. The address, city, and ZIP Code are all text inputs that use the v-model directive to bind the input.

Choosing a state is a little different. Instead of using a text box, we'll use a select drop-down control. The `v-model` has been added to the select element.

You might wonder how we can easily add more states to our select drop-down control. For this simple example, hard-coding all four states is fine. But if we were to add all 50 states, we'd probably want to dynamically generate the select box. In the next section, we'll look at using value bindings to help generate dynamic options.

Before we move on, let's not forget to add our new properties to the data object in the Vue instance.

**Listing 4.4   Updating the Vue instance data object with new properties:
chapter-04/data-new-properties.js**

```
data: {
  sitename: "Vue.js Pet Depot",
  showProduct: true,
  order: {
    firstName: '',
    lastName: '',
    address: '',
    city: '',
    zip: '',
    state: ''
  },
```

As we saw in figure 4.3, if any of these properties are changed within any of the form elements, these values are updated in the `<pre>` tag at the bottom. Reload the browser and your new form should look like figure 4.4.

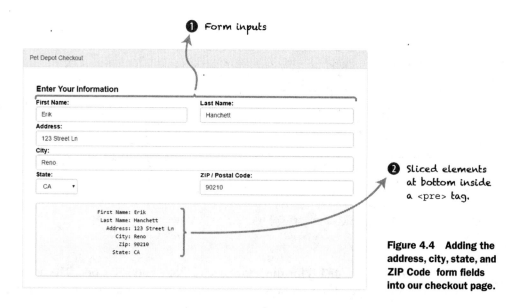

Figure 4.4   Adding the address, city, state, and ZIP Code form fields into our checkout page.

Our form checkout page is looking good, but we need to add in a couple more things. Let's allow our customer an option to ship items as a gift. To do this, we'll add a simple check box. If the check box is selected, we'll ship the items as a gift. If it isn't, selected items won't be shipped as a gift. To keep track of the binding we'll use the `order` `.gift` property.

Next up, we need to allow our customer an option to ship to a home or business address. Let's add a radio button to our code for this purpose. In Vue, we must set the `v-model` directive in both check boxes to the same value, otherwise the radio buttons won't update after they're clicked.

Finally we'll need to update the `<pre>` tag with `order.method` and `order.gift`, as shown in the following listing. Add this HTML after listing 4.3 in the index.html file.

Listing 4.5   Adding check boxes and radio buttons: chapter-04/adding-buttons.html

```
<div class="form-group">
  <div class="col-md-6 boxes">
    <input type="checkbox"
 id="gift"
 value="true"
 v-model="order.gift">               ◁——┐  Adds checkbox
    <label for="gift">Ship As Gift?</label> │  with v-model
  </div>
</div>
<div class="form-group">
  <div class="col-md-6 boxes">
    <input type="radio"
      id="home"
      value="Home"
      v-model="order.method">          ◁——┐
    <label for="home">Home</label>         │
    <input type="radio"                    │  Adds radio
      id="business"                        │  button v-model
      value="Business"                     │
      v-model="order.method">          ◁——┘
    <label for="business">Business</label>
  </div>
</div>
<div class="col-md-12 verify">
  <pre>                                  ◁——┐  Updates <pre> tag with
    First Name: {{order.firstName}}     │  order.method and order.gift
     Last Name: {{order.lastName}}
       Address: {{order.address}}
          City: {{order.city}}
           Zip: {{order.zip}}
         State: {{order.state}}
        Method: {{order.method}
          Gift: {{order.gift}}
  </pre>
</div>
```

Let's add our properties to our data object by adding this code.

Listing 4.6   Adding more properties to our Vue data object: chapter-04/more-props.js

```
data: {
  sitename: "Vue.js Pet Depot",
  showProduct: true,
  order: {
    firstName: '',
    lastName: '',
    address: '',
    city: '',
    zip: '',
    state: '',
    method: 'Home',
    gift: false
  },
```

You may have noticed that we added default values for both `method` and `gift`. The reason behind this is simple. By default, the method radio button is selected, and the check box isn't selected. Therefore, it would be clever of us to set a default value in this code for now.

One last thing we need to do is add a Place Order (submit) button. For now, we'll mock out the button so we can use it the future. You have a couple of ways to create a Place Order button. You could attach an action to a form element that encompasses all our inputs. (We'll look at this more in chapter 6 on Events.) Instead, let's use the `v-on` directive that we first learned about in chapter 3. The `v-on` directive can bind functions to DOM elements in the application. Add it to the click event on the Place Order button. This HTML code can be added after listing 4.5.

Listing 4.7   Adding the `v-on` directive to the click event: chapter-04/adding-v-on.html

```
<div class="form-group">
  <div class="col-md-6">
    <button type="submit"
      class="btn btn-primary submit"
      v-on:click="submitForm">Place Order</button>
  </div>
</div>
```

> The Place Order button is attached to the v-on directive.

In future chapters, we'll add functionality to our Place Order button. For our purposes now, let's create a simple function and verify that the button works by adding an alert popup. Add the `submitForm` function to the method's object that exists in the index.html file, as shown in this listing.

Listing 4.8   Creating the new `submitForm` method: chapter-04/submit.js

```
methods: {
  submitForm() {
    alert('Submitted');
...
  }
},
```

Inside the Vue constructor is the
methods object which holds all our
functions that can be triggered in
the application. The submitForm
function will display an alert popup
when triggered. In the browser,
click the Place Order button and
you'll see this popup (figure 4.5)
that was triggered by the submit-
Form function.

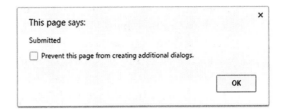

Figure 4.5   This popup was triggered by the
submitForm function.

Now that we have the form in place with a Place Order button, it should look like
figure 4.6 when it's all put together.

Place Order
button added.

Figure 4.6   Completed checkout page with all form elements included.

Each property in the form is bound to our Vue.js model! Now let's see if we can make
our input bindings a little better.

4.2   A look at value binding

The v-model directive has been useful in binding properties for us so far. We've used
it to bind many basic inputs. We have a problem, though. How do you bind the value for

check boxes, radio buttons, and select drop-down controls? If you remember, we hard-coded the values for both check boxes and radio buttons. For our select box control, we left the values blank. All the HTML elements can, and sometimes should, have a value associated with the selected option. Instead of using hard-coded values, let's rewrite our select box, check box, and radio buttons to use properties from our data object. Let's begin by updating our check box with values by using the `v-bind` directive.

4.2.1   *Binding values to our check box*

In our first example, our check box was bound to the `order.gift` property. We could set it to be either `true` or `false`. With that said, our customers don't want to see true or false. They'd rather see a message that lets them know if the order will be shipped as a gift. We can add that.

The `v-bind` directive binds values to attributes in our HTML elements. In this case, we're binding the `true-value` attribute to a property. The `true-value` attribute is unique to the `v-bind` directive, and it allows us to bind properties based on the check box being checked or not, either `true` or `false`. This will change the value of the `order.gift`. In listing 4.9, the `true-value` binds to the `order.sendGift` property. Likewise, the `false-value` binds to the `order.dontSendGift` property. When the check box is checked, the `order.sendGift` message displays. If the check box isn't checked, the `order.dontSendGift` property displays. Add this HTML after listing 4.8 in the index.html.

> **Listing 4.9   Binding `true` and `false` values to the gift check box: chapter-04/true-false.html**

```
<div class="form-group">
  <div class="col-md-6 boxes">
    <input type="checkbox"
      id="gift" value="true"
      v-bind:true-value="order.sendGift"        ◁──┐  Sets the order.sendGift
      v-bind:false-value="order.dontSendGift"   ◁─┐│  property when the
      v-model="order.gift">                      ││  checkbox is checked
    <label for="gift">Ship As Gift?</label>      ││
  </div>                           Binds order.gift│└─ Sets the order.dontSendGift
</div>                             to the input    │   property when the
                                                   └── checkbox isn't checked
```

To make this binding work as we expect, we'll need to add in these new properties to our `order` object, as shown in the next listing. Update the `order` object in the index.html values with the `sendGift` and `dontSendGift` properties.

> **Listing 4.10   Adding the `sendGift` property to the `order` object: chapter-04/prop-gift.js**

```
order: {
  firstName: '',
  lastName: '',
  address: '',
```

```
    city: '',
    zip: '',
    state: '',
    method: 'Business',
    gift: 'Send As A Gift',
    sendGift: 'Send As A Gift',
    dontSendGift: 'Do Not Send As A Gift'
},
```

The default value of checkbox defaults to the Send As A Gift check box.

The order.sendGift property is a text message that displays when the check box is checked.

The order.dontSendGift property is a text message that displays when the check box isn't checked.

Our data object is getting bigger! We can now assign text values if the check box is checked or not checked. Refresh the page and uncheck the Ship As Gift check box. Look at our box at the bottom (figure 4.7); we'll see the new values represented in the {{order.gift}} property in the UI.

First Name. Erik
Last Name: Hanchett
Address: 123 Street Ln
City: Reno
Zip: 90210
State: NV
Method: Home
Gift: Do Not Send Gift

{{order.gift}} property in UI displayed.

Figure 4.7 The {{order.gift}} property is displayed.

Toggling the check box changes the values from the Do Not Send As A Gift to the Send As A Gift string. Note that because we set the order.gift property value to Send As A Gift, it will default the check box to checked. If needed, we could assign it to the other value. This would cause the check box to display as unchecked.

4.2.2 *Working with value bindings and radio buttons*

Like check boxes, we can assign values to radio buttons. We can do this by binding the value directly. This could be a useful feature for our application. Let's display to the user the home address if the user selects the Home radio button and the business address if the user selects the Business radio button. Add this HTML to the index.html after the previous check box code.

Listing 4.11 Binding values to our radio buttons: chapter-04/radio-bind.html

```
<div class="form-group">
  <div class="col-md-6 boxes">
    <input type="radio"
      id="home"
```

```
      v-bind:value="order.home"
      v-model="order.method">
   <label for="home">Home</label>
   <input type="radio"
     id="business"
     v-bind:value="order.business"
     v-model="order.method">
   <label for="business">Business</label>
 </div>
</div>
```

> ◁─┐ **Sets the v-bind directive to the value attribute on the input element for the first radio button**

> ◁─┐ **Sets the v-bind directive to the value attribute on the input element for the second radio button**

The v-bind directive binds order.home to the first radio button and order.business to the second radio button. This can be powerful, because we can dynamically change these values at any time.

To finish this example, let's add these new properties to the order object in data in the index.html, as shown in the following listing.

Listing 4.12   Updating the order object with business and home: chapter-04/update-order.html

```
order: {
  firstName: '',
  lastName: '',
  address: '',
  city: '',
  zip: '',
  state: '',
  method: 'Home Address',
  business: 'Business Address',
  home: 'Home Address',
  gift:'Send As A Gift',
  sendGift: 'Send As A Gift',
  dontSendGift: 'Do Not Send As A Gift'
},
```

> **Sets the default value to the 'Home Address' radio button** ◁─

> **Displays the order.business property text message when the first radio button is selected** ◁─

> ◁─ **Displays the order.home property text message when the second radio button is selected**

This new order object now has a couple of new properties—home and business—that are bound to the radio buttons. If we select either one, the value at the bottom will toggle between Home Address and Business Address (figure 4.8).

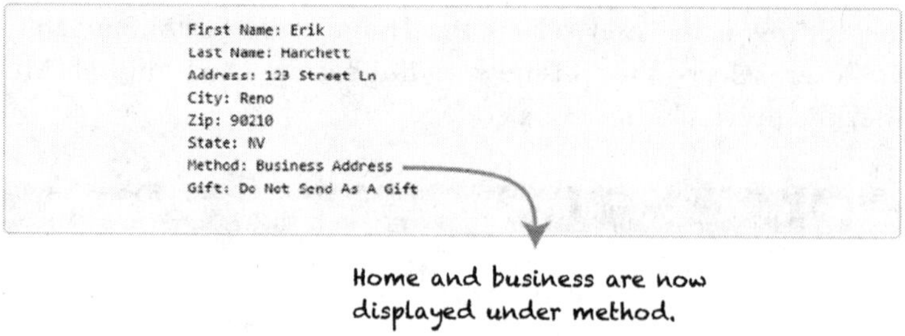

```
First Name: Erik
Last Name: Hanchett
Address: 123 Street Ln
City: Reno
Zip: 90210
State: NV
Method: Business Address
Gift: Do Not Send As A Gift
```

Home and business are now displayed under method.

Figure 4.8   Method is updated from the radio button.

Our customer can see that they have a package being delivered to a business address (Erik Hanchett at 123 Street Ln, Reno, NV) and it won't be shipped as a gift! Binding properties to any attribute value in our form makes things much cleaner and easier. We now need to look at the US states select box control in the next section.

4.2.3   *Learning the v-for directive*

Our select box control lists US states that our customer can choose from. We need to update the select drop-down control so the state shows in our box when we refresh the page. Let's look at how we can bind the state values. Replace the state drop-down in the index.html after the city input with the markup shown in the following listing.

Listing 4.13   Binding values to our select box: chapter-04/bind-select.html

```
<div class="form-group">
  <div class="col-md-2">
    <strong>State:</strong>
    <select v-model="order.state" class="form-control">
      <option disabled value="">State</option>
      <option v-bind:value="states.AL">AL</option>
      <option v-bind:value="states.AR">AR</option>
      <option v-bind:value="states.CA">CA</option>
      <option v-bind:value="states.NV">NV</option>
    </select>
  </div>
</div>
```

Assigns the v-bind directive value attribute to states.AL property

The v-bind directive value attribute is assigned to the states.AR property.

The v-bind directive value attribute is assigned to the states.CA property.

The v-bind directive value attribute is assigned to the states.NV property.

As we saw before, the v-bind directive is assigning our value attribute. This time we've created a new data property called states. Inside that states property, I've listed US states. The states object holds four values. We can access them inside our select box by using the v-bind directive. Update the index.html file and add the states object to the data object.

Listing 4.14   Adding the states property to the Vue instance data object: chapter-04/states.html

```
states: {
  AL: 'Alabama',
  AR: 'Arizona',
  CA: 'California',
  NV: 'Nevada'
},
```

After everything is updated, we should see these values inside our text box in our template at the bottom of the page (figure 4.9). As you can see, the state is spelled out, making it clear what's happening.

Earlier in this chapter, I mentioned a critical problem with our drop-down. In this example, only four states are listed. As we grow our list of states, we'll need to create

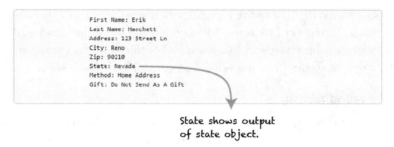

State shows output
of state object.

Figure 4.9   State text property is displaying the correct state selected.

an option> tag for each one. This could be tedious and repetitive. Luckily, Vue has something that can help us with this. It's called the v-for directive.

The v-for directive makes it easy to loop over values in a list or object, which is perfect for our situation. To make this work, we'll define all our states in the state object. We'll then iterate over every state while using the v-bind directive so everything matches. Let's give it a shot!

Many things are happening here, so I'll break it down. The v-for directive requires a special syntax in the form of state in states. states is the source data array, while the state is an alias for the array element that is being iterated on. In this case, state is Alabama, Arizona, California, and so on. Replace the state drop-down in the index.html after the city input with the HTML as shown here.

> **Listing 4.15   Updating the select drop down with v-for:**
> **chapter-04/select-drop-down.html**

```
<div class="form-group">
  <div class="col-md-2">
    <strong>State:</strong>                          The v-for directive
    <select v-model="order.state"                    iterating through the
      class="form-control">                           state object with
      <option disabled value="">State</option>        each key and value.
      <option v-for="(state, key) in states"                         The v-bind directive value
          v-bind:value="state">                                      attribute is assigned to
        {{key}}                                                      the state property.
      </option>            The key property
    </select>              is displayed.
  </div>
</div>
```

The key value is an optional argument that specifies the index of the current item. This is important in our select drop-down control because our key value can be used as the abbreviated state, while the actual value is the full state name.

The v-bind directive binds the value of state to the value on the <option> tag, as shown in listing 4.16. After replacing this code in your application, peek at the

HTML that is generated by opening up your web browser and looking at the source of the index.html. The <option> tag will show every state in the states property.

Listing 4.16 HTML generated by the v-for directive: chapter-04/options.html

```
<option value="Alabama">
  AL
</option>
<option value="Alaska">
  AK
</option>
<option value="Arizona">
  AR
</option>
<option value="California">
  CA
</option>
<option value="Nevada">
  NV
</option>
```

This is good news for our application. Because we can now bind the values and iterate over them with v-for, we no longer need to hard-code every US state. Our select box can grow dynamically based on how we create the states object.

4.2.4 The v-for directive without the optional key

I mentioned that the key value is optional, so what would a v-for directive look like without the key value? Taking a quick detour and seeing how that works, let's start from an empty detour.html file and create a brand-new application. Create a Vue constructor and add in a data object with a states array.

Listing 4.17 Updating the states object in data: chapter 04-/detour.html

```
<div id="app">
  <ol>
    <li v-for="state in states">        ◁──┐  The v-for directive using
      {{state}}                            │  the state in states syntax.
    </li>
  </ol>
</div>
<script src="https://unpkg.com/vue/dist/vue.js"></script>
<script type="text/javascript">
var webstore = new Vue({
  el: '#app',
  data: {
    states: [
      'Alabama',
      'Alaska',
```

```
        'Arizona',
        'California',
        'Nevada'
      ]
    }
  }
})
</script>
```

MORE The states array has five values. Let's create an ordered list to display each item. We don't have any keys, so we don't need to worry about that. To create our list, we'll use the `<ol>` and `<li>` tags. Add these tags to the top of the new detour.html file.

The `v-for` directive iterates through the states array and displays each state in the list. Keep in mind that state is an alias to the array element being iterated on, whereas states is the array item. It's easy to get this confused; remember the alias always comes first, then the optional key, then the array or object being iterated on.

When rendered, we'll see a list of ours states in an ordered numbered list, as follows:

1 Alabama
2 Alaska
3 Arizona
4 California
5 Nevada

We can now grow our list by adding values to our states object without having to change the template.

NOTE You may run into a situation where you need to directly manipulate the DOM, and you may not want to use the `v-model` directive. In this instance Vue.js offers us `$el`. You can use `$el` inside your Vue instance with `this.$el`. This will be the root DOM element that the Vue instance is managing. From there you can run any type of `Document` method, like `query-Selector()`, to retrieve any element you'd like. Remember, if you can, try to use the built-in Vue.js directives when working with the DOM. They are there to make your job easier! For more information on `$el` and other APIs check out the official API documentation at https://vuejs.org/v2/api/.

4.3   *Learning modifiers with the application*

As mentioned earlier in the chapter, the `v-model` directive can bind to our input values. These values update with each input event. We can use modifiers with the `v-model` directive to change that behavior. We can, for example, typecast values to numbers using .number and use .trim with our inputs (for more information about modifiers, go to https://vuejs.org/v2/guide/forms.html#Modifiers). We can also chain modifiers by adding one after the other (for example, `v-model.trim.number`). Let's add several of these modifiers to our checkout page on the application.

4.3.1 Using the .number modifier

The .number modifier is used to automatically typecast values in the v-model directive as a number. This will be useful in our ZIP input box (we'll assume ZIP Codes in our app don't start with a zero, otherwise the .number modifier removes the leading zero). Let's update the ZIP Code in the index.html file to use the .number modifier and see what effect it has in the following listing.

Listing 4.18 The .number modifier on the ZIP form element: chapter-04/number-mod.html

```
<div class="form-group">
  <div class="col-md-6 col-md-offset-1">
    <strong>Zip / Postal Code:</strong>
    <input v-model.number="order.zip"        ◁─── Shows the v-model directive
      class="form-control"                         with the .number modifier
      type="number"/>
  </div>
</div>
```

HTML inputs always return as strings, even if you add in type="number". Adding the .number modifier prevents this behavior and instead returns as a number. To verify this, let's update the index.html with the typeof operator while displaying the order.zip property in the template.

Listing 4.19 Using the typeof operator on order.zip: chapter-04/type-of.html

```
<div class="col-md-12 verify">
    <pre>
      First Name: {{order.firstName}}
      Last Name: {{order.lastName}}
      Address: {{order.address}}
      City: {{order.city}}
      Zip: {{typeof(order.zip)}}        ◁─── The JavaScript typeof operator returns
      State: {{order.state}}                 the type of the unevaluated operand.
      Method: {{order.method}}
      Gift: {{order.gift}}
    </pre>
</div>
```

Before we added the .number modifier, it would have displayed as a string. Now it returns as a number. Type a number into the ZIP input box and re-render the page to see the new output< as seen in figure 4.10.

You can see the ZIP column shows number in figure 4.10. Because we wrapped the ZIP Code in the typeof operand, it shows us the type of that property. We'll be using this feature later; for now we'll remove the typeof operand so it returns the ZIP Code. Delete the typeof operand from the order.zip property so all that remains is the property {{order.zip}}.

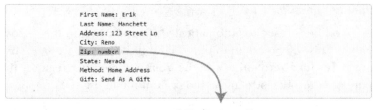

ZIP displays the
type of number.

Figure 4.10   Type of value entered into the zip property.

4.3.2   *Trimming the input values*

When extracting form information, we often have no use for preceding whitespace or whitespace after the text has been entered. If a user accidentally enters a few spaces before typing their name, we need to remove them. Vue.js gives us a nice modifier to trim the space automatically from our inputs.

In our application, we use input-string text boxes for the first name, last name, address, and city. In the following listing, let's update the first name and last name in the index.html to see how the .trim modifier works.

Listing 4.20   The .trim modifier on first and last name: chapter-04/trim-mod.html

```
<div class="form-group">
  <div class="col-md-6">
    <strong>First Name:</strong>
    <input v-model.trim="order.firstName"          ◁──┐  The v-model directive uses
      class="form-control" />                           the .trim modifier for the
  </div>                                                 order.firstName property.
  <div class="col-md-6">
    <strong>Last Name:</strong>
    <input v-model.trim="order.lastName"           ◁──┐  The v-model directive uses
      class="form-control" />                           the .trim modifier for the
  </div>                                                 order.lastName directive.
</div>
```

To add the .trim modifier all we need to do is add .trim to the end of the v-model directive. This will now trim our whitespace automatically for us! Now we can add it to the address and city inputs in the index.html.

Listing 4.21   The .trim modifier on the address and city: chapter-04/trim-mod-add.html

```
<div class="form-group">
  <div class="col-md-12"><strong>Address:</strong></div>
  <div class="col-md-12">
    <input v-model.trim="order.address"            ◁──┐  The v-model directive uses
class="form-control" />                                 the .trim modifier for the
  </div>                                                order.address property.
```

```
</div>
<div class="form-group">
  <div class="col-md-12"><strong>City:</strong></div>
  <div class="col-md-12">
    <input v-model.trim="order.city"
      class="form-control" />
  </div>
</div>
```

◁─┐ **The v-model directive uses the .trim modifier for the order.city directive.**

If we look at the output at the bottom of the page after browser refresh, we'll notice that the whitespace is removed (figure 4.11).

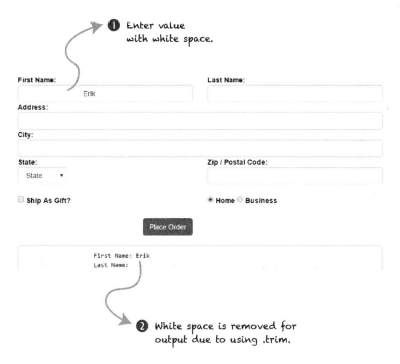

Figure 4.11 An example of using the .trim modifier on the v-model directive.

The first name input text box has the name Erik in it with many preceding whitespaces. With that said, the output at the bottom has the trimmed value on display. In fact, if we click outside the box, the value in the first name box syncs to the trimmed value. This is the power of the .trim modifier.

4.3.3 The .lazy v-model modifier

There is one last modifier that is known as the .lazy modifier. As I mentioned earlier, the v-model directive syncs after each input event. In practice, this occurs in a text box after each letter is typed. The value is synced on each keystroke. The .lazy modifier will sync on change events instead. Change events occur in a variety of situations depending on the form element used. A check box or radio button will trigger a change event when it's clicked. An input text box will trigger a change event when it loses focus. Different browsers might not trigger change events on the same interactions, so keep that in mind.

Typically, a .lazy modifier will look like the following when added to a v-model directive:

```
<input v-model.lazy="order.firstName" class="form-control" />
```

Exercise

Use your knowledge from this chapter to answer these questions:

How does two-way data binding work? When should you use it in your Vue.js application?

See the solution in appendix B.

Summary

- The v-model directive can be used to bind input, select, text areas, and components. It creates a two-way data binding on form input elements and components.
- The v-for directive renders data multiple times based on the data that it's given. You can use an alias in the expression on the current element being iterated on as well.
- The v-model directive has the .trim, .lazy, and .number modifiers. The .trim modifier eliminates whitespace while the .number modifier typecasts strings as numbers. The .lazy modifier changes when data is synced.

Conditionals, looping, and lists

This chapter covers

- Working with the conditionals `v-if` and `v-if-else`
- Looping using `v-for`
- Looking at array changes

In the previous chapter, we saw the power of the `v-model` directive and how we can use it to bind inputs to our application. We constructed a checkout page that displayed all the input forms we needed to gather from the user. To display this page, we used a conditional statement.

In chapter 3, we created a checkout button bound to a click event method. This method toggles a property called `showProduct`. In our template, we used the `v-if` directive and the `v-else` directive. If `showProduct` was `true`, the product page was displayed; if `showProduct` was `false`, the checkout page was displayed. By clicking the checkout button, users can easily switch between these pages. In later chapters, we'll look at refactoring this code to use components and routes, but for now this will work.

To expand our app, we'll look at other types of conditionals. For example, we need to add a new feature that displays messages to the user based on available inventory levels. In addition, we need to add more products to our product page. We'll look at that more closely in section 5.2.

5.1   Show an available inventory message

Every time an additional item is added to our shopping cart, the `cartItemCount` computed property is updated. What if we want to let the user know how many are available? Let's display a few messages when the available inventory is almost out. We'll use the `v-if`, `v-else-if`, and `v-else` directives to make this possible.

5.1.1   Adding how many are left with v-if

Before we begin, let's add more inventory. This will make it easier to display a message to the user as they put more items into their cart. To add inventory, we can update our product property in the data object. Edit the `availableInventory` product property in index.html. Let's change it from 5 to 10, as shown in listing 5.1. That should be enough for now.

If you've been following along from previous chapters, you should have an index.html file. If not, you can always download the completed chapter 4 index.html file that's included with this book as a starting point, along with any code snippets and CSS. As always, each listing is broken into its own file. Make sure to add each snippet into index.html as you continue.

> **Listing 5.1   Updating the inventory: chapter-05/update-inventory.js**

```
product: {
  id: 1001,
  title: "Cat Food, 25lb bag",
  description: "A 25 pound bag of <em>irresistible</em>, organic goodness
  for your cat.",
  price: 2000,
  image: "assets/images/product-fullsize.png",        Adds
  availableInventory: 10                               inventory
},
```

Now that the inventory has been updated, let's add a conditional to the template when the available inventory is low. We'll display a message showing the remaining inventory that the user can add to their cart. In listing 5.2 we can see the new span tag with the `v-if` directive. A class called `inventory-message` was also added to this span. This CSS makes the message stand out better and positions it correctly. I've added basic formatting to make our message look a little nicer. The `v-if` directive is flexible. You'll notice that we aren't using a specific property the way we did in chapter

3 with `showProduct`. Instead, we're using an expression. This is a nice touch that Vue.js allows us to do.

When the Add to cart button is clicked, the checkout number at the top increments. When the inventory reaches fewer than 5 (`product.availableInventory` – `cartItemCount`), a message appears that displays the amount of remaining inventory. This count continues to decrement as the button is pressed until the inventory reaches zero.

Locate the `addToCart` button in our template. Add a new span tag with our `v-if` directive in the index.html file, as shown here.

> **Listing 5.2   Adding a new message based on inventory: chapter-05/add-message.html**

```
<button class="btn btn-primary btn-lg"
  v-on:click="addToCart"
  v-if="canAddToCart">Add to cart</button>
  <button disabled="true" class="btn btn-primary btn-lg"
    v-else >Add to cart</button>
  <span class="inventory-message"
v-if="product.availableInventory - cartItemCount < 5">
Only {{product.availableInventory - cartItemCount}} left!
  </span>
```

Span class adds a message and adds an inventory-message class

The v-if directive will only display if the expression is true.

REMINDER   Keep in mind the source code, including this app.css file, is available to download for this chapter and all other chapters from Manning at www.manning.com/books/vue-js-in-action.

We could have used a computed property in this `v-if` directive but for the sake of simplicity, using an expression like this will work. Keep in mind that if your expressions are getting too long inside your template, you're probably better off using a computed property.

A quick look at v-show

The `v-show` directive is a close relative of the `v-if` directive. The use of both is similar: `<span v-show=" product.availableInventory - cartItemCount < 5">Message</span>`. The only real difference is that the `v-show` directive will always be rendered in the DOM. Vue.js uses a simple toggle in CSS to display the element. If you're confused about which one to use, use `v-if` if it's followed by `v-else` or `v-else-if`. Use `v-show` if it's more likely to be shown/rendered in most cases or if it's likely that the visibility of the element will be changed more than once during the lifetime of the page. Otherwise, use `v-if`.

Let's look at what we have so far (figure 5.1).

New display that shows number of items
left. Created with the v-if directive.

**Figure 5.1   Product
page with only four
items left, the result
of using the** v-if
directive.

5.1.2   *Adding more messaging with v-else and v-else-if*

We have a slight problem. When the inventory reaches 0, the message displays "Only 0 left!" Obviously, that doesn't make sense, so let's update the code so it outputs a better message when the inventory reaches 0. Add a message that encourages the user to buy now. This time we'll introduce the v-else-if and v-else directives! Let's break down what we want to do and how we'll do it. The v-if directive will display if the inventory count, minus the cart item count, equals zero. If we add all the items to the cart, the product inventory is all gone.

In figure 5.2, we see the completed functionality that shows a message (All Out) when the inventory is sold out.

Message displayed when
inventory runs out.

Figure 5.2   Product page shows All Out! after the inventory is exhausted.

If the product isn't sold out, we continue to the `v-else-if` directive. If the available inventory is close to selling out and fewer than five are left, we'll display a message, as you can see in figure 5.3.

Figure 5.3 shows the Buy Now! message. When you click the Add to cart button, you should see the message change. When the inventory is fewer than 5, you'll see figure 5.1. After the inventory runs out, you'll see figure 5.2.

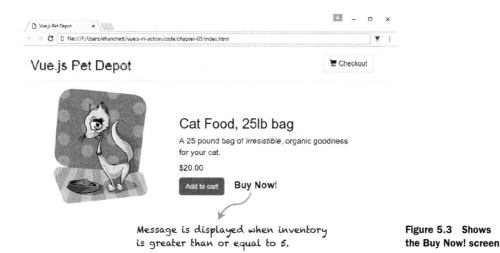

Message is displayed when inventory is greater than or equal to 5.

Figure 5.3 Shows the Buy Now! screen

The last `else` triggers only if both the `v-else` and `v-else-if` are false. The `v else` directive is a catch all when everything else falls through. If this occurs, we want a Buy Now message to appear next to the cart button. Update the span tag we added with the following code in the index.html file.

Listing 5.3 Adding multiple inventory messages: chapter 05/multiple-inventory.html

```
<button class="btn btn-primary btn-lg"
  v-on:click="addToCart"
  v-if="canAddToCart">Add to cart</button>
  <button disabled="true" class="btn btn-primary btn-lg"
  v-else >Add to cart</button>
  <span class="inventory-message"
    v-if="product.availableInventory - cartItemCount === 0">All Out!
  </span>
  <span class="inventory-message"
    v-else-if="product.availableInventory - cartItemCount < 5">
    Only {{product.availableInventory - cartItemCount}} left!
  </span>
  <span class="inventory-message"
    v-else>Buy Now!
  </span>
```

Shows the v-if directive that will only display if the inventory runs out

This directive will only trigger if the first v-if fails.

The v-else will trigger if both v-if and v-if-else fail.

Working with conditionals

When working with `v-if`, `v-else`, and `v-else-if`, we must be aware of a few things. Any time you use `v-else`, it must immediately follow a `v-if` or `v-else-if`. You cannot create extra elements in between. Like `v-else`, a `v-else-if` must also immediately follow a `v-if` or `v-else-if` element. Failure to do this causes the `v-else-if` or `v-else` not to be recognized.

Keep in mind that the `v-else-if` directive can be used more than once in the same block. For example, in our application we could have included multiple messages when the item was close to selling out. This would have been possible with the `v-else-if` directive.

With all that said, be careful with using too many conditionals and putting too much logic in the template. Instead, use computed properties and methods when needed. This will make your code easier to read and more understandable.

5.2   *Looping our products*

Since we introduced our pet depot store in chapter 2, we've been working with only one product. This has worked well up to now with the examples in previous chapters, but once we add more products, we'll need a way to display them all in our template. In addition, we want to show a simple star rating at the bottom of each product. The versatile `v-for` directive can handle both scenarios.

5.2.1   *Adding a star rating with v-for range*

Vue.js has the `v-for` directive to loop through items, as we saw briefly in chapter 4. It's worth mentioning that we can use it with objects, arrays, or even components. One of the simplest ways of using the `v-for` directive is by giving it an integer. When added to an element, it will be repeated that many times, which is sometimes referred as a `v-for` range.

Let's begin by adding a five-star rating system to our product. To keep it simple, let's use a span tag and add the `v-for` directive to it. The `v-for` syntax is always in the form of `item in items`. The `items` refers to the source array data being iterated on. The `item` is an alias element being iterated on. As you can see in figure 5.4, the `v-for` directive uses the `item` as an alias of `items`. The `items` is an array.

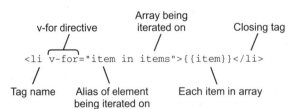

Figure 5.4 **Diagram showing how `v-for` alias works.**

When using v-for ranges, the source data is the upper inclusive limit of the range. This signifies how many times an element will be repeated. In figure 5.5 you can see that n is iterated on five times.

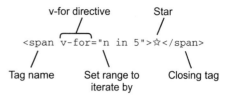

Figure 5.5 Diagram showing how v-for ranges works.

In listing 5.4, we're going to repeat the ☆ symbol five times. We also add in a div with a class called rating. (Remember to download the ap.css for this book; you'll find more information in appendix A.) Add this span as shown in the following listing inside the index.html below the inventory messages we added in section 5.1.

Listing 5.4 Adding star symbol using v-for: chapter 05/star-symbol.html

```
<span class="inventory-message"
  v-else>Buy Now!
</span>
<div class="rating">
  <span v-for="n in 5">☆</span>        Repeats the star symbol
</div>                                   five times
```

Once we add the stars to the template, refresh your browser. It should look like figure 5.6.

As you can see, there isn't much to show with our star rating: each star is empty. We'll need a way to dynamically bind a class to our CSS so we can show a filled-in star.

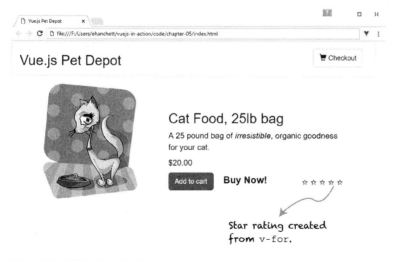

Figure 5.6 With star rating

5.2.2 *Binding an HTML class to our star rating*

Vue.js gives us a way to dynamically add or remove classes to HTML elements in our template. We can pass data objects, arrays, expressions, methods, or even computed properties to help determine which classes appear.

Before we can get started, we need to edit the product data object property and add a rating. This rating will determine how many stars each product should display. Open the index.html file and find the `product` property under order. Add the rating to the bottom of the product property, as shown in the following listing.

Listing 5.5 Adding to the `product` property: chapter 05/add-product.js

```
product: {
  id: 1001,
  title: "Cat Food, 25lb bag",
  description: "A 25 pound bag of <em>irresistible</em>, organic goodness
for your cat.",
  price: 2000,
  image: "assets/images/product-fullsize.png",
  availableInventory:10,
  rating: 3                              │  Adds a new
},                                       ◄──┘ rating property
```

Next, we need to display the star rating on the screen. The easiest way of doing this is with CSS and a little bit of JavaScript. We'll add simple CSS that creates a black star when the class is added to our span element. For our example, we'll need the first three stars to appear black. The last two remaining stars will appear as white. Figure 5.7 is an example of what it should look like when we're done.

As I mentioned, we can use a method to help determine whether a class should appear. Because we're using a `v-for` range, we'll need to pass in the range to a method.

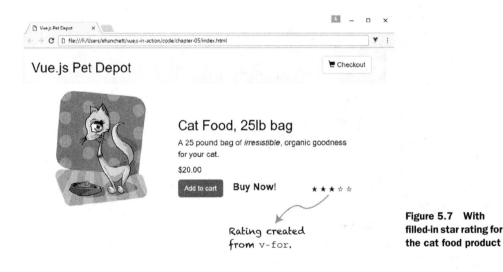

Figure 5.7 With filled-in star rating for the cat food product

Let's add a new method that reads the rating from the product and then returns `true` if the class should be added or not to the span. The class will make the star black.

To make this work, we must pass in a variable n to the method. The passed-in variable n comes from the v-for range directive `<span v-for="n in 5">`>☆`</span>`. Although we didn't display it in our template, n increments from 1 to 5. The first loop's n is 1, the next loop's n is 2, and so on. We know that as n loops it will increment from 1, 2, 3, 4, to 5. We can use simple math to determine if the star should be filled in.

In our example the first iteration n should be 1 and `this.product.rating` will always be 3. *3 – 1 = 2* is greater or equal to 0 so we return `true` and the class is added. The next iteration n will be 2. *3 – 2 = 1* is greater than or equal to 0 so it evaluates to `true` again. The next iteration n will be 3. *3 – 3 = 0*, so the class is added again. The next iteration n will be 4. *3 – 4 = -1* and therefore the method returns `false`. It's that simple. Add a new method called `checkRating` at the top of the method object in the index.html file, as shown here.

> **Listing 5.6 Adding a method to check if class should be added: chapter 05/check.js**

```
methods: {
  checkRating(n) {
    return this.product.rating - n >= 0;
  }
},
```
| **Returns true or false**
    depending on rating and *n*

To put our new star rating all together, we need to add the v-bind:class syntax to our span element. It will add our new class, `rating-active`, if the method returns `true`. Otherwise it will be ignored. In this example, we're passing an object to the v-bind:class. The truthiness of the `checkRating` method will determine if the `rating-active` class is added. Because this is in a loop, we must also pass in the value n, as we discussed before, which iterates with every loop.

Update the rating span in index.html and add the new v-bind:class directive to it, as shown in the next listing. Make sure to add the quotes around `rating-active`. Otherwise, you'll get an error in the console.

> **Listing 5.7 Adding class binding: chapter 05/add-class-bind.html**

```
<span class="inventory-message"
  v-else>Buy Now!
</span>
<div class="rating">
  <span  v-bind:class="{'rating-active': checkRating(n)}"
v-for="n in 5"☆>
  </span>
</div>
```
The binding of rating-active is determined by checkRating.

These are the basics of binding HTML classes. Vue.js allows you to add multiple classes and use arrays and components. For more information on how to bind classes, check out the official Vue.js guides on classes and style bindings at https://vuejs.org/v2/guide/class-and-style.html.

5.2.3 *Setting up our products*

Until now we've worked with only one product. A real pet store app would have hundreds if not thousands of products. We won't go that far! Let's see what it takes to add in five new products and what we could use to loop through those products on our product page.

To get started, we'll look at our product object. It's already taking up space in our index.html file and at this point it will be easier to put it in a separate file.

We need to create a new products.json file and add it to the chapter-05 folder. That way, we can more easily organize our data from our main application. If you want, you can add your own products, the way you did in the data object. But if you don't want to type all this, you can grab the products.json file from the code that's included with the book and copy it to the chapter-05 folder. You can find instructions on how to download the code for this book in appendix A. This listing shows the products in the products.json file.

Listing 5.8 Products in the products.json file: chapter 05/products.json

```
{
    "products":[                        ← ─┐  Shows the products
        {                                  │  array in JSON
            "id": 1001,         ─ ─ ▷       Shows the
            "title": "Cat Food, 25lb bag",  first product
            "description": "A 25 pound bag of <em>irresistible</em>, organic
goodness for your cat.",
            "price": 2000,
            "image": "assets/images/product-fullsize.png",
            "availableInventory": 10,
            "rating": 1
        },
        {                                          ┌─  Shows the
            "id": 1002,            ← ─┘               second product
            "title": "Yarn",
            "description": "Yarn your cat can play with for a very
<strong>long</strong> time!",
            "price": 299,
            "image": "assets/images/yarn.jpg",
            "availableInventory": 7,
            "rating": 1
        },
        {                                          ┌─  Shows the
            "id": 1003,            ← ─┘               third product
            "title": "Kitty Litter",
            "description": "Premium kitty litter for your cat.",
            "price": 1100,
            "image": "assets/images/cat-litter.jpg",
            "availableInventory": 99,
            "rating": 4
```

```
    },
    {                                              | Shows the
      "id": 1004,                                 ⊲—┘ fourth product
      "title": "Cat House",
      "description": "A place for your cat to play!",
      "price": 799,
      "image": "assets/images/cat-house.jpg",
      "availableInventory": 11,
      "rating": 5
    },
    {                                              | Shows the
      "id": 1005,                                 ⊲—┘ fifth product
      "title": "Laser Pointer",
      "description": "Drive your cat crazy with this <em>amazing</em>
product.",
      "price": 4999,
      "image": "assets/images/laser-pointer.jpg",
      "availableInventory": 25,
      "rating": 1
    }
  ]
}
```

After you've added or downloaded the products.json file and moved it to the chapter 5 root folder, you'll need to do additional refactoring. If you're following along, there's a good chance you're loading up everything locally from your hard drive instead of using a web server. This is perfectly fine and works great, except for one thing. Due to security concerns from browser creators, we can't easily load our products.json file. To do this right, we need to create a web server.

> **LOOKING AHEAD** When you run a site using a local web server, it can load JSON files from your hard drive with no problem, and you won't have any security concerns. In later chapters, we'll use the Vue CLI. This command-line tool will create a web server for us. Until we get there, we can use an npm module called http-server. You can find instructions on how to install npm in appendix A. This lightweight module makes it a snap to create a simple web server for our app.

We'll use npm to create a web server. Open a terminal window and run the following command from the command prompt to install the http-server module:

```
$ npm install http-server -g
```

After the installation completes, change directories to the chapter 5 folder. Run the command to start a server running your index.html on port 8000:

```
$ http-server -p 8000
```

If you receive any errors after running this command, verify that you don't have any other programs running on port 8000. You may want to try 8001 as the port number instead.

Once it starts, open your favorite web browser and head over to http://localhost:8000 to display your web page. If the page doesn't display, double-check the command line for errors. You may want to try changing the port if port 8000 is already taken.

5.2.4 *Importing products from product.json*

Remember in chapter 2 when we learned about Vue.js lifecycle hooks? We need to load our JSON file as soon as the webpage loads. One of those hooks would be perfect in this situation. Do you know which one? If you said the created lifecycle hook you are correct! The created lifecycle hook is called after the instance is created. We can use this hook to load the JSON file. To make this work we'll need another library.

Axios is a promise-based HTTP client for the browser and Node.js. It has several helpful features such as automatic transforms of JSON data that will come in handy. Let's add this library to our project. Inside the index.html, add a new script tag for Axios in the head tag, as shown in the following listing.

Listing 5.9 Adding Axios script tag: chapter 05/script-tags.html

```
   <link rel="stylesheet"
href="https://maxcdn.bootstrapcdn.com/bootstrap/3.3.7/css/bootstrap.min.css
" integrity="sha384-
BVYiiSIFeK1dGmJRAkycuHAHRg32OmUcww7on3RYdg4Va+PmSTsz/K68vbdEjh4u"
crossorigin="anonymous">
   <script src="https://cdnjs.cloudflare.com/ajax/libs/axios/0.16.2/axios.js">
</script>         ◁┐  Shows a CDN script
</head>              │  tag for Axios
```

After this tag is added, we can use Axios in our created lifecycle hook. Insert the created hook in the index.html file right after the filters object. We'll need to add in code that retrieves the products.json file from the hard drive and overwrites our existing product data. Update the index.html and add the Axios code.

Listing 5.10 Adding Axios tag to create a lifecycle hook: chapter 05/axios-lifecycle.js

```
...
},
created: function() {                     │ Retrieves the
  axios.get('./products.json')       ◁─┘ products.json file
    .then((response) =>{
      this.products=response.data.products;    ◁┐  Adds the response
      console.log(this.products);               │  data to products
    });
},
```

The `axios.get` command takes in a location, in our case the local file. It then returns a promise that has a `.then` method. The promise is fulfilled or rejected and returns a response object. Per Axios documentation, this object has a data property. We copy the `response.data.products` reference to `this.products` (this refers to the Vue instance). To make sure everything is okay, we also console-logged the output.

If you look closely at the code in listing 5.10, you may realize that we're assigning the data from the JSON file to `this.products`, not `this.product`. We need to create a new `products` property on our data object because it helps clean up the code.

Open the index.html file and look for the data object near the middle of the file. Add the new `products` property and then replace the `product` property because we no longer need it, as shown in the following listing.

> **Listing 5.11** `product` property, add `products`: chapter 05/product-delete.js

```
business: 'Business Address',        ⊲┐  Orders object
home: 'Home Address',                 │   without any changes
gift:'',
sendGift: 'Send As A Gift',
dontSendGift: 'Do Not Send As A Gift'
},
products: [],                         ┐  Shows the new products array
                                     ⊲┘  that replaces product object
```

At this point, if you try to refresh your browser you'll get an error because we removed the product object. We'll fix that when we add the `v-for` directive to loop through all the products.

5.2.5 Refactoring our app with the v-for directive

Before we can start looping through our products, we'll need to make slight changes to the `div` classes that control our CSS. Because we're using Bootstrap 3, we want each row to be a product because we must now accommodate more than one product. When we get done, it will look like figure 5.8.

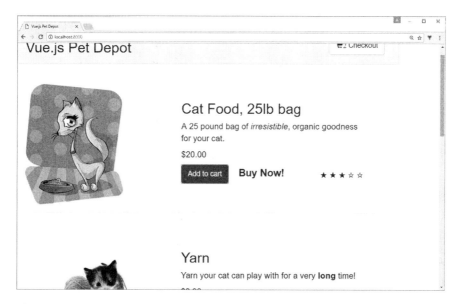

Figure 5.8   Final update of products.

Update index.html and locate the `v-else` directive that displays the checkout page. Add another `div` tag for a new row, as shown in the following listing.

Listing 5.12   Fixing CSS for Bootstrap: chapter 05/bootstrap-fix.html

```
<div v-else>
  <div class="row">
```
Shows the new
Bootstrap row

We'll need to move the `div` with the class `row` that's right before the `showProduct` `v-if` directive. Move the `div` class to the position below `showProduct`, as seen in the following listing. Update the index.html so it matches.

Listing 5.13   Fixing CSS for bootstrap: chapter 05/bootstrap-fix-v-if.html

```
<div v-if="showProduct">
  <div class="row product">
```
Moves div for row
below showProduct

Now that we have the minor issues with the CSS/HTML resolved, we can add our `v-for` directive that loops through all the products. This will display all the products on our page. In our example, we'll use the syntax `product in products`. `products` is the object that we loaded earlier; it is now an alias to each individual product in `products`. We'll also update the column widths using Bootstrap so that our products are displayed a little nicer.

Inside index.html, add the `v-for` directive below the `showProduct` `v-if` directive. Make sure to end the `div` tag at the bottom of the page, as shown here.

Listing 5.14   Adding the `v-for` directive for `products`: chapter 05/v-for-product.html

```
<div v-if="showProduct">
  <div v-for="product in products">
    <div class="row">
     <div class="col-md-5 col-md-offset-0">
       <figure>
          <img class="product" v-bind:src="product.image">
       </figure>
     </div>
      <div class="col-md-6 col-md-offset-0 description">
 ...
    </div><!-- end of row-->
    <hr />
  </div><!-- end of v-for-->
</div><!-- end of showProduct-->
```
Loops through all the products
using the v-for directive

Changes column width
to 5 without offset

Changes column
width without offset

Adds horizontal
rule tag

Shows the closing
tag for v-for directive

We've added the `v-for` directive but we have a few small problems. The `checkRating` method and the `canAddToCart` computed property are still referencing `this.product`. We need to change this so it references the `this.products` array instead.

This can be a little tricky. Let's begin by fixing the checkRating method. This method helps us determine how many stars each product has. We can fix it by passing the product alias into the method. Inside index.html, update the checkRating method, as shown here.

Listing 5.15 Updating checkRating with product info: chapter 05/check-rating.js

```
methods: {
  checkRating(n, myProduct) {
    return myProduct.rating - n >= 0;
},
```

←⎤ **Shows the new checkRating**
  ⎟ **method that accepts a product**

We now need to update the template and pass in the product to our updated method. Update the index.html and look for the checkRating method below the inventory messages. Add product to the checkRating method, as shown next.

Listing 5.16 Updating template for ratings: chapter 05/update-template.html

```
<span class="inventory-message"
  v-else>Buy Now!
</span>
<div class="rating">
  <span  v-bind:class="{'rating-active': checkRating(n, product)}"
    v-for="n in 5" >☆
  </span>
</div>
```

Updates the checkRating
method so it accepts a product

If you haven't done so, grab the pictures from the chapter in the assets/images folder and copy them to your local assets/images folder. Also grab the app.css file, if you haven't already, and copy it to your assets/css folder.

One of the last things we need to do to finish refactoring our app is to fix the canAddToCart computed property. This property greys out the Add to Cart button after the available inventory exceeds the amount in the cart.

You may be wondering how we can accomplish this. Before, we had only one product, so it was easy to figure out if that product's inventory had been exceeded. With multiple products, we need to loop through every product in the cart and calculate whether or not we can add another item.

This is easier than you might think. We need to move the canAddToCart computed property and make it a method. Then we need to update the method so it can accept a product. Finally, we'll update the conditional so it retrieves the count.

To retrieve the count, we'll use a new method called cartCount that accepts an ID and returns the number of items for that ID. The cartCount method uses a simple for loop to iterate through the cart array. For every match, it increments the count variable. It then returns that variable at the end.

Update index.html with the new canAddToCart method. You can move it from the computed property section to methods. Create a cartCount method as well.

Listing 5.17   Updating `canAddToCart` and adding `cartCount` method: chapter 05/update-carts.js

> Returns whether the available inventory is greater than the count of items in the cart

```
canAddToCart(aProduct) {
  return aProduct.availableInventory > this.cartCount(aProduct.id);
},
cartCount(id) {
  let count = 0;
  for(var i = 0; i < this.cart.length; i++) {
    if (this.cart[i] === id) {
      count++;
    }
  }
  return count;
}
```

> Shows the new cartCount method that returns the number of items in the cart for ID

> Shows the loop that checks every item in the cart

To complete our updates to `canAddToCart`, we must update our template and pass the product to it. At the same time, let's update the `addToCart` method and make sure it also accepts a product. Update index.html and pass in the product alias to the `canAddToCart` and `addToCart` methods.

Listing 5.18   Updating `canAddToCart` template: chapter 05/update-can-add-cart.html

```
<button class="btn btn-primary btn-lg"
v-on:click="addToCart(product)"
v-if="canAddToCart(product)">Add to cart</button>
```

> Updates addToCart so it accepts product

> Updates canAddToCart so it accepts product

This was a simple update to both methods. Because we've updated the template to `addToCart`, we must also update the method to push the ID of the product. For this we'll use the push mutation method, shown in listing 5.19.

Mutation methods

Vue has many mutation methods that you can use with your arrays. Vue, by convention, wraps arrays in observers. When any changes occur to the array, the template is notified and updated. Mutation methods mutate the original array they're called upon. These mutation methods include push, pop, shift, unshift, splice, sort, and reverse.

Be careful: there are certain changes to arrays that Vue cannot detect. These include directly setting an item, `this.cart[index] = newValue` and modifying the length, `this.item.length = newLength`. To learn more about mutations, see the official guide at https://vuejs.org/v2/guide/list.html#Mutation-Methods.

```
addToCart(aProduct) {                           Pushes the product
  this.cart.push( aProduct.id );            ◁──┘ ID into the cart
},
```

Now we can click the Add to cart button without any problems. Every time the button is clicked, the product ID will be pushed into the cart and the cart count will be updated automatically at the top of the screen.

The last step of our refactor is to fix the product inventory messages that we created earlier. The problem is that we're still using the total cart item count to determine which messages to display. We need to change this code so that we now calculate the message based on the cart item count of only that item.

To fix this issue, let's change from the `cartItemCount` method to our new `cartCount` method, which will accept a product ID. Update the index.html and locate the inventory messages. Update the `v-if` and `v-else-if` directives with the new expression that uses `cartCount`, as shown here.

```
                                             Lists the new expression for
                                             v-if directive with cartCount

<span class="inventory-message"
  v-if="product.availableInventory - cartCount(product.id) === 0">   ◁──┐
All Out!                                                                 │
</span>
<span class="inventory-message"
  v-else-if="product.availableInventory - cartCount(product.id) < 5">  ◁──┐
  Only {{product.availableInventory - cartCount(product.id)}} left!
</span>                                                   Lists the new
<span class="inventory-message"                    expression for v-else-if
  v-else>Buy Now!                                   directive with cartCount
</span>
```

That's it! We can now load our page and see the results. Make sure that you have the http-server running `http-server -p 8000` and reload your web browser. You should see the updated webpage with all the items listed that were pulled from the products.json file. Figure 5.9 shows our completed refactored app using the `v-for` directive to loop through our `products` object.

In your browser, make sure that everything works as you expect. Click the Add to cart button and see the messages change. Verify that the button is disabled when the item count reaches zero. Try to change the products.json file and reload the browser. Everything should update accordingly.

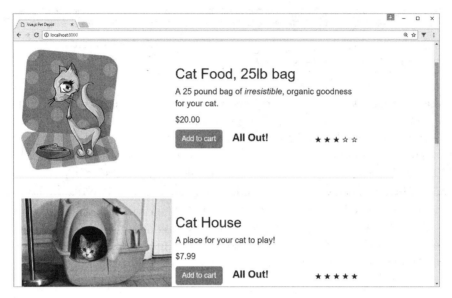

Figure 5.9   Showing several items that are being looped through the product.json file

5.3   Sorting records

Often when working with arrays, or objects in our case, you may want to sort the values when displaying them using the v-for directive. Vue makes this easy to do. In our case, we'll need to create a computed property that returns our sorted results.

In our app, we load the product list from the JSON file. The order displayed matches the order in the file. Let's update the sort order so products are listed alphabetically by product title. To do this, we'll create a new computed property called sortedProducts. We first need to update the template.

Update the index.html file and find the v-for directive in the template that lists our products. Change the v-for to use sortedProducts instead of the products object.

Listing 5.21   Adding sorting to the template: chapter 05/add-in-sort.html

```
<div v-if="showProduct">
  <div v-for="product in sortedProducts">          ◁─┐ Adds new sortedProducts
    <div class="row">                                 │ computed property
```

Now that we've sortedProducts in place in the template, we need to create the computed property. But we've a problem to solve. We'll need to be aware that the data for this.products may not be available right away because information from the products.json file is loaded from a promise in the create lifecycle hook as the app loads. To make sure this isn't a problem, we'll surround our code with an `if` block that verifies the products exist.

Let's define our own compare function that will sort on the title, as shown in the following listing. Then we'll use JavaScript's array sort, with our passed-in compare function, to alphabetically sort by title.

Listing 5.22 `sortedProducts` computed property: chapter 05/sort-products-comp.js

```
sortedProducts() {
  if(this.products.length > 0) {
    let productsArray = this.products.slice(0);        ◁── Converts object to array
    function compare(a, b) {                                using JavaScript's slice
      if(a.title.toLowerCase() < b.title.toLowerCase())   ◁── Compares function
        return -1;                                             that will compare
      if(a.title.toLowerCase() > b.title.toLowerCase())       based on title
        return 1;
      return 0;
    }
    return productsArray.sort(compare);     ◁── Returns new
  }                                             product array
}
```

That should do it. Refresh the browser and you should see an alphabetical list of all the products by title. Figure 5.10 shows the output of our sorted array. If you scroll down, all products should be listed. Double-check to verify that the functionality works as expected.

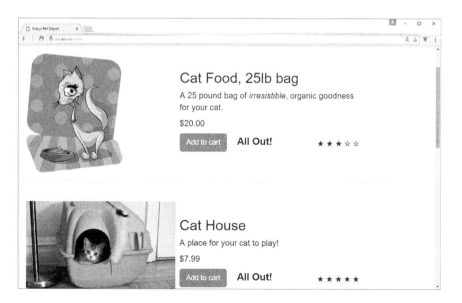

Figure 5.10 Sorted products array

Exercise

Use your knowledge from this chapter to answer this question.

What's a v-for range and how does it compare to a normal v-for?

See the solution in appendix B.

Summary

- Conditionals in Vue are created using the v-if, v-else-if, and v-else directives. Occasionally we'll use the v-show directive but not often.
- The v-for directive is very versatile. It can be used to iterate over a range of positive integers (that is, starting at 1), array elements, or object property values and keys to replicate HTML markup, Vue templates, or Vue components. Any type of expression can be used to loop through items.
- We can easily sort values with computed properties. Computed properties can be used with the v-for directive to sort output

Working with components

6

In the previous chapters, we learned about conditionals, looping, and lists. Instead of repeating code, we used loops to simplify things. We used conditionals to show different messages depending on the user action. This works, but you may have noticed that our application has grown to more than 300 lines of code. The index.html file we've been updating every chapter has computed properties, filters, methods, lifecycle hooks, and data properties in it. With all this information, it's not easy finding things.

To help solve this, we need to separate our code and componentize it. Each part of the code should be reusable and allow properties and events to be passed to it.

Vue.js components can help us accomplish this. Before we begin, let's look at several of the fundamentals of components and a few examples of how they work.

Then we'll look at local and global registration of components. Afterward, we'll see a few examples on how to pass props and how to validate them. We'll end the chapter with defining our templates and custom events.

You maybe be wondering what happened to our pet store application. Don't worry, we'll look at this in the next chapter when we look at single-file components, build tools, and Vue-CLI.

6.1   *What are components?*

Components in Vue.js are a powerful construct that reduce and simplify our code base. Most Vue.js apps consist of one or more components. With components, we can pull out repeated parts of our code and separate them into smaller logical parts that make more sense to us. We can reuse each component throughout our application. Components are defined as a collection of elements that can be accessed through a single element. In certain cases, they can appear as a native HTML element using a special `is` attribute (we'll look at that operator later in this chapter).

Figure 6.1 is a simple example of converting a few HTML tags into one component. All of the HTML inside the opening and closing `<div>` tags are encapsulated in the one component: `my-component`. It's worth mentioning that you can also have a self-closing tag, `<my-component/>` if your web browser supports it or you're using single-file components that we'll discuss later in the chapter.

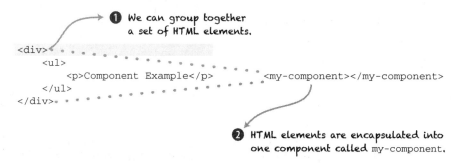

Figure 6.1 Example of encapsulating code into a component

6.1.1   *Creating components*

Before we can create our first Vue component we must create a Vue.js root instance, and then we must decide how to structure our application. Vue.js gives us the option to register our components either locally or globally. Global components can be used throughout the application, while local components can only be used in the Vue.js instance that created it. Let's create a global component first.

Global components, as we mentioned earlier, can be used in all Vue.js instances. In this example, we're creating a global component called `my-component`. Vue.js allows much flexibility in naming our components. Keep in mind that Vue.js doesn't enforce any rules for component names, the way other frameworks do. It's good practice to name all your components lowercase with hyphens.

6.1.2 *Global registration*

To create a global component, we must place it before the Vue instance. As you can see from listing 6.1, the global component (`my-component`) is defined right before it's created with `new Vue`.

To display information in our component, we must add a template property. The template is where the HTML resides. Keep in mind that all templates must be surrounded by a tag. In our example, we've surrounded it in a `<div>` tag; otherwise, you'll see an error in the console, and the template won't render on the screen.

The last thing we need to do to get our component to render is to add it to the parent's template. To get this working, we add the `<my-component></mycomponent>` custom tag inside the parent entry point of our app, `<div id="app">`, as shown in the following listing. While going through this chapter, try these examples for yourself. Make sure to save them as a .HTML file and load them in your web browser.

> **Listing 6.1 Creating our first global component**
> **chapter-06/global-component-example.html**

```
<!DOCTYPE html>
<html>
<head>
<script src="https://unpkg.com/vue"></script>      ⟵  Adds script
</head>                                                 tag to Vue.js
  <body>
  <div id="app">
    <my-component></my-component>      ⟵  Adds component
  </div>                                   to template
  <script>
  Vue.component('my-component', {      ⟵  Registers global Vue
    template: '<div>Hello From Global Component</div>'   to component
  });                                                ⟵  Renders template
                                                        for component
  new Vue({              ⟵  Instantiates
    el: "#app"              Vue instance
  });
  </script>
  </body>
</html>
```

It goes without saying that our application isn't too useful. If you open this file in a web browser, you'll see a message on the page, "Hello From Global Component." This is a trivial example on how components work so you can understand the fundamentals. Let's look at local registration and see how that differs.

> **The is special attribute**
> You have special restrictions when using components in our DOM. Certain HTML
> tags—`<ul>`, `<ol>`, `<table>`, and `<select>`—have restrictions on the type of ele-
> ments that can appear inside them. This is due to how the DOM hoists components
> out as invalid content. The workaround is to use the `is` attribute. Instead of putting
> the component inside those HTML tags, you can add the component to the element
> itself—for example, `<table> <tr is="my-row"></tr></table>`. The `tr` ele-
> ment will now be associated with the `my-row` component. We can create our own `tr`
> component to match whatever functionality we like. This limitation doesn't apply to
> inline, x-templates, or .vue components. For more information on this attribute, check
> out the official guides at http://mng.bz/eqUY.

6.1.3   Local registration

Local registration restricts scope to only one Vue instance. We can do this by registering it with the component's instance option. After the component is registered locally,
it can only be accessed by the Vue instance that registered it.

In listing 6.2 we see a simple example of a local component. It looks similar to the
global component that we registered before. The biggest difference is that we have a
new instance option called `components`.

The components instance option declares all components needed for that Vue
instance. Each component is a key-value pair. The key is always the name of the component that you'll reference later inside the parent template. The value is the component definition. In listing 6.2 the name of the component is `my-component`. The
value is `Component`. Component is a `const` variable that defines what's inside the
component.

In the following listing, we name our component `my-component` and the variable
`Component`. You can name these whatever you like, although, as mentioned earlier,
try to name the component using hyphens and lowercase, also known as kebab case.
It's good practice.

> **Listing 6.2   Registering a local component: chapter-06/local-component-example.html**

```
<!DOCTYPE html>
<html>
<head>
<script src="https://unpkg.com/vue"></script>
</head>
  <body>
  <div id="app">
    <my-component></my-component>
  </div>
  <script>
      const Component = {
          template: '<div>Hello From Local Component</div>'
      };
```

Shows the const variable
that has the component
declaration in it

This is the template
that will be displayed
for this component.

```
new Vue({
    el: '#app',
    components: {'my-component': Component}      ⊲─┐  Shows the components
    });                                              │  instance option that
  </script>                                          │  declares components
  </body>
</html>
```

Load the web page in a browser and you'll see "Hello From Local Component." If not, double-check the console for any errors. It's easy to leave a typo in, forget to surround the template in the `<div>` tag, or forget to close all your HTML tags.

Kebab case vs. camelCase

Although you can name your components whatever you like, there's one caveat. Inside your HTML templates you must use the *kebab case* (lowercase with hyphens) equivalent to the name you chose. Let's say you register your component "myComponent". When using camelCase, your HTML templates must be in kebab case. Therefore, the component would be named <my-component>. This is also true for PascalCase. If you name your component, MyComponent, then your HTML template must be in kebab case, <my-component> as well. This rule also applies to props, which we'll learn about later.

Later, when we look at single-file components, this won't be a problem. Until then, stick with kebab case. You can learn more about camelCase versus kebab case in the official documentation at http://mng.bz/5q9q.

6.2 Relationships in components

Imagine you're designing a commenting system. The system should display a list of comments from each user. Each comment needs to contain the username, time and date, and the comment. Each user of our system can delete and edit each of their own comments.

Your first thought might be to use the `v-for` directive. This worked well in the last chapter when it was used to iterate through our inventory list. That could work, but let's say our requirements change, and now we need to add a way to show threaded comments, or a new upvote and downvote system is needed. The code will become complicated very quickly.

Components can help solve this problem. In such a relationship, comments will be displayed in a comment-list component. The parent (the Vue.js root instance) is responsible for the rest of the app. The parent also contains a method to retrieve all the comment data from a backend. The parent passes down the data it retrieved to the child component, `comment-list`. The `comment-list` component is responsible for displaying all the comments passed down to it.

Keep in mind that each component has its own isolated scope, so it should never access the parent's data directly. That's why we always pass that data down. In Vue.js, the data that's passed down is called *props*. This is short for properties; but inside Vue.js you must refer to it as props. Child components must explicitly state each prop it expects to receive using the props option. This option will reside in the Vue.js instance and will contain an array in the form like this: props: ['comment']. In this example, 'comment' is a property that will be passed down into the component. If we had multiple props, then we'd separate each with a comma. Props are one-way from the parent component to the child component (figure 6.2).

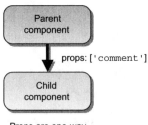

Props are one-way

Figure 6.2   A parent component can send data to a child component.

In chapter 4, we discussed how the v-model directive creates a two-way data binding on form inputs and text area elements. Changes to v-model elements update the data properties in the Vue.js instance and vice versa. But components form a one-way data binding. When the parent updates properties, it flows down to the child component and not the other way around. This is an important distinction because it prevents the child from accidentally mutating the parent's state. If you mutate state, you'll see an error in your console, like the one in figure 6.3.

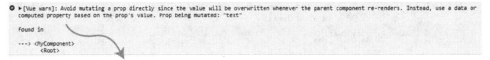

Error when mutating state shown in console.

Figure 6.3   Error in console warns against mutating props directly.

Note that all values are passed by reference. If an object or array is mutated in the child, it will affect the parent state. This isn't always the desired outcome and should be avoided. Instead you should make the changes in the parent only. Later in this chapter we'll see how we can use events to update data from the child to the parent.

6.3   *Using props to pass data*

As mentioned, props are used to pass data from the parent to the child components. Props are intended for one-way communication only. You can think of props as variables the component has that can only be assigned from the parent.

Props also can be validated. We can make sure the values passed in follow a certain type of validation. We'll look at this too.

6.3.1   *Literal props*

The easiest to use type of props are literal props. They're plain strings that we can pass in to the component. Inside the template, we create the component in the usual manner, but we add our new prop within the angle brackets of our component as an additional attribute, `<my-component text="World"></my-component>`. This text will be passed down as a string to the text prop we created. The template will interpolate it within the curly braces.

Be aware, this is a common mistake by many beginners: oftentimes, you might want to pass in a real value into the prop, not only a string. You might accidentally pass in a string instead of passing in a value. To pass in a value, you'll need to make sure you use the `v-bind` directive as we'll see in the next section.

In listing 6.3 we see an example of passing in a literal prop. Copy this example into your editor and try it out for yourself. You'll see that `my-component` has the passed-in value of `"World"`. You can display that value using the `text` prop inside the template, as shown here.

Listing 6.3 Using literal props in our component: chapter 06/literal-props.html

```html
<!DOCTYPE html>
<html>
<head>
<script src="https://unpkg.com/vue"></script>
</head>
  <body>
  <div id="app">
    <my-component text="World"></my-component>          ◁─┐ Shows the component
  </div>                                                     │ with passed-in text literal
  <script>
  const MyComponent= {
    template:'<div>Hello {{text}}! </div>',  ◁─┐ The template displays Hello
    props:['text']                              │ and the passed-in prop
  };
  new Vue({
    el: "#app",
    components: {'my-component': MyComponent}
  });
  </script>
</html>
```

6.3.2 Dynamic props

Dynamic props are props that are passed in from the parent that are bound to a property that can change (unlike literal props, that are static text). We can use the `v-bind` directive to make sure it's passed in correctly. Let's update our example from the previous section and pass in the message to our new prop named `text`.

The component `<my-component v-bind:text="message"></my-component>` has a new `v-bind` directive attribute. This will bind the prop `text` to our new `message`. The `message` is a property from our data function.

If you've been following along in previous chapters, you may have noticed that data, in our Vue.js instance, is no longer an object `data: { }` as you can see in listing 6.4. This is an intentional choice. Components behave a little differently, and data must be represented as a function, not an object.

If I add a data object to `my-component`, an error displays in the console. To stay consistent, we'll use `data` as a function for both our components and the root Vue instance for the rest of the book.

This listing is an example of using dynamic props. Copy this into an editor and try it for yourself.

Listing 6.4   Using dynamic props: chapter 06/dynamic-props.html

```
<!DOCTYPE html>
<html>
<head>
<script src="https://unpkg.com/vue"></script>
</head>
  <body>
  <div id="app">
    <my-component v-bind:text="message"></my-component>      ⟵——  Uses the v-bind
  </div>                                                            directive to bind
  <script>                                                          message from parent
  const MyComponent = {                                            to text in child
    template: '<div>Hello {{text}}! </div>',    ⟵——  This is the template that
    props: ['text']                                   displays the text prop.
  };
  new Vue({
    el: "#app",
    components: {'my-component': MyComponent},
    data() {
      return {
        message: 'From Parent Component!'      ⟵——  The data function that
      }                                               returns the message
    }
  });
  </script>
</html>
```

Before we move on, let's imagine that we need to update our program to add three counters. Each counter needs to start at zero and increment independently. Each counter is represented by a button that you can click to increment. How can we do this with components?

Let's take the code from listing 6.4 and update it. Add a data function to `MyCom-ponent` and a counter. Your first thought might be to add a global variable. Let's try that and see what happens.

As you can see from listing 6.5, we added the component three times. We created a global `const` object called counter, and it's initialized to zero. In our template, we created a simple binding to the click event using the `v-on` directive. The counter variable will increment by one on every click.

Listing 6.5   Dynamic props with global counter: chapter 06/dynamic-props-counter.html

```
<!DOCTYPE html>
<html>
```

```
<head>
<script src="https://unpkg.com/vue"></script>
</head>
  <body>
  <div id="app">
  <my-component></my-component>
  <my-component></my-component>          Lists component three times
  <my-component></my-component>
  </div>
  <script>
  const counter = {counter: 0};                         Shows the global
  const MyComponent= {                                  variable counter
    template:'<div><button v-on:click="counter +=
  1">{{counter}}</button></div>',                       The counter increments
    data() {                                            on every click.
      return counter;          The data function returns
    }                          the global counter.
  },
// ...
  </script>
</html>
```

Open your browser to the code you wrote. Click the button on the page a few times and see what occurs (figure 6.4).

Figure 6.4   Dynamic props example in a browser.

You might be surprised to see that every counter increments when we click any of the buttons. This is certainly not what we want, although it's a good illustration on how to share scope.

Take the listing from 6.5 and update it so we can correct this problem, as shown in listing 6.6. Remove the const counter and update the data function. Instead of having the data function return the global counter, have it return its own counter. This counter is scoped locally for the component, and therefore isn't shared with other components.

**Listing 6.6   Updating counters with correct return object:
chapter 06/dynamic-props-counter-correct.html**

```
<!DOCTYPE html>
<html>
<head>
```

```
<script src="https://unpkg.com/vue"></script>
</head>
  <body>
  <div id="app">
    <my-component></my-component>
    <my-component></my-component>
    <my-component></my-component>
  </div>
  <script>
  const MyComponent= {
    template: '<div><button v-on:click="counter +=
➡ 1">{{counter}}</button></div>',
    data() {
      return {
        counter: 0                  ◁──┐  The data function
      }                                 │  returns a counter.
    }
  };
// ...
  </script>
</html>
```

Fire up your browser and open the updated code you wrote. Click a few of the buttons and observe the counter (figure 6.5).

Figure 6.5   Dynamic props with a local scope counter example.

This time things look correct! As we click each button, the counter increments by itself only and doesn't affect the other counters.

6.3.3   *Prop validation*

Vue.js has a nice feature called *prop validation* that ensures that the props that we receive from the parent pass validation. This can be particularly useful when working on a team, where multiple people use the same component.

Let's begin by checking the type of our props. Vue.js provides the following native constructors to make this possible:

- String
- Number
- Boolean
- Function

- Object
- Array
- Symbol

In listing 6.7, you can see the use of prop validation. We'll first create a component called `my-component` and pass in values to it. The component will display those values in its template.

Instead of creating a prop array, `prop: ['nameofProp']`, we create an object. Each object is named after the `prop`. We then create another object to specify the type; we can add either required or default. *Default* refers to the default value if no value is passed in to the `prop`. If the type of property is an object, it must have a default value assigned. The *required* property, as the name suggests, requires the property to be added to the component during creation in the template.

The last thing you'll notice from listing 6.7 is the even `prop`. This is called a custom validator. In this case, we're checking whether or not the value is even. If it's even, it'll return `true`. If it's not even, then an error will be shown in the console. Keep in mind that custom validators can perform any type of function you like. The only rule is that they must return `true` or `false`.

Keep in mind also that a single colon (:) by itself is shorthand for `v-bind`. This is similar to the way the at symbol (@) is shorthand for `v-on`.

Listing 6.7 Validating props: chapter 06/props-example.html

```
<!DOCTYPE html>
<html>
<head>
<script src="https://unpkg.com/vue"></script>
</head>
  <body>
  <div id="app">
    <my-component :num="myNumber" :str="passedString"
         :even="myNumber" :obj="passedObject"></my-component>
  </div>
  <script>
  const MyComponent={
    template:'<div>Number: {{num}}<br />String: {{str}} \
         <br />IsEven?: {{even}}<br/>Object: {{obj.message}}</div>',
    props: {
      num: {
        type: Number,
        required: true
      },
      str: {
        type: String,
        default: "Hello World"
      },
      obj: {
        type: Object,
        default: () => {
```

Passes in values to my-component

The MyComponent template is used to display all the properties.

Number validation must be present.

String validation includes a default value.

Object validation has a default message.

```
          return {message: 'Hello from object'}
        }
      },
      even: {
        validator: (value) => {                    Custom validator has to
          return (value % 2 === 0)                 check whether or not the
        }                                          number is even.
      }
    }
  }
};
new Vue({
  el: '#app',
  components:{'my-component': MyComponent},
  data() {
    return {
      passedString: 'Hello From Parent!',
      myNumber: 43,
      passedObject: {message: 'Passed Object'}
    }
  }

});
</script>
</body>
</html>
```

Open a browser and run the code in this example. The output is shown in figure 6.6.

Figure 6.6   Validation number, string, and object using prop validation.

This is what we expect! But is there a problem? If you look at the code, you'll notice our custom validator checks whether a number is even or odd. If it's odd, it returns `false`. Why don't we see `false` where it shows `IsEven`?

In fact, Vue.js does show it as `false`! But it's not in the template. By default, prop validations don't prevent passed-in values from showing up in the template. Vue.js checks the validation and emits warnings in the console. Open the Chrome console and look. Your console should look similar to figure 6.7.

The error shows that our custom validator failed for prop `even`. This is good to know, and we should change the passed in number to an even number. Keep this type of error in mind while using prop validations.

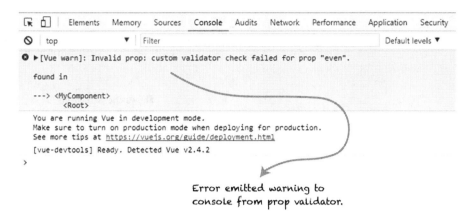

Error emitted warning to
console from prop validator.

Figure 6.7   Error showing validation failure.

6.4   Defining a template component

Until now, we've used local and global registration to define our components. Templates in each of our components have been defined as a string. This can be problematic as our components get larger and more complicated. The template strings aren't the easiest to work with due to different development environments that may cause issues with syntax highlighting. In addition, multiline template strings need escape characters, which clutter our component definition.

Vue.js has multiple ways to display templates that can help fix this. We'll discuss this and how we can use ES2015 literals to make our component templates easier to use.

6.4.1   Using inline template strings

One of the simplest ways of working with a template is to use it inline. To make this work, we need to include the template information inside the component when it's added to the parent template.

In listing 6.8, you can see that we declare the component as `<my-component :my-info="message" inline-template>` in the template. The `inline-template` tells Vue to render the contents of the component within the opening and closing of the `my-component` tag.

One downside of using inline templates is that they separate the template from the rest of the definition of the component. For smaller applications, this will work, although it's not recommended for use in larger applications. In larger applications, you should look into the single-file components that we'll discuss in the next chapter.

Listing 6.8   Using templates inline: chapter 06/inline-component-example.html
---

```
<!DOCTYPE html>
<html>
<head>
<script src="https://unpkg.com/vue"></script>
```

```
</head>
<body>
  <div id="app">
    <my-component :my-info="message" inline-template>
      <div>
          <p>
             inline-template - {{myInfo}}
          </p>
      </div>
    </my-component>
  </div>
  <script>
  const MyComponent = {
    props: ['myInfo']
  };

  new Vue({
      el: '#app',
      components: {'my-component': MyComponent},
      data() {
        return {
          message: 'Hello World'
        }
      }
  });
  </script>
</body>
</html>
```

The inline template displays HTML.

Shows the passed-in property

6.4.2 *Text/x-template script elements*

Another way of defining a template in our component is by using text/x-template script elements. In this case, we create a script tag with the type text/x-template.

In listing 6.9, we use the text/x-template to define the template for my-component. The thing to remember here is that you must define the script as type="text/x-template", otherwise it won't work.

Once again, we run into the same downside as with the inline templates. The biggest problem is that we're separating the component definition from the template. This will work, but it's useful only in smaller applications and not in larger ones.

> Listing 6.9 Working with text/x-templates: chapter 06/x-template-example.html

```
<!DOCTYPE html>
<html>
<head>
<script src="https://unpkg.com/vue"></script>
</head>
<body>
<div id="app">
  <my-component></my-component>
</div>
<script type="text/x-template" id="my-component">
  <p>
```

Shows the x-template script

```
      Hello from x-template
    </p>
  </script>
  <script>
  const MyComponent = {
    template: '#my-component'
  };
  new Vue({
    el: '#app',
    components: {'my-component': MyComponent}
  });
  </script>
  </body>
</html>
```

6.4.3 *Using single-file components*

Earlier in our examples, we used strings to represent our templates in our components. With ES2015 template literals, we can help eliminate several problems we had using strings. In ES2015, if you surround a string with a backtick (`` ` ``), it becomes a template literal. Template literals can be multiline without having to escape them. They can have embedded expressions in them, too. This makes writing our templates much easier.

With all that said, ES2015 template literals still have several of the same drawbacks as strings. It still looks a little cluttered in your component definition, and certain development environments won't have syntax highlighting. You have one more option to help fix all these problems: single-file components.

Single-file components combine your template and definitions into one .vue file. Each one has its own scope, and you don't have to worry about forcing unique names for every component. CSS is also scoped for each component, which is helpful in those larger applications. To top it all off, you no longer have to worry about dealing with string templates or having to work with unusual script tags.

In the following listing, you can see that the HTML is surrounded by the template tag, unlike in our previous examples. The .vue file uses ES2015 export to return the data for the component.

> **Listing 6.10 Single-file components: chapter 06/single-file-component.vue**

```
<template>
  <div class="hello">        ◁⎯⎤ The template displays
    {{msg}}                       │ information for the component.
  </div>
</template>

<script>
  export default {
  name: 'hello',             ◁⎯⎤ Shows the ES2015
  data () {                      │ export of the data
    return {
      msg: 'Welcome to Your Vue.js App'
    }
  }
}
```

```
}
</script>

<!-- Add "scoped" attribute to limit CSS to this component only -->
<style scoped>
</style>
```

To use single-file components, you'll have to get familiar with several modern build tools. You'll need to use a tool such as Webpack or Browserify to build the .vue code. Vue.js has made this process easy with its own scaffolding generator called Vue-CLI. It contains all the necessary build tools. We'll discuss tools in the next chapter. For now, know that there are many ways to work with templates and that single-file components are the way to go for larger applications.

6.5   *Working with custom events*

Vue.js has its own event interface. Unlike normal events that we saw in chapter 3, custom events are used when passing events from parent to child components. The event interface can listen to events using the `$on(eventname)` and trigger events using `$emit(eventName)`. Typically, `$on(eventname)` is used when sending events between different components that aren't parent and child. For parent and child events, we must use the `v-on` directive. We can use this interface so parent components can listen directly to child components.

6.5.1   *Listening to events*

Imagine you're creating a counter. You want to have a button on the screen that increments the counter by 1 every time it's clicked but you'd like to have that button in a child component and the counter in a parent Vue.js instance. You don't want the counter to mutate inside the child component. Instead, it should notify the parent that the counter should be updated. On every button click, the counter in the parent needs to update. Let's look at how to do this.

Let's start by creating a component. When we add it to our template, we'll need to use the v-on directive and create a custom event. As you can see in listing 6.11, we've added the component and created a custom event called `increment-me`. This custom event is bound to the `incrementCounter` method that we defined in the parent Vue instance. We'll also add a normal button that's bound to the click event that triggers `incrementCounter`, too. This button resides in the parent's template.

Inside the definition of our component, we'll need to add a button. We'll again use the v-on directive bound to the click event. This triggers the `childIncrement-Counter` method that we defined in the child component.

The `childIncrementCounter` has only one responsibility, and that's to emit the custom event we created earlier. This is where it might get confusing. We'll use `this.$emit('increment-me')` to trigger the bound event, `incrementCounter`, defined in the parent methods. We're triggering the parent Vue.js instance `incrementCounter` method, which will increment the counter. This is powerful and allows us to modify values in the parent while keeping the one-way data principle intact.

Listing 6.11 Incrementing a parent counter using `$emit`**: chapter 06/event-listen.html**

```html
<!DOCTYPE html>
<html>
<head>
<script src="https://unpkg.com/vue"></script>
</head>
  <body>
  <div id="app">
    {{counter}}<br/>
    <button v-on:click="incrementCounter">Increment Counter</button>
    <my-component v-on:increment-me="incrementCounter"></my-component>
  </div>
  <script>
  const MyComponent = {
    template: `<div>
      <button v-on:click="childIncrementCounter"
        >Increment From Child</button>
    </div>`,
    methods: {
      childIncrementCounter() {
        this.$emit('increment-me');
      }
    }
  };
  new Vue({
    el: '#app',
    data() {
      return {
        counter: 0
      }
    },
    methods: {
      incrementCounter() {
        this.counter++;
      }
    },
    components: {'my-component': MyComponent}
  });
  </script>
  </body>
</html>
```

- Shows the button to increment the counter from the parent ◁
- Indicates the component that sets the increment me event to incrementCounter ◁
- Indicates the component button that triggers the childIncrementCounter method
- Emits the increment-me event ◁
- Shows the method to increment the counter by 1 ◁

If we load the Chrome browser, you'll see two buttons. Both will increment the counter setup in the parent and be displayed in the component (figure 6.8).

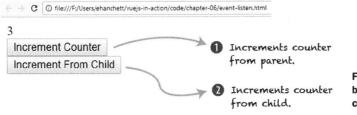

← → C ⓘ file:///F:/Users/ehanchett/vuejs-in-action/code/chapter-06/event-listen.html

3

Increment Counter — ❶ Increments counter from parent.

Increment From Child — ❷ Increments counter from child.

Figure 6.8 Shows two buttons; both increment the counter from the parent.

6.5.2   *Modifying child props using .sync*

In most situations, we don't want to have the child component mutate a prop from the parent. We'd rather have the parent do it. This is one of the fundamental rules of the one-way data flow that we mentioned earlier in the chapter. Vue.js allows us to break this rule, though.

The .sync modifier allows us to modify values in a parent component from inside a child component. It was introduced in Vue 1.x and removed from Vue 2.0 but the Vue.js core team decided to reintroduce it in 2.3.0+. With all that said, be cautious when using it.

Let's create an example that shows how .sync can update a value. Modify the code in listing 6.11 by updating my-component and childIncrementCounter. To begin, we'll look at the .sync modifier. To use the .sync modifier you can attach it to any prop on the component. In listing 6.12, it's attached at <my-component :my-counter.sync="counter">. The my-counter prop is bound to counter.

The .sync modifier is syntactic sugar for this <my-component :my-counter ="counter" @update:my-counter="val => bar = val"></my-component>. The new event created is called update. That event will take the my-counter prop and assign it to whatever variable is passed in .

To make this work, we still need to emit our new event that was created and pass in the value we want the counter to be updated to. We'll use this.$emit to do this. The this.myCounter+1 is the first argument that will be passed to the update event.

> **Listing 6.12   Working with .sync to modify props from child
> chapter 06/event-listen-sync.html**

```
. . .
<my-component :my-counter.sync="counter"></my-component>      ⬅─┐ Shows the component
  . . .                                                          setup with the
  const MyComponent = {                                          .sync modifier
    template: `<div>
      <button v-on:click="childIncrementCounter"
>Increment From Child</button>
    </div>`,
    methods: {
      childIncrementCounter() {
        this.$emit('update:myCounter', this.myCounter+1);   ⬅─┐ Emits to update event
      }                                                         followed by a comma
    },
    props:['my-counter']
```

If we load the browser, you'll see two buttons. If we click either one, it updates the counter (figure 6.9).

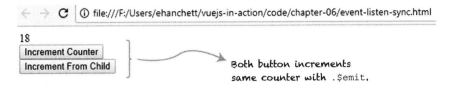

Figure 6.9 This example uses `.sync` to modify the counter.

Exercise

Use your knowledge from this chapter to answer these questions:

How do you pass information from a parent to a child component? What do you use to pass information from a child component back to a parent component?

See the solution in appendix B.

Summary

- Local registration for components has local scope. It can be created by using the components option when constructing a new Vue instance.
- Global registration for components uses the `Vue.components` instance operator where the component is defined.
- Components use one-way data binding between the parent and child component.
- Props are used in components to define what can be passed to them.
- Single-file components combine all template and script information into one file.
- You can use `$emit` to send information to the parent component.

Advanced components and routing

This chapter covers

- Working with slots
- Using dynamic components
- Implementing async components
- Using single-file components with Vue-CLI

Now that we've looked at components and how they can be used to break applications into smaller parts, let's look deeper into components and explore more of their advanced features. These features will help us create more dynamic and robust applications.

We'll look at slots first. *Slots* interweave the parent's content with the child components template, making it easier to dynamically update content inside components. Then we'll move on to dynamic components, which offer the ability to switch out components in real time. This feature makes it easy to change out whole components based on user action. For example, you might be creating an admin panel that displays multiple graphs. You can easily swap out each graph with dynamic components based on user action.

We'll also look at async components and how to divide an application into smaller chunks. Each chunk will load only when needed—a nice addition when our application grows large and we need to be sensitive to how much data we load when the application starts up.

While we're here, we'll look at single-file components and Vue-CLI. With Vue-CLI we can set up and create an application within seconds without having to worry about learning complicated tooling. We'll take everything we've learned from this chapter and refactor our pet store application to take advantage of Vue-CLI!

Finally, we'll look at routing and how we can use it to create route parameters and child routes. Let's begin!

7.1 Working with slots

When working with components, we occasionally need to weave in parent content with the child content, meaning that you'll need data passed into your component. Imagine you have a custom form component that you'd like to use on a book-publishing site. Inside the form are two text input elements, named author and title. Preceding each text input element is a label that describes them. Each label's title is already defined inside the root Vue.js instance data function.

You may have noticed when working with components that you can't add content in between the opening and closing tags. As you can see in figure 7.1, any content in between the opening and closing tags will be replaced.

```
<my-component>
    Information here will not be displayed by default.
</my-component>
```

Figure 7.1 Information inside component tags will be discarded.

The easiest way to make sure content is shown is to use the slot element, as we'll see next. This can be accomplished with Vue's *slot* element, a special tag that Vue.js uses to represent where data that's added in between the opening and closing tags of a component should be shown. In other JavaScript frameworks, this process is also known as *content distribution*; in Angular, it's called *transclusion* and it's similar to React's child components. No matter the name or framework being used, the idea is the same. It's a way to embed content from the parent to the child without passing it in.

At first, you may think of passing the values down from the root Vue.js instance to the child component. This will work, but let's see if we run into any limitations. We'll take each property and pass it down to the component.

Create a new file for this example and create a local component called form-component and a simple form inside it. The goal here is to create two simple props that the component will accept: title and author. In the root Vue.js instance, pass in the props to the component, as you can see in listing 7.1. This is similar to the prop passing we learned in chapter 6.

For the next few examples we'll create smaller standalone examples. Feel free to copy, or type, this into your text editor and follow along.

Listing 7.1 Creating a normal parent/child component with props: chapter-07/parent-child.html

```
<!DOCTYPE html>
<html>
<head>
<script src="https://unpkg.com/vue"></script>
</head>
<body>
  <div id="app">
    <form-component
      :author="authorLabel"          ⊲⎯ Passes in author label
      :title="titleLabel">                to form component
    </form-component>              ⊲⎯ Passes in title label to
  </div>                               form component
<script>
const FormComponent ={
  template: `
  <div>
    <form>
      <label for="title">{{title}}</label>     ⊲⎯ Displays passed
        <input id="title" type="text" /><br/>     in element title
      <label for="author">{{author}}</label>   ⊲⎯ Displays passed in
        <input id="author" type="text" /><br/>    element author
      <button>Submit</button>
    </form>
  </div>

  `,
  props: ['title', 'author']
}
new Vue({
  el: '#app',
  components: {'form-component': FormComponent},
  data() {
    return {
        titleLabel: 'The Title:',
        authorLabel: 'The Author:'
    }
  }

})
</script>
</body>
</html>
```

As I mentioned, the code will work, but as the form scales, we'll need to deal with passing in several attributes. What if we added in ISBN, date, and year to the form? We need to add more props and more attributes to the component. This can become tedious and means many properties to keep track of, which can lead to errors in your code.

Instead, let's rewrite this example to use slots. To begin, add text that can be displayed at the top of the form. Instead of passing the value in as props, we'll use a slot to display it. We won't need to pass everything into the component as a property. We can display whatever we want directly inside the opening and closing brackets of the component. When the form is completed, it should look like figure 7.2.

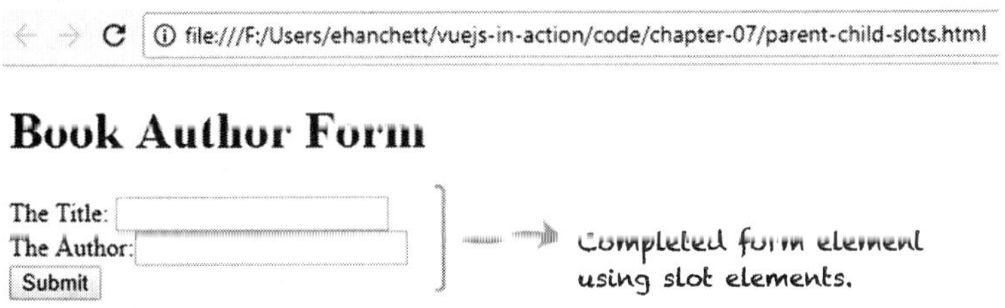

Figure 7.2 Book form page example.

Copy and paste listing 7.1 into a file and change the data function and add a new property called header. (Remember you can always download the code for this book at my GitHub at https://github.com/ErikCH/VuejsInActionCode.) As you can see in figure 7.2, we'll add a new header property that displays the Book Author Form. Next, find the opening and closing form-component that's declared in the parent's Vue.js instance. Add the header property in between those tags. Finally, we need to update the form component itself. Immediately after the first `<form>`, add the `<slot></slot>` elements. This tells Vue to add whatever is in between the opening and closing tags of the form-component. To run this example, update the code from listing 7.1 with the new updates in this listing.

Listing 7.2 Adding in the `slot` element: chapter-07/parent-child-slots-extract.html

```
. . .
<body>
  <div id="app">
    <form-component
      :author="authorLabel"
      :title="titleLabel">
      <h1>{{header}}</h1>          Shows header variable added
    </form-component>              inside form-component
  </div>
<script>
const FormComponent ={
  template: `
  <div>
    <form>
```

```
        <slot></slot>
        <label for="title">{{title}}</label>
     <input id="title" type="text" /><br/>
        <label for="author">{{author}}</label>
           <input id="author" type="text" /><br/>
        <button>Submit</button>
      </form>
    </div>
    `,
    props: ['title', 'author']
}
new Vue({
    el: '#app',
    components: {'form-component': FormComponent},
    data() {
       return {
           titleLabel: 'The Title:',
           authorLabel: 'The Author:',
           header: 'Book Author Form'
       }
    }

})
</script>
</body>
</html>
```

Inserts slot element from parent ←

Adds new header property ←

7.2 A look at named slots

As of now, we've added only one slot element to our component. But, as you may have guessed, this isn't too flexible. What if we had multiple props we wanted to pass in to a component and each prop needed to be displayed at different locations? Once again, passing in every single prop can be tedious, so what if we decided to use slots instead? Is there a way to do it?

This is where *named slots* come in. Named slots are like normal slots except they can be specifically placed inside a component. And unlike unnamed slots, we can have multiple named slots in our components. We can place these named slots anywhere in our components. Let's add two named slots to our example app. To add them, we need to define exactly where we want them added in our child component. In listing 7.3 we'll add two named slots—`titleSlot` and `authorSlot`—to the form-component.

We'll begin by replacing the `form-components` template with the new slot names. To do this, we must add a new `named-slot` element into the HTML. Take the completed code listing from 7.2 and move the label elements from the `form-component` to the parent's template as seen in listing 7.3. Make sure to change the name of the property in the label from `title` to `titleLabel` and from `author` to `authorLabel`.

Next, add two new slot elements. Each will replace the label in the form component's template. It should look like this: `<slot name="titleSlot"></slot>` and `<slot name="authorSlot"></slot>`.

Inside the parent's template, update the label we moved over and add a new attribute called slot to it. Each label should have a slot attribute like this: `<label for="title" slot="titleSlot">`. This tells Vue.js to make sure that the contents of this label are added to the corresponding named slot. Because we're no longer using the passed-in props, we can delete them from the form component. This is the completed code listing.

Listing 7.3   Using named slots: chapter-07/named-slots.html

```
<!DOCTYPE html>
<html>
<head>
<script src="https://unpkg.com/vue"></script>
</head>
<body>
  <div id="app">
    <form-component>
      <h1>{{header}}</h1>
      <label for="title" slot="titleSlot">{{titleLabel}}</label>
      <label for="author" slot="authorSlot">{{authorLabel}}</label>
    </form-component>
  </div>
<script>
const FormComponent ={
  template: `
  <div>
    <form>
      <slot></slot>
      <slot name="titleSlot"></slot>
        <input id="title" type="text" /><br/>
      <slot name="authorSlot"></slot>
        <input id="author" type="text" /><br/>
      <button>Submit</button>
    </form>
  </div>
  `

}
new Vue({
  el: '#app',
  components: {'form-component': FormComponent},
  data() {
    return {
        titleLabel: 'The Title:',
        authorLabel: 'The Author:',
        header: 'Book Author Form'
    }
  }

})
</script>
</body>
</html>
```

Displays the label using the slot titleSlot →

Displays the label for the author linked to slot authorSlot

Inserts the named slot for titleSlot ←

Inserts the named slot for authorSlot

The named slots make it much easier to insert elements from the parent into the child component in various places. As we can see, the code is a little shorter and cleaner. In addition, there are no more props passing, and we no longer have to bind attributes when declaring the `form-component`. As you design more complicated applications, this will come in handy.

> **Compilation scope with slots**
>
> In listing 7.3 we added a data property from the root Vue.js instance within the opening and closing tags of our form component. Keep in mind that the child component doesn't have access to this element because it was added from the parent. It's easy to accidentally mistake the correct scope for elements when using slots. Remember that everything in the parent template is compiled in the parent's scope. Everything compiled in the child template is compiled in the child scope. This is good to memorize because you might run into these problems in the future.

7.3   Scoped slots

Scoped slots are like named slots except they're more like reusable templates that you can pass data to. To do this, they use a special template element with a special attribute called `slot-scope`.

The `slot-scope` attribute is a temporary variable that holds properties that are passed in from the component. Instead of passing values into a child component, we can pass values from the child component back to the parent.

To illustrate this, imagine you have a web page that lists books. Each book has an author and title. We want to create a book component that holds the look and feel of the page, but we want to style each book that's listed inside the parent. In this case, we'll need to pass the book list from the child back to the parent. When all is said and done, it should look like figure 7.3.

This is a bit of a contrived example, but it shows the power of scoped slots and how we can easily pass data back and forth from child components. To create this app, we'll create a new book component. Inside the component we'll display a header

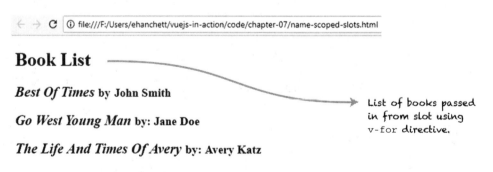

Figure 7.3   List of books and authors in the book list.

using a named slot, and we'll create another named slot for each book. As you can see in listing 7.4, we'll add a `v-for` directive that will loop through all the books and bind values to each one.

The books array is created in the root Vue.js instance. It's basically an array of objects, each having a title and author. We can pass that books array into the book-component using the `v-bind` directive `:books`.

Inside the parent's template we've add the new `<template>` element. We must also add the `slot-scope` attribute to the template tag for this to work. The `slot-scope` attribute binds the passed-in value from the child component. In this case, `{{props.text}}` is equal to `{{book}}` from the child component.

Inside the template tags, we can now access the `{{props.text}}` as if it were `{{books}}`. In other words, `{{props.text.title}}` is the same as `{{book.title}}`. We'll add special styling to each title and author to make it stand out.

Open your code editor and try to copy the code yourself from listing 7.4. What you'll see is that we took the books array and passed it into the book component. We then displayed each book in a slot that got passed into a template that the parent displayed to the user.

Listing 7.4   Scoped slots: chapter-07/name-scoped-slots.html

```
<!DOCTYPE html>
<html>
<head>
<script src="https://unpkg.com/vue"></script>
</head>
<body>
  <div id="app">
    <book-component :books="books">          Shows book component
                                             with passed-in books
      <h1 slot="header">{{header}}</h1>      Shows header text using named slot header
      <template slot="book" slot-scope="props">   Inserts template element with slot-scope of props
        <h2>
Displays text     <i>{{props.text.title}}</i>
for each          <small>by: {{props.text.author}}</small>
individual book  </h2>
      </template>
    </book-component>
  </div>
<script>
const BookComponent ={
  template: `
  <div>
      <slot name="header"></slot>          Inserts named slot that
      <slot name="book"                    binds the v-for directive
        v-for="book in books"
        :text="book">                      Passes in alias book
      </slot>                              from book in books
  </div>
  `,
  props: ['books']
```

```
}
new Vue({
  el: '#app',
  components: {'book-component': BookComponent},
  data() {
    return {
      header: 'Book List',
      books: [{author: 'John Smith', title: 'Best Of Times' },
              {author: 'Jane Doe', title: 'Go West Young Man' },
              {author: 'Avery Katz', title: 'The Life And Times Of Avery' }
             ]
    }
  }

})
</script>
</body>
</html>
```

> **Sets an array of books**

This might be a little confusing at first, but using scoped slots is powerful. We can take values from our component and display them in our parent to do special styling. As you're dealing with more complicated components with lists of data, this is a nice tool to have.

7.4   Creating a dynamic components app

Another powerful feature of Vue.js is *dynamic components*. This feature lets us dynamically change between multiple components using the reserved <component> element and the is attribute.

Inside our data function, we can create a property that will determine which component will display. Then, inside our template, we need to add the component element with the is attribute which points to the data property we created. Let's look at a practical example.

Imagine that we're creating an app with three different components. We need to add a button so we can cycle through each one. One component will list our books, another will list a form to add books, and the last will display header information. When we get it all done, it should look like figure 7.4.

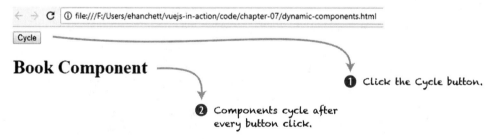

Figure 7.4   Dynamic book component cycle that displays each component after clicking the Cycle button.

Clicking the Cycle button displays the next component. The Cycle button triggers simple JavaScript that rotates through the book component to the form component then to the header component.

Open your text editor and create a new Vue.js application. Instead of creating one component, we'll create three. In each template, we'll display text letting the user know which component is activated. You can see an example of this in listing 7.5.

The data function will have one property called `currentView`. This property will point to the `BookComponent` at the start of the application. Next, create a method called `cycle`. This will update the `currentView` property on every click so it cycles through all the components.

As a final step, in the root Vue.js instance we'll add our button, with a click event attached like this: `<button @click="cycle">Cycle</button>`. Under the button we'll add an `<h1>` tag with our new component element. The component element will have one attribute, `is`, which will point to `currentView`. This is how you can dynamically change the component. The `currentView` property will update on every button click. To run this example, create a dynamic-components.html file. Add in this code.

Listing 7.5 Dynamic components: chapter-07/dynamic-components.html

```
<!DOCTYPE html>
<html>
<head>
<script src="https://unpkg.com/vue"></script>
</head>
<body>
  <div id="app">
    <button @click="cycle">Cycle</button>
    <h1>
      <component :is="currentView"></component>
    </h1>
  </div>
<script>
const BookComponent ={
  template: `
  <div>
    Book Component
  </div>
  `
}

const FormComponent = {
  template: `
  <div>
    Form Component
  </div>
  `
}

const HeaderComponent = {
  template: `
```

On every button click, the cycle method is triggered that changes currentView.

Shows the component element that's dynamically bound to currentView

```
      <div>
        Header Component
      </div>
      `
    }

  new Vue({
    el: '#app',
    components: {'book-component': BookComponent,        ◁──┐ Lists all components
                'form-component': FormComponent,               created
                'header-component': HeaderComponent},
    data() {
      return {
        currentView: BookComponent        ◁──┐ This is the property that's
      }                                        assigned initially to the
    },                                         BookComponent.
    methods: {                                              ┐ Shows the method to cycle
        cycle() {                              ◁────────────┘ through all three components
          if(this.currentView === HeaderComponent)
            this.currentView = BookComponent
          else
            this.currentView = this.currentView === BookComponent ?
            FormComponent : HeaderComponent;
        }
      }
  })
  </script>
  </body>
  </html>
```

You've learned how you can use one button to cycle through three different components. It's also possible to do this example using multiple `v-if` and `v-else` directives
but this is much easier to understand and works better.

7.5   Setting up async components

When working with larger applications, there might be times when we need to divide
the app into smaller components and load only parts of the app when needed. Vue
makes this easy with asynchronous components. Each component can be defined as a
function that asynchronously resolves the component. Furthermore, Vue.js will cache
the results for future re-renders.

Let's set up a simple example and simulate a server load. Going back to our book
example, let's say we're loading a book list from a backend, and that backend takes a
second to respond. Let's resolve this using Vue.js. Figure 7.5 is how it will look when
we're all done.

The function has a resolve and reject callback and we must set up our component
to handle the situations. Create an app and new book component, as seen in listing 7.6.

This simple component displays text on the screen after it resolves. We'll create a
timeout so it will take 1 second. The timeout is used to simulate network latency.

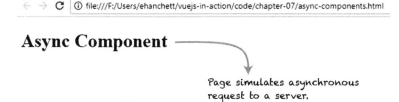

Figure 7.5 **Async component rendered after 1 second onscreen.**

The most important thing to do when creating an async component is to define it as a function with a resolve and reject callback. You can trigger different actions to occur, depending on whether the callback is resolved or rejected.

To run this example, create a file called async-components.html. Copy the code in the following listing to see it in action. You should see a simple asynchronous component. We're simulating a server that takes 1 second to respond. We could have also created a reject as well that would have resolved if the call failed.

Listing 7.6 Async components; chapter-07/async-components.html

```html
<!DOCTYPE html>
<html>
<head>
<script src="https://unpkg.com/vue"></script>
</head>
<body>
  <div id="app">
    <book-component></book-component>                Displays book
  </div>                                             component in template
<script>
                                                     Shows an asynchronous
                                                     book component that
const BookComponent = function(resolve, reject) {    must resolve or reject
  setTimeout(function() {
    resolve({                                        Shows a timeout that
      template: `                                    simulates a server and
      <div>                                          resolves after 1000 ms
        <h1>
          Async Component
        </h1>
      </div>
      `
    });

  },1000);

}

new Vue({
  el: '#app',
  components: {'book-component': BookComponent }
```

```
})
</script>
</body>
</html>
```

Advanced async components

Since Vue 2.3.0, you can now create more advanced async components. In these components, you can set up loading components that will display when the component is loaded. You can set error components and set timeouts. If you'd like to learn more about these components, check out the official guides at http://mng.bz/thlA.

7.6   *Converting the pet store app using Vue-CLI*

Until now, we've built our applications using one file. This has proved challenging because our pet store application has grown. One thing that would make our code base cleaner is to break the application into separate components.

As we saw in chapter 6, there are many ways to break up our application. One of the most powerful ways is using single-file components, which have many advantages over the other ways of creating components. The most important advantages are component-scoped CSS, syntax highlighting, ease of reuse, and ES6 modules.

Component-scoped CSS lets us scope CSS per component. This can help us easily make specific styles for each component. Syntax highlighting is improved because we no longer have to worry about our IDE not recognizing our component's template text since it no longer has to be assigned to a variable or property. ES6 modules make it easier to pull in our favorite third-party libraries. Each has advantages that make writing Vue.js applications a little easier.

To take full advantage of single-file components, we'll need to use a build tool such as Webpack that helps bundle all our modules and dependencies. In addition, we can use tools such as Babel to transpile our JavaScript so we can ensure that it's compatible with every browser. We could try to do this all ourselves, but Vue.js has given us Vue-CLI to make this process much easier.

Vue-CLI is a scaffolding tool to help jumpstart your Vue.js applications. It comes with all the glue needed to get started. The CLI has a number of official templates, so you can start your application with the tools you prefer. (You can learn more about Vue-CLI from the official GitHub page at https://vuejs.org/v2/guide/installation .html.) The following is a list of the most common templates:

- *webpack*—A full-featured Webpack build with Vue loader, hot reload, linting testing, and CSS extraction.
- *webpack-simple*—A simple Webpack + Vue loader for quick prototyping.
- *browserify*—A full-featured Browserify + Vuetify setup with hot reload, linting, and unit testing.
- *browserify-simple*—A simple Browserify + Vuetify setup for quick prototyping.
- *pwa*—A PWA (Progressive Web Application) template based on Webpack.

- *Simple*—The simplest possible Vue setup in a single HTML file.

To create an application, you'll need to install Node and Git, and then install Vue-CLI. (If you haven't done this yet, please refer to appendix A for more information.)

> **NOTE** As of this writing Vue-CLI 3.0 is still in beta. This chapter was written with the latest version of Vue-CLI, 2.9.2. If you're using Vue-CLI 3.0, several of these options will be different. Instead of creating the application with `vue init`, you'll use `vue create <project name>`. It will then ask you a new set of questions. You can either select a set of default presets or the features you want from a list. These include TypeScript, Router, Vuex, and CSS pre-processors, to name a few. If you're following along, make sure to select the same options as you see in listing 7.7. You can then skip ahead to section 7.6.2. For more information on Vue-CLI 3.0, check out the official readme at https://github.com/vuejs/vue-cli/blob/dev/docs/README.md.

7.6.1 Creating a new application with Vue-CLI

Let's create an application using Vue-CLI for our pet store. Open your terminal and type in `vue init webpack petstore`. This command tells Vue-CLI to create an application using the Webpack template.

As of this writing the latest Vue-CLI version is 2.9.2. If you're using a later version don't worry, the questions should be similar and self-explanatory. If you run into any issues, follow the official guides on the installation and use of Vue-CLI at https://vuejs.org/v2/guide/installation.html - CLI.

After you run the command, you're prompted with a few questions. The first asks for a name, then a description and author. Type in the name as `petstore` and put in any description and author you like. The next few questions prompt you whether to run Vue.js with a runtime only or runtime and compiler. I recommend running with the runtime and compiler together. This makes it easier when we're creating our templates; otherwise all templates are allowed in only .vue files.

The next question asks about installing the vue-router. Type `yes`. After this, it asks if you want to use ESLint. This is a linting library that will check your code on every save. For our purposes, we'll say no here because this isn't important to our project. The last two questions are about testing. In later chapters, I'll show you how to create test cases using the vue-test-utils library, but for now you can answer yes to both. Follow along with the this listing and create a new Vue-CLI application for our pet store app.

Listing 7.7 Terminal commands

```
$ vue init webpack petstore                      ◁──────────     Shows the init command that
? Project name petstore                                          creates a new application
? Project description Petstore application for book
? Author Erik Hanchett <erikhanchettblog@gmail.com>
? Vue build standalone
? Install vue-router? Yes
? Use ESLint to lint your code? No
```

```
? Setup unit tests with Karma + Mocha? Yes
? Setup e2e tests with Nightwatch? Yes

    vue-cli · Generated "petstore".                    Lists setup questions
                                                       and answers
    To get started:

      cd petstore
      npm install
      npm run dev

    Documentation can be found at https://vuejs-templates.github.io/webpack
```

After the application is created and the template is downloaded, you need to install all the dependencies. Change directories to petstore and run npm install, or YARN, to install all the dependencies by running the following commands at the prompt:

```
$ cd petstore
$ npm install
```

This will install all the dependencies for your application. This could take several minutes. After all the dependencies are installed, you should now be able to run the server with the following command:

```
$ npm run dev
```

Open your web browser and navigate to localhost:8080, where you should see the Welcome to Your Vue.js App window as seen in figure 7.6. (While the server is running, any changes will be hot reloaded in your browser.) If the server doesn't start, make sure another application isn't running on the default 8080 port.

We're now ready to move to our pet store application.

Figure 7.6 Default welcome screen for Vue-CLI

7.6.2   *Setting up our routes*

Vue-CLI comes with an advanced routing library called *vue-router*, the official router for Vue.js. It supports all sorts of features, including route parameters, query parameters, and wildcards. In addition, it has HTML5 history mode and hash mode with auto-fallback for Internet Explorer 9. You should have the ability to create any route you need with it and not have to worry about browser compatibility.

For our pet store app, we'll create two routes called `Main` and `Form`. The `Main` route will display the list of products from our products.json file. The `Form` route will be our checkout page.

Inside the app we created, open the src/router/index.js file and look for the routes array. You may see the default `Hello` route in it; feel free to delete this. Update the routes array so it matches listing 7.8. Every object in the array has at a minimum a path and a component. The path is the URL that you'll need to navigate to inside the browser to visit the route. The component is the name of the component we'll use for that route.

Optionally we can also add a name property. This name represents the route. We'll use the route name later. Props is another optional property. This tells Vue.js if the component should expect props being sent to it.

After updating the array make sure to import the `Form` and `Main` components into the router. Any time we refer to a component, you must import it. By default, Vue-CLI uses the ES6 import style. If the components aren't imported, you'll see an error in the console.

Finally, by default the vue-router uses hashes when routing. When navigating to `form` in the browser, Vue will construct the URL as `#/form` instead of `/form`. We can turn this off by adding `mode: 'history'` to the router.

> **Listing 7.8   Adding routes: chapter-07/petstore/src/router/index.js**

```
import Vue from 'vue'
import Router from 'vue-router'
import Form from '@/components/Form'      ◁──┐ Imports the components
import Main from '@/components/Main'          │ Form and Main

Vue.use(Router)

export default new Router({
  mode: 'history',                         ◁──┐ Shows history mode with
  routes: [                                   │ routes without hashes
    {
      path: '/',
      name: 'iMain',                       ◁──┐ Shows iMain
      component: Main,                        │ route at /
      props: true
    },
    {
      path: '/form',                          ┌ Shows Form
      name: 'Form',                        ◁──┘ route at /form
```

```
      component: Form,
      props: true
    }

  ]
})
```

It's a good idea to start any new application with your routes first. It gives you a good indication on how you want to construct the app.

7.6.3   *Adding CSS, Bootstrap, and Axios to our application*

Our pet store app uses a handful of different libraries that we need to add to our CLI project. We can handle this in different ways.

One way is to use a Vue.js-specific library. As Vue has grown, so has the ecosystem. New Vue.js-specific libraries are popping up all the time. For example, BootstrapVue, is a Vue.js-specific library to add Bootstrap to our project. Vuetify is a popular material-design library. We'll be looking at several of these libraries in the future, but not right now.

Another common way of adding libraries is to include them in the index file. This is useful when there isn't a Vue.js-specific library available.

To get started, open the index.html file in the root folder of our pet store application. To stay consistent with our original application from chapter 5, we'll add a link to Bootstrap 3 and Axios CDN in this file, as shown in the following listing. By adding these libraries in this file, we now have access to it throughout the application.

Listing 7.9   Adding Axios and Bootstrap: chapter-07/petstore/index.html

```
<!DOCTYPE html>
<html>
  <head>
    <meta charset="utf-8">                                      Denotes Axios
    <script                                                      library CDN
src="https://cdnjs.cloudflare.com/ajax/libs/axios/0.16.2/axios.js">  ◁

</script>

    <title>Vue.js Pet Depot</title>
    <link rel="stylesheet"
href="https://maxcdn.bootstrapcdn.com/bootstrap/3.3.7/css/bootstrap
➥ .min.css" crossorigin="anonymous">              ◁
                                                   Shows Bootstrap 3
  </head>                                          library CDN
  <body>
    <div id="app"></div>
    <!-- built files will be auto injected -->
  </body>
</html>
```

We have a few ways we can add in the CSS. As we'll see later, one way to add CSS is to scope it to each component. This is a helpful feature if we have specific CSS we want to use for a component.

We can also specify CSS that will be used throughout the site. To keep things simple, let's add our CSS to our pet store app so it can be accessed by all components inside it. (Later, we'll look at using scoped CSS.)

Open the src/main.js file. This is where the root Vue.js instance lives. From here we can import the CSS we'd like to use for our application. Because we're using Webpack we'll need to use the `require` keyword with the relative path to the asset.

> **FYI** For more information on how Webpack and assets work, check out the documentation at https://vuejs-templates.github.io/webpack/static.html.

Copy the app.css file into the src/assets folder, as shown in the next listing. You can find a copy of the app.css with the included code for the book in the appendix A.

Listing 7.10 Adding CSS: chapter-07/petstore/src/main.js

```
import Vue from 'vue'
import App from './App'
import router from './router'
require('./assets/app.css')            ◁──┐  Adds the app.css
                                           │  to the application
Vue.config.productionTip = false

/* eslint-disable no-new */
new Vue({
  el: '#app',
  router,
  template: '<App/>',
  components: { App }
})
```

After the CSS is added to the application, every component will use it.

7.6.4 Setting up our components

As we discussed previously, components make it easy to break our application into smaller reusable parts. Let's break our pet store app into a few smaller pieces so we can more easily work with our application. For the pet store we'll have a `Main`, `Form`, and `Header`. The `Header` component will display our site name and navigation, `Main` will list all our products, and `Form` will display the checkout form.

Before we begin, delete the HelloWorld.vue file in the src/components folder. We won't use this. Create a file called Header.vue in this folder instead. This file is where we'll put in our header information.

Most .vue files follow a simple pattern. The top of the file is usually where the template resides. The template is surrounded by an opening and closing `template` tag. As we've seen before, you must also include a root element after the template tag. I usually put a `<div>` tag in but a `<header>` tag will work too. Keep in mind a template can only have one root element.

After the template is a `<script>` tag. This is where we'll create our Vue instance. After the `<script>` tag is a `<style>` tag, which is where we can optionally put in our CSS code and scope it to the component. (You'll see this in listing 7.12.)

Go ahead and copy the code from listing 7.11 for the template. This code is similar to the code in chapter 5 for the header. You'll notice that we have a new element in the template called `router-link`, which is a part of the vue-router library. The `router-link` element creates internal links in our Vue.js application between routes. The `<router-link>` tag has an attribute called `to`. We can bind that attribute to one of our named routes. Let's bind it to the `Main` route.

> **Listing 7.11 Header template: chapter-07/petstore/src/components/Header.vue**

```
<template>
<header>
  <div class="navbar navbar-default">
    <div class="navbar-header">
      <h1><router-link :to="{name: 'iMain'}">        ◁─┐ This links to the
          {{ sitename }}                                 │ iMain route.
              </router-link>
                  </h1>
    </div>
    <div class="nav navbar-nav navbar-right cart">
      <button type="button"
class="btn btn-default btn-lg"
v-on:click="showCheckout">
        <span class="glyphicon glyphicon-shopping-cart">
              {{cartItemCount}}</span> Checkout
      </button>
    </div>
  </div>
</header>
</template>
```

Next, we need to create the logic for this component. We'll copy and paste from our previous pet store application into the Header.vue file. We'll need to make a few changes though. When we last updated the pet store application in chapter 5, we used a `v-if` directive to determine whether or not to display the checkout page. We created a method that toggled `showProduct` when the Checkout button was clicked.

Let's replace that logic so that instead of toggling `showProduct` we switch to the Form route we created earlier. As you can see in listing 7.14, this is done with `this.$router.push`. Similar to the `router-link`, we need to provide the router with the name of the route we want to navigate to. For this reason, we'll have the Checkout button navigate to the Form route.

Because we changed the `sitename` variable to a link using `router-link`, it now looks a little different than it did before. We should update the CSS for our new anchor tag by putting it in the `<style>` section. Because we added the keyword `scoped` to it, Vue.js will make sure the CSS will be scoped for this component only.

Also, you may notice from listing 7.12 that we're no longer using the Vue.js instance initializer that we used in previous chapters. The CLI doesn't require it. Instead we use a simpler syntax, the ES6 module default export (`export default { }`). Put all your Vue.js code in here.

In our CSS, we'll turn off text decorations and set the color to black. Combine listings 7.11 and 7.12 into one file.

> **Listing 7.12 Adding the script and CSS:**
> **chapter-07/petstore/src/components/Header.vue**

```
<script>
export default {
  name: 'my-header',
  data () {
    return {
    sitename: "Vue.js Pet Depot",
    }
  },
  props: ['cartItemCount'],
  methods: {
    showCheckout() {
      this.$router.push({name: 'Form'});          ◁─┐ Navigates Vue.js app
    }                                                │ to the Form route
  }
}
</script>

<!-- Add "scoped" attribute to limit CSS to this component only -->
<style scoped>                                       ◁─┐
a {                                                   │ Shows
  text-decoration: none;                              │ scoped CSS
  color: black;
}
</style>
```

From there you should be all set with this component. You may have also noticed that our header accepts a prop called `cartItemCount`. Our main component will pass this information in, as we'll see when we create the Main component. The `cartItemCount` will keep track of how many items we've added to our cart.

7.6.5 Creating the Form component

The `Form` component is where the checkout page resides. It will remain close to what we created in chapter 5. The biggest difference is that we're now referencing the new `my-header` component at the top of the template. We'll also pass in the `cartItemCount` into the header.

Create a component in the src/components folder and call it Form.vue. As you can see in listing 7.13, the HTML code in the template is almost exactly what we saw in chapter 5. The only change is that we've added a new component at the top for the header. I won't copy it all here, so I suggest that you download the code for chapter 07 (download instructions are in appendix A).

> **Listing 7.13 Creating the form component:**
> **chapter-07/petstore/src/components/Form.vue**

```
<template>
  <div>
    <my-header :cartItemCount="cartItemCount"></my-header>          ◁┐  The header
      <div class="row">                                              │  component shows
        <div class="col-md-10 col-md-offset-1">                      │  a passed-in value
          ...                                                        │  of cartItemCount.

      </div><!--end of col-md-10 col-md-offset-1-->
    </div><!--end of row-->
  </div>
</template>
```

The script code for this component resembles that from chapter 5. One difference is that now it accepts a prop called cartItemCount. In addition, we must define the Header component so it can be used in the template, as shown in this listing.

> **Listing 7.14 Adding the script tag: chapter-07/petstore/src/components/Form.vue**

```
<script>
import MyHeader from './Header.vue';          ◁┐  Imports Header
export default {                                │  component
  name: 'Form',
  props: ['cartItemCount'],          ◁┐  Passes-in the prop
  data () {                            │  cartItemCount
    return {
      states: {
...
      },
      order: {
        ...
      }

    }
  },
  components: { MyHeader },
  methods: {
    submitForm() {
      alert('Submitted');
    }
  }
}
</script>
```

Combine listings 7.13 and 7.14 and you should be all set. In later chapters we'll add more logic for inputs, but for now this will work.

7.6.6 *Adding the Main component*

The `Main` component of the pet store application will display all our products. It's where we'll add products to our cart and see the star ratings. We've already written all the logic for this, so the only thing we really need to do is get it into one .vue file.

As with the `Form` component, we'll add the `my-header` component to the top of the file and pass in the `cartItemCount` to it. Create a file called Main.vue in the src/ components folder. Add the following code into it.

Listing 7.15 Creating the main template:
chapter-07/petstore/src/components/Main.vue

```
<template>
  <div>
  <my-header :cartItemCount="cartItemCount"></my-header>          <———  The my-header component
  <main>                                                                 is added to the code.
  <div v-for="product in sortedProducts">
    <div class="row">
      <div class="col-md-5 col-md-offset-0">
        <figure>
          <img class="product" v-bind:src="product.image" >
        </figure>
      </div>
      <div class="col-md-6 col-md-offset-0 description">
        <h1 v-text="product.title"></h1>
        <p v-html="product.description"></p>
        <p class="price">
        {{product.price | formatPrice}}
        </p>
        <button class=" btn btn-primary btn-lg"
                v-on:click="addToCart(product)"
                v-if="canAddToCart(product)">Add to cart</button>
        <button disabled="true" class=" btn btn-primary btn-lg"
                                 v-else >Add to cart</button>
        <span class="inventory-message"
         v-if="product.availableInventory - cartCount(product.id)
         === 0"> All Out!
        </span>
        <span class="inventory-message"
        v-else-if="product.availableInventory - cartCount(product.id) < 5">
          Only {{product.availableInventory - cartCount(product.id)}} left!
        </span>
        <span class="inventory-message"
              v-else>Buy Now!
        </span>
        <div class="rating">
          <span  v-bind:class="{'rating-active' :checkRating(n, product)}"
             v-for="n in 5" >☆
          </span>
```

```
        </div>
      </div><!-- end of col-md-6-->
    </div><!-- end of row-->
    <hr />
  </div><!-- end of v-for-->
  </main>
  </div>
</template>
```

After you add the template, we'll need to add the Vue.js code. Add a new `MyHeader` import statement at the top of the file, as seen in listing 7.16. You'll also need to declare the component by referencing `components: { MyHeader }` after the data function.

Before we add the rest of the code, make sure to copy the image folder and the products.json files into the petstore/static folder. You can find these files and the code for chapter 7 at https://github.com/ErikCH/VuejsInActionCode.

When using the CLI, we can store files in two places—either the assets folder or the static folder. Asset files are processed by Webpack's url-loader and file-loader. The assets are inlined/copied/renamed during the build, so they're essentially the same as the source code. Whenever you reference files in the assets folder, you do so by using relative paths. The ./assets/logo.png file could be the location of the logo in the assets folder.

Static files aren't processed by Webpack at all; they're directly copied to their final destination as is. When referencing these files, you must do so using absolute paths. Because we're loading all our files using a products.json file, it's easier to copy the files to a static folder and reference them from there.

Go ahead and update the Main.vue file in the src/components folder. (Filters and methods are excluded in listing 7.16.) Grab the Vue.js instance data, methods, filters, and lifecycle hooks from the pet store application and add it to the Main.vue file below the template.

**Listing 7.16 Creating the script for Main.vue:
chapter-07/petstore/src/components/Main.vue**

```
<script>
import MyHeader from './Header.vue'        ◁─┐ Imports MyHeader
export default {                             │ into project
  name: 'imain',
  data () {
    return {
      products: {},
      cart: []
    }
  },
  components: { MyHeader },
  methods: {

    ...
```

```
  },
  filters: {
    ...

  },
  created: function() {
    axios.get('/static/products.json')
    .then((response) =>{
      this.products=response.data.products;
      console.log(this.products);
    });
  }
}
</script>
```

JSON products file is located in the static folder with the absolute path.

After copying the file, delete the styles and logo.png <img> tag in the App.vue file. If you like, you can also delete the logo.png file in the assets folder. Make sure to restart the Vue-CLI server by running npm run dev, if you haven't already. You should see the pet store application launch, where you can navigate to the checkout page by clicking the Checkout button (figure 7.7). If you receive any errors, double-check the console. For example, if you forgot to import the Axios library inside index.html as we did in listing 7.9, you'll get an error.

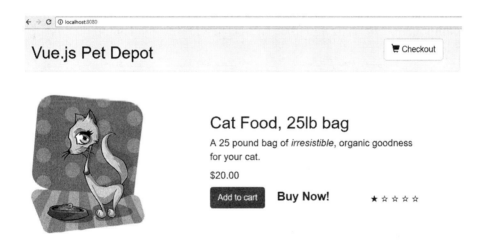

Figure 7.7   Pet store application opened with Vue-CLI.

7.7   Routing

Now that we have our app using Vue-CLI, let's take a deeper look at routing. Earlier in the chapter, we set up a couple of routes. In this section, we'll add a couple more.

In any single-page application such as Vue.js, routing helps with the navigation of the app. In the pet store, we have a Form route. When you load the application and go to /form, the route is loaded. Unlike traditional web apps, data doesn't have to be sent from the server for the route to load. When the URL changes, the Vue router intercepts the request and displays the appropriate route. This is an important concept because it allows us to create all the routing on the client side instead of having to rely on the server.

Inside this section, we'll look at how to create child routes, use parameters to pass information between routes, and how to set up redirection and wildcards. We aren't going to cover everything, so if you need more information, please check out the official Vue router documentation at https://router.vuejs.org/en/.

7.7.1 Adding a product route with parameters

In our application, we have only two routes, Main and Form. Let's add another route for our product. Let's imagine we've been given a new requirement for our pet store app. We've been told to add a product description page This can be achieved with dynamic route matching, using route *parameters*. Parameters are dynamic values sent inside the URL. After we add the new product description route, you'll look up a product page using the URL, as shown in figure 7.8. Notice how the URL at the top is product/1001? This is the dynamic route.

We designate dynamic routes with a colon (:) inside the router file. This tells Vue.js to match any route after /product to the Product component. In other words, both routes /product/1001 and /product/1002 would be handled by the Product component. The 1001 and 1002 will be passed into the component as a parameter with the name id.

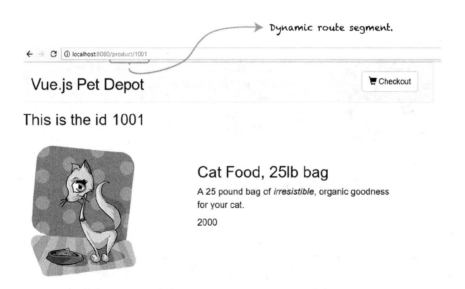

Dynamic route segment.

Figure 7.8 Dynamic segment for product 1001.

Inside the pet store app, look for the src/router folder. The index.js file has our existing routes. Copy the snippet of code from the following listing and add it to the routes array in the src/router/index.js file. Make sure to import the Product component at the top. We'll create that next.

Listing 7.17   Editing the router file: chapter-07/route-product.js

```
import Product from '@/components/Product'
...
    },
    {
        path: '/product/:id',            ◁─┐ Shows the dynamic
        name: 'Id',                         │ route segment called id
        component: Product,
        props: true
    }
...
```

We have a dynamic segment with a parameter named id. We set the name of the route to Id so we can easily look it up later using the router-link component. As mentioned, let's create a Product component.

Inside the Product component is a single product that we'll retrieve from the route params. Our purpose is to display that product information inside the component.

Inside the product template, we'll have access to the $route.params.id. This will display the id passed into the parameter. We'll display the id at the top of the component to verify that it was passed in correctly.

Copy the following code into a new file at src/components/Product.vue. This is the top of the file for the component.

Listing 7.18   Adding the product template: chapter-07/product-template.vue

```
<template>
  <div>
    <my-header></my-header>
    <h1> This is the id {{ $route.params.id}}</h1>   ◁─┐ The $route.params.id
    <div class="row">                                   │ shows the passed-in id.
      <div class="col-md-5 col-md-offset-0">
        <figure>
          <img class="product" v-bind:src="product.image" >
        </figure>
      </div>
      <div class="col-md-6 col-md-offset-0 description">
        <h1>{{product.title}}</h1>
        <p v-html="product.description"></p>
        <p class="price">
          {{product.price }}
        </p>
      </div>
    </div>
  </div>
```

```
      </div>
    </template>
...
```

The template was straightforward but the bottom of the component, where the logic and script live, is a little more complex. To load the correct product for the template, we need to find the correct product using the `id` that was passed in.

Luckily, with simple JavaScript we can do exactly that. We'll use the Axios library again to access the products.json flat file. This time we'll use the JavaScript filter function to return only the products whose ID matches `this.$route.params.id`. The filter should return only one value because all the IDs are unique. If for any reason this doesn't occur, double-check the products.json flat file and make sure each ID is unique.

Last, we'll need to add a fo/' character in front of the `this.product.image` that's returned from our flat file (listing 7.19). This needs to be done because we're using dynamic route matching and relative paths to files can cause problems.

Copy the code in this listing and add it to the bottom of the src/components/ Product.vue file. Make sure that the code from both listings 7.18 and 7.19 are present in the file.

Listing 7.19   Product script: chapter-07/product-script.js

```
...
  <script>
  import MyHeader from './Header.vue'         ◁── Imports Header
  export default {                                 component into file
    components: { MyHeader },
    data() {
    return {
      product: ''
    }                       Retrieves the static file
  },                        with the Axios library
    created: function() {                                           Filters the
      axios.get('/static/products.json')    ◁───────               response data
      .then((response) =>{
        this.product = response.data.products.filter(    ◁──
            data => data.id == this.$route.params.id)[0]
        this.product.image = '/' + this.product.image;   ◁──┐
      });                        Adds a '/' to the front of      Adds only data
    }                            product.image to help           that matches the
  }                              with the relative path          route params to
  </script>                                                      this.product
```

With the product component in place, we can now save the file and open our web browser. We don't have a way to access the route directly yet, but we can type the URL inside the browser at http://localhost:8080/product/1001. This will display the first product.

TROUBLESHOOTING   If the route doesn't load, open the console and look for any errors. Make sure you saved the data inside the router file; otherwise, the route

won't load. It's also easy to forget to add the '/' in front of this.product
.image.

7.7.2 Setting up a router-link with tags

Routes can be useless unless we add links to them inside our app. Otherwise, our users
would have to memorize each URL. With Vue router, we can make routing to a path
easy. One of the easiest ways, which we saw earlier in the chapter, is using the router-
link component. You can define the route you want to navigate to by using the :to
property. This can be bound to a specific path or object that defines the name of the
route to navigate to. For example, <router-link :to="{ name: 'Id' }">Prod-
uct</router-link> will route to the named route Id. In our app, it's the Product
component.

The router-link component has a few other tricks up its sleeve. This component has many additional props that add more functionality. In this section, we'll
focus on the active-class and tag props.

Let's imagine we've been given another requirement for our pet store app. We
want the Checkout button to appear like it's been clicked when the user navigates to
the Form route. When the user leaves the route, the button must return to its normal
state. We can do this by adding a class named active to the button when the route is
activated and remove the class when the user is not on the route. We also need to add
a way for the user to click the title of any product and have it route to the product
description page.

When all is done, our app will appear like figure 7.9 after the user clicks the Checkout button. Notice the button's appearance when the user is on the checkout page.

Let's add the link to our new product page. Open the src/Main.vue file and look
for the h1 tag that displays {{product.title}}. Delete it and add a new router
link. Inside the router-link, add a tag prop. The tag prop is used to convert the
router-link to the tag listed. In this case, the router-link will display as an h1 tag
in the browser.

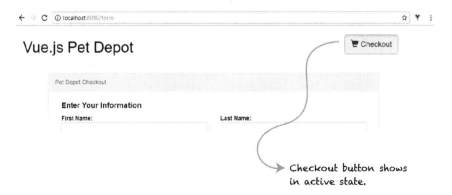

Figure 7.9 Checkout button updated with new style.

The `to` prop is used to denote the target route of the link. It has an optional descriptor object that we can pass to it. To send a `param`, use the `params: {id: product.id}` syntax. This tells Vue router to send the `product.id` as the `id` to the dynamic segment. For example, if the `product.id` was 1005, the route would be /product/1005.

Open the src/Main.vue file and update the component with the code in the following listing. Notice how the `:to` has two different props, `name` and `params`. You can separate each prop with a comma.

Listing 7.20   Updating router-link in main: chapter-07/route-link-example.html

```
                                        Starts router-link        Converts router-
...                                                                link to show up
<div class="col-md-6 col-md-offset-0 description">                 as an h1 tag
  <router-link
 tag="h1"
         :to="{ name : 'Id', params: {id: product.id}}">          The target of the
         {{product.title}}                        This will be    route is Id and the
  </router-link>                                   the clickable   params is passed.
  <p v-html="product.description"></p>             text.
...
```

Save and open the browser after running the command, `npm run dev`. You can now click the title of any product to navigate to the Product component. The `id` param will be sent to the Product route and used to display the product.

> **Query parameters**
>
> Query parameters are another way we can send information between routes. Parameters are appended to the end of the URL. Instead of using a dynamic route segment, we could send the product ID using a query parameter. To add a query parameter with Vue router, all you need to do is add a query prop to the descriptor object like this:
>
> ```
> <router-link  tag="h1":to=" {name : 'Id', query:
>  {Id: '123'}}">{{product.title}}</router-link>
> ```
>
> Multiple query parameters can be added, but each one must be separated by a comma; for example, `{Id: '123', info: 'erik'}`. This will show up in the URL as `?id=123&info=erik`. You can access queries inside the template with `$route.query.info`. If you want more information on query parameters, check out the official documentation at https://router.vuejs.org/en/api/router-link.

7.7.3   Setting up a router-link with style

One of our requirements is to find a way to activate the Checkout button after the user navigates to the `Form` route. The `active-class` prop makes this easy. When the route is active, the `router-link` will automatically add whatever value we assign to `active-class` to the tag. Because we're using Bootstrap, the class name `active` will make the button look like it's been activated.

Open the src/components/Header.vue file and update the button element for {{cartItemCount}}. Delete the existing button and add the router-link instead, as in this listing. You can also delete the showCheckout method because it will no longer be needed.

Listing 7.21 Updating header links when route is active: chapter-07/header-link.html
---

Notes the router-link element that will navigate to the checkout page

The active-class prop will add the active class.

```
...
<div class="nav navbar-nav navbar-right cart">
    <router-link
active-class="active"
tag="button"
class="btn btn-default btn-lg"
:to="{name: 'Form'}">
        <span
            class="glyphicon glyphicon-shopping-cart">
            {{ cartItemCount}}
        </span> Checkout
...
```

Converts route-link to h1 tag

Navigates to the Form route

Bootstraps classes for button

Save the changes to the header component and navigate the app. If you open the browser console, you'll see how the active class is added to the checkout button inside the header after each time it's clicked. When you navigate to the Main route again, the active class is removed. The active class is added to the button only if the route is active. When the user navigates away from the Form route, the active class is removed.

As of Vue 2.5.0+, a new CSS class was added whenever the user changes route. This is called the router-link-exact-active class. We can use this class out of the box and define functionality. Let's say we wanted to change the link to the color blue whenever the class was active.

Inside the src/components/Header.vue, add a new CSS selector at the bottom: copy the snippet from this listing. This class will be added to only the router-link element when the route is active.

Listing 7.22 Router-link-exact-active: chapter-07/route-link.css
---

```
...
.router-link-exact-active {
  color: blue;
}
...
```

Sets element to blue when route is active

Save the file and try navigating around in the browser. You'll notice that the Checkout button text in the header changes to blue when the route is active. For the rest of this book, we'll change this CSS selector to black, because blue doesn't look as nice as black. It's nice knowing it's there if we need it.

7.7.4   Adding a child edit route

The new Id route displays each individual product, but let's suppose we need to add a way to edit each product. Let's add another route that will display inside the Product route that's triggered whenever the user clicks the Edit Product button.

> **NOTE**   For the sake of simplicity, we won't implement the edit functionality. With our current implementation, there's no way we can save changes to our static file. Rather, we'll focus on how to add a child route and save the implementation of changing the product for the future.

Child routes are nested routes. They're perfect for situations where you need to edit or delete information within a current route. You can access these routes by adding a router-view component within the parent route, as we'll see.

When we have everything wired together, the new Edit route should look like figure 7.10. Take notice of the URL, product/1001/Edit.

Figure 7.10   The child Edit route of a product.

Let's begin by adding a new component. Inside the src/components folder, add a new file and call it EditProduct.vue. Copy this listing and add it to the src/components/EditProduct.vue file.

Listing 7.23   Adding the `EditProduct` component: chapter-07/edit-comp.vue

```
<template>
  <div>
    <h1> Edit Product Info</h1>
```

```
    </div>
</template>
<script>
    export default {
        //future                    ◁── Gives a future implementation
    }                                   for editing the product
</script>
```

Inside the `Product` component, add a `router-view` component. This component is internal to Vue router and is used for the endpoint for new routes. When this route is activated, the `EditProduct` component will display inside where the `router-view` component is located.

Copy the code snippet in the following listing and edit the src/components/Product.vue file to add a new button at the bottom and the router-view component. The button will trigger the new edit method. This pushes the `Edit` route and activates it.

Listing 7.24 Adding the `Edit Product` button: chapter-07/edit-button.vue

```
. . .
  </p>
  <button @click="edit">Edit Product</button>   ◁──┐ Shows the button that
  <router-view></router-view>   ◁── The router-view component is    triggers the edit method
</div>                              the entry point for the route.
. . .
methods: {
    edit() {                                    The $router.push
      this.$router.push({name: 'Edit'})   ◁── activates the Edit route.
    }
},
```

Now we have everything in place to update the router file. Add a new array called `children` inside the `Id` route. Inside the children array, we'll add the `Edit` route and the component `EditProduct`.

Take the code from the next listing and update the src/router/index.js file. Update the `Id` route and add the new `children` array. Make sure to also import the `EditProduct` component at the top.

Listing 7.25 Updating the router with the new child route: chapter-07/child-route.js

```
import EditProduct from '@/components/EditProduct'
import Product from '@/components/Product'
. . .
{
    path: '/product/:id',
    name: 'Id',
    component: Product,
    props: true,                          Defines a new child route that will
    children: [                       ◁── only appear inside the Id route.
      {
        path: 'edit',
        name: 'Edit',
```

```
            component: EditProduct,
            props: true
        }
    ]
},
...
```

Save the index.js file and check out the new route in your browser. Click the Edit Product button and you should see the Edit Product Info message. If the route isn't loading, double-check for errors in the console and verify the index.js file again.

7.7.5 *Using redirection and wildcards*

The last features of Vue router I want to cover are *redirection* and *wildcard routes*. Let's imagine we're given one final requirement for our pet store app. We need to make sure that if anyone accidentally enters the wrong URL, it routes them back to the main page. This is done with wildcard routes and redirection.

When creating a route, we can use a wildcard, also known as the * symbol, to catch any routes that aren't already covered by the other routes. This route must be added at the bottom of all the other routes.

The `redirect` option redirects the browser to another route. Go ahead and edit the src/routes/index.js file. At the bottom of the route, add this snippet of code.

> **Listing 7.26 Adding wildcard for route: chapter-07/wildcard-route.js**

```
...
{                              Catches all
  path: '*',         ◄──┘
  redirect:"/"                  Redirects
}                       ◄──┐    to "/"
...
```

Save the file and try to browse to /anything or /testthis. Both URLs will route you back to the main "/" route.

Navigation guards

Navigation guards, as the name suggests, guard navigation by redirecting or canceling routes. This might be particularly helpful if you're trying to validate a user before letting them enter a route. One way to use navigation guards is to add a `before-Enter` guard directly in the route configuration object. It might look like this:

```
beforeEnter (to, from, next) => { next() }
```

You can also add a `beforeEnter(to, from, next)` hook inside any component. This is loaded before the route loads. The `next()` tells the route to continue. A `next(false)` will stop the route from loading. If you'd like more information, see the official documentation at https://router.vuejs.org/guide/advanced/navigation-guards.html.

For reference, this listing shows the full src/routes/index.js file.

Listing 7.27 Full router file: chapter-07/petstore/src/router/index.js

```
import Vue from 'vue'
import Router from 'vue-router'
import Form from '@/components/Form'
import Main from '@/components/Main'
import Product from '@/components/Product'
import EditProduct from '@/components/EditProduct'
Vue.use(Router)

export default new Router({
  mode: 'history',
  routes: [
    {
      path: '/',
      name: 'iMain',
      component: Main,
      props: true,
    },
    {
      path: '/product/:id',          Notes the dynamic
      name: 'Id',                    route segment for id
      component: Product,
      props: true,                   Shows the child route
      children: [                    inside Id route
        {
          path: 'edit',
          name: 'Edit',
          component: EditProduct,
          props: true
        }
      ]
    },
    {
      path: '/form',
      name: 'Form',
      component: Form,
      props: true
    },                               Catches all at the bottom of
    {                                routes that redirect to "/"
      path: '*',
      redirect:"/"
    }
  ]
})
```

Lazy loading

The Vue-CLI uses Webpack to bundle the JavaScript code. This bundle can become quite big. This could affect load times in larger applications or for users with slow internet connections. We can use vue.js async component features and code splitting

(continued)
with lazy loading to help decrease the size of our bundles. This concept is beyond this book, but I strongly suggest you look up the official documentation for more information on it. You can find it at https://router.vuejs.org/guide/advanced/lazy-loading .html.

Routes are fundamental to most Vue applications. Anything beyond a simple "Hello World" app will need them. Make sure to take time and map out your routes accordingly so they make logical sense. Use child routes to specify things such as adding or editing. When passing information between routes, don't be afraid to use parameters. If you're stuck on a routing issue, don't forget to check out the official documentation at http://router.vuejs.org/en.

Exercise

Use your knowledge of this chapter to answer the following question:

Name two ways you can navigate between different routes.

See the solution in appendix B.

Summary

- Using slots makes an application more dynamic when passing information into components.
- You can use a dynamic component to switch between components within an application.
- Adding asynchronous component to an application improves speed.
- You can use Vue-CLI to convert an application.
- You can pass values using props between components.
- Child routes can be used to edit information inside parent routes.

Transitions and animations

This chapter covers

- Understanding transition classes
- Using animations
- Adding JavaScript hooks
- Updating the pet store application

In chapter 7 we looked at advanced components and discussed how we could use single-file components to break our application into smaller parts. In this chapter we'll look at transitions and animations using Vue.js. We'll create simple transitions and animations using these built-in animation/transition classes. After this, we'll use JavaScript hooks to create animations. We'll then look at transitions between components. At the end of the chapter we'll update our pet store application and add transitions and animations to it.

8.1 Transitions basics

To create a transition in Vue.js, you must first understand the `<transition>` component element. This is a special element that signifies to Vue.js that you want to transition or animate one or more elements. The `<transition>` element wraps a conditional, a dynamic component, or a component root node.

The transition component is either inserted or removed from the DOM, depending on certain conditions. For example, a `v-if` directive may add or remove an element that it surrounds. The transition component can recognize if there are any CSS transitions or animations when this action occurs. It will then either remove or add the CSS classes at the appropriate time to create the transition or animation. You can also add special JavaScript hooks to the component to create more complex scenarios. If no CSS transitions or animations are found, the DOM operations for insertion and removal will happen immediately; otherwise, the transition or animation occurs. Let's look at an example.

Imagine you're creating a website with a list of book titles. You want the user to toggle the description on or off by clicking the title. As we've learned in previous chapters, we can use a `v-if` directive to do this.

But you want the description to slowly fade in after clicking the title. You then need it to fade out after clicking the title again. You can do this in Vue.js using CSS transitions and the `<transition>` element.

Open your editor and create an application, as you see in listing 8.1. To begin, create a simple application that shows a fictitious title of an imaginary book as an `<h2>` tag at the top of the page. We'll surround this element by a `<div>` tag and attach a click event to it using `@click`. The purpose of this click event is to toggle a variable named `show`. If `show` is `true`, and the user clicks the button, it toggles it to `false`. If it's `false`, it will toggle to `true`.

Inside the body tag you'll need to add your new transition element. Transition elements can also have a `name` attribute. Set the name to `fade`. Wrapped inside the transition element is the `v-if` directive. This directive will toggle the description. At the bottom of our application, add the Vue constructor with the data function. This will hold all the variables for our application.

Listing 8.1   Creating a description transition: chapter-08/transition-book-1.html

```html
<!DOCTYPE html>
<html>
<head>
  <script src="https://unpkg.com/vue"></script>
</head>
<body>
  <div id="app" >
    <div @click="show = !show">          Denotes the div tag that toggles
      <h2>{{title}}</h2>                  variable show to be true or false
    </div>
    <transition name="fade">            Shows the new transition
      <div v-if="show">                  element that's named fade
        <h1>{{description}}</h1>
      </div>                            Shows the v-if directive that
    </transition>                       toggles showing the
                                        description or not
```

```
    </div>
    <script>
    new Vue({                                     Notes the Vue.js
      el: '#app',                                 constructor
      data() {                                    Shows the data
        return {                                  function with variables
          title: 'War and Peace',
          description: 'Lorem ipsum dolor sit amet,
consectetur adipiscing elim',
          show: false
        }
      }

    });
    </script>
  </body>
</html>
```

Load the application in a browser and open it. You should see a page that looks like figure 8.1. If you click the title, the description will pop up below it. This example has no transition at all. Clicking the title toggles the description either off or on. To add the transition, we must add the transition classes.

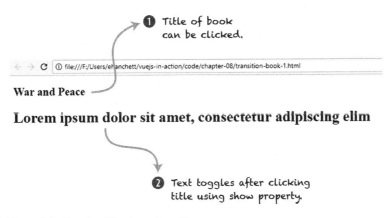

1 Title of book can be clicked.

War and Peace

Lorem ipsum dolor sit amet, consectetur adipiscing elim

2 Text toggles after clicking title using show property.

Figure 8.1　Toggle without any transition

Using listing 8.1, add a style tag inside the head element. For the purposes of simplicity, we'll inline the CSS inside the style tags in our example. That way, we don't have to worry about adding a separate CSS file.

There are six Vue.js CSS classes that can be applied to the enter and leave transitions. In this example we'll use four: `v-enter-active`, `v-leave-active`, `v-enter`, and `v-leave-to`. The other two we'll use later are `v-enter-to` and `v-leave`.

In listing 8.1, we didn't add any animation classes. As I mentioned earlier, if no CSS classes are present, the `v-if` directive conditional fires immediately and there are no

CSS transitions. We'll need to add CSS transition classes to make the fade effect work. First, let's look at what each of these classes does and when they're added or deleted from the DOM. Be aware that a frame is an array-like property that represents all elements in the current window. Table 8.1 shows all the CSS transition classes that you should be aware of.

Table 8.1 CSS transition classes

Transition class	Description
v-enter	This is the first state. It is added before the element is inserted and removed one frame after the element is inserted.
v-enter-active	This class is added to the element as long as the element is entering the DOM. It's inserted before the element is inserted and removed when the transition/animation is finished. This is where you enter in the duration, delay, and easing curve for the entire transition.
v-enter-to	This class was introduced in Vue.js 2.1.8+. This is added one frame after the element is inserted and removed when the transition/animation is finished.
v-leave	This class is added as soon as the element is leaving, or being removed, from the DOM. It's removed after one frame.
v-leave-active	This is the active state for the leave animation/transition. This is similar to the v-enter-active. You can use it to set the duration, delay, and easing curve of the leaving transition/animation. It's added immediately when the leave transition is triggered and removed when the transition/animation finishes.
v-leave-to	This is similar to the v-enter-to and was added after Vue.js 2.1.8+. This is the ending state for the leave. It's added one frame after a leaving transition is triggered and removed when the animation/transition is finished.

Each of these classes is added and removed at different times when elements in the DOM are added or removed. We can use these elements to construct transitions and animations. For more information on the transition classes, check out the official documentation at http://mng.bz/5mb2.

Let's add the transitions in the style element inside the head. Before we add these classes, you may have noticed in listing 8.1 that we added a name attribute to the transition element. Because we added a name attribute, the CSS class names will begin with the name we added, fade, instead of v-. If we chose not to add the name attribute to the transition element, the names of the classes would have remained: v-enter-active, v-leave-active, and so on. Instead, the class names will start with fade, fade-enter-active, and fade-leave-active, for example.

Add the fade-enter-active and fade-leave-active CSS transition classes inside the style tag in the application code from the previous listing. As mentioned, active classes are where we put the CSS transitions with the delay. In this example we'll set opacity, 2.5 seconds, and ease-out. This will create a nice fade effect that will take 2.5 seconds to complete.

Next, we'll add a `fade-enter` and `fade-leave-to`. This will set our initial opacity to 0. This will make sure that the fade occurs correctly with the opacity at 0. Update the previous example with the new style and see how it works. For the sake of simplicity, I've removed the other code, and because it's the same as listing 8.1. You can always consult the completed code that's included with the book.

> **Listing 8.2   Description transition with fade: chapter-08/transition-book.html**

```
...
  <style>
  .fade-enter-active, .fade-leave-active {      ⟵─  Active states show the duration
    transition: opacity 3.0s ease-out;              and easing of transition.

  }

  .fade-enter, .fade-leave-to {                 ⟵─  Enters and leaves
    opacity: 0;                                     states for opacity 0

  }
  </style>
...
```

Load this in your browser and open the development tools. You may notice something interesting when you click the title of the book and look at the source. For 3.0s you'll see a new class that surrounds the description, `fade-enter-active` and `fade-enter-to`. You can see it in figure 8.2.

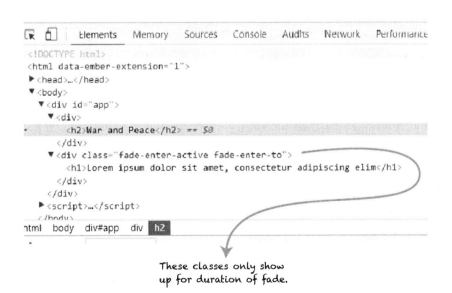

Figure 8.2   Classes when element is being added to the DOM

These classes will show up only for the duration of the fade. Afterward, the classes will be removed. If we click the title again, it will begin fading out the text. You can see in the browser `fade-leave-active` and `fade-leave-to` are added to the HTML node during the transition in figure 8.3.

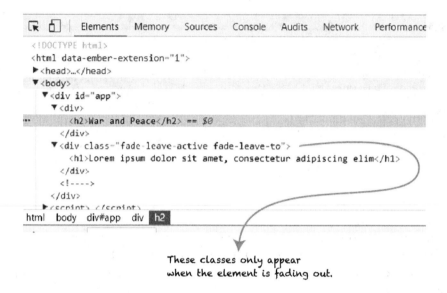

These classes only appear
when the element is fading out.

Figure 8.3   Classes shown when the element is removed from the DOM.

These classes are added momentarily while the element is being removed from the DOM. This is how Vue.js creates its animations and transitions. By adding and removing classes at different times, elements in Vue.js can create neat transitions and animations.

8.2   Animations basics

Animations are another important feature that Vue.js is good at. You may be wondering what the difference is between animations and transitions. Transitions are moving from one state to another, whereas animations have multiple states. In the last example, we went from seeing the text to fading the text. We also saw a transition from no text on the page to fading the text back in.

Animations are a bit different. You can have multiple states for each animation that can be within one declaration. You can do neat stuff with animations, such as create complex movements and chain multiple animations together. Animations can act like transitions too, but they aren't transitions.

Let's take the same example from listing 8.2 and add an animation. We'll use the same code, except this time we'll add a nice bounce effect using CSS keyframes. We want the animation to fade in and scale when the title is clicked. When the title is clicked again, we want the animation to scale and fade out. Open your text editor and copy listing 8.2. Update the transition name to bounce, as seen in listing 8.3.

Listing 8.3   Animation with scale: chapter-08/animation-book-1.html

```
<div @click="show = !show">
  <h2>{{title}}</h2>
</div>
<transition name="bounce">          ⊲┐  Shows the bounce
  <div v-if="show">                     │  transition
    <h1>{{description}}</h1>
  </div>
</transition>
```

Now we need to add our new animation. This animation needs the enter-active and leave-active classes. Begin by deleting the old CSS transition elements. Then add the bounce-enter-active and the bounce-leave-active classes. Add a CSS animation with a bounceIn of 2s inside the bounce-enter-active class. Add the same to the bounce-leave-active class and add a reverse.

Next create the CSS keyframes. Use @keyframes and add 0%, 60%, and 100%. We'll use CSS transform with a scale of .1 for 0%, 1.2 for 60%, and 1 for 100%. We'll also change the opacity from 0 to 1. Add this into the style as shown here.

Listing 8.4   Animation with scale full: chapter-08/animation-book.html

```
...
  <style>
  .bounce-enter-active {             ⊲┐  Enters active state that
  animation: bounceIn 2s;               │  uses keyframe bounceIn
  }
  .bounce-leave-active {             ⊲┐  Leaves active state that
  animation: bounceIn 2s reverse;       │  uses keyframe bounceIn
  }

  @keyframes bounceIn {              ⊲─────  Shows the keyframes
  0% {                              ⊲┐          for animation
    transform: scale(0.1);           │  0% animation transforms the scale
    opacity: 0;                         to 0.1 and sets the opacity at 0.
  }
  60% {                             ⊲┐  60% animation transforms the scale
    transform: scale(1.2);            │  to 1.2 and sets the opacity at 1.
    opacity: 1;
  }
  100% {                            ⊲┐  Final animation at 100%
    transform: scale(1);              │  transforms the scale to 1.
  }
  </style>
```

Open the file in your browser and check out the animation. You should see the fade in and scale occur when you click the title of the book. If you click it again, it will fade away. Figure 8.4 is a screenshot of the animation halfway through.

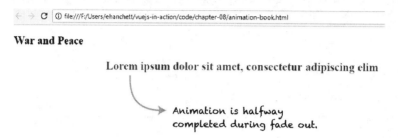

Figure 8.4   Screenshot of transition

The animation creates an effect where the text gets bigger and shrinks at the end.

8.3   *JavaScript hooks*

The transition and animation classes Vue.js provides should cover most basic transitions and animations you need, but Vue.js gives us an even more robust solution if we need it. We can set JavaScript hooks to do even more complex transitions and animations. We do this by combining the hooks with JavaScript that manipulate and direct CSS.

These hooks may remind you of the hooks we discussed in an earlier chapter for the Vue.js lifecycle. These JavaScript hooks are similar but are used for only transitions/animation. Remember a few things before using these hooks. First, we must always use the done callback when using the enter and leave hooks. Otherwise, they'll be called synchronously and the transition will finish right away. In addition, it's a good idea to add v-bind:css="false" when using JavaScript-only transitions so that Vue can skip all the CSS detection for that transition. One last thing to remember is that all hooks have the el, or element parameter, passed in except for enter and leave, which also passes done as a parameter. Don't worry if this is a little confusing; I'll show you in the next section how this works.

The JavaScript hooks that we can use when entering are beforeEnter, enter, afterEnter, and enterCancelled. When a transition is leaving, there's before-Leave, leave, afterLeave, and leaveCancelled. All these hooks are triggered at various times of the animation.

Let's imagine we're updating our book example to use the same sort of animations we were using earlier, except this time, we want to use JavaScript hooks instead of the CSS classes. How can we do this? Let's begin by taking our program from listing 8.4 and deleting the bounce-enter-active and the bounce-leave-active classes. We'll leave the keyframes in. Instead, we'll use the JavaScript hooks for enter and leave to do the animation in JavaScript.

Let's change the transition element so it has all the JavaScript hooks listed. To do this we'll need to use the v-on directive or use the @ sign for short. Add the JavaScript hooks for before-enter, enter, before-leave, leave, after-leave, after-enter, enter-cancelled, and leave-cancelled.

Listing 8.5   JavaScript hooks transition: chapter-08/jshooks-1.html

```
<transition name="fade"                          Shows all the hooks
    @before-enter="beforeEnter"                  for the transition
    @enter="enter"
    @before-leave="beforeLeave"
    @after-enter="afterEnter"
    @enter-cancelled="enterCancelled"
    @leave="leave"
    @after-leave="afterLeave"
    @leave-cancelled="leaveCancelled"
    :css="false">
```

Next, we'll need to add the JavaScript hooks in our methods object inside the Vue instance. To make this work correctly, we'll need to detect when the animation is completed. That way, we can clear the style and run done on the event. done is the parameter that's used in the enter and leave JavaScript hooks. done must be executed in these hooks. To do that, we'll create a new event listener.

The event listener waits until the animation completes by looking for animationend. When the animation completes, the callback will reset the style and execute done. We'll add this code above the Vue constructor in your HTML file, as shown here.

Listing 8.6   JavaScript hooks event listener: chapter-08/jshook-2.html

```
function addEventListener(el, done) {
    el.addEventListener("animationend", function() {      The Event listener watches
        el.style="";                                      for the animation to end.
        done();
    });
};
```

Even though we're using only leave and enter, let's add all the JavaScript hooks to our program. Each hook will write to the console log so you can get a better idea when they're triggered.

Add a new methods object to your Vue.js instance. Add all the JavaScript hooks that you added to the transition to that methods object. Inside the enter method, add a function to call the addEventListener that was created earlier and make sure to pass in the element and done, as you can see in listing 8.7. Next, we'll use JavaScript to set up the animation. The el.style.animationName is the name of the keyframe animation we created inside the style. The el.style.animationDuration will be set to 1.5 s.

Inside the leave hook, add the same animationName and animationDuration. We'll also add an el.style.animationDirection and set it to reverse. This will reverse the animation when the element is leaving the DOM.

Listing 8.7   JavaScript hooks methods: chapter-08/jshooks.html

```
...
  methods: {
      enter(el, done) {
          console.log("enter");
          addEventListener(el,done);
          el.style.animationName = "bounceIn"
          el.style.animationDuration = "1.5s";
      },
      leave(el, done) {
          console.log("leave");
          addEventListener(el,done);
          el.style.animationName = "bounceIn"
          el.style.animationDuration = "1.5s";
          el.style.animationDirection="reverse";
      },
      beforeEnter(el) {
          console.log("before enter");
      },
      afterEnter(el) {
          console.log("after enter");
      },
      enterCancelled(el) {
          console.log("enter cancelled");
      },
      beforeLeave(el) {
          console.log("before leave");
      },
      afterLeave(el) {
          console.log("after leave");
      },
      leaveCancelled(el) {
          console.log("leave cancelled");
      }
    }
  });
...
```

◁ The enter hook

◁ Inside the enter hook is a call to the addEventListener function.

◁ The leave hook

◁ Inside the leave hook is a call to the addEventListener function.

◁ The beforeEnter hook

◁ The afterEnter hook

◁ The enterCancelled hook

◁ The beforeLeave hook

◁ The afterLeave hook

◁ The leaveCancelled hook

After running this example, it should behave exactly like the book example in listing 8.4. Click the title and the animation will begin. If you click again, the animation will start in reverse. Keep an eye on the console. When you first click the title, you'll see a few messages, before enter, enter, and then after enter, as seen in figure 8.5.

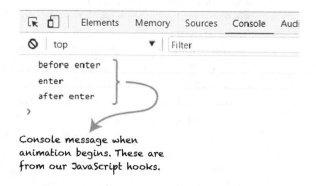

Console message when animation begins. These are from our JavaScript hooks.

Figure 8.5   Hooks triggered after clicking title

This is the order the hooks are executed. The `after enter` doesn't fire until the animation is completed. After clicking the title button again, we can see the order in which the hooks are triggered. First is `before leave`, then `leave`, and finally `after leave`, as you can see in figure 8.6.

Console messages appear when animation transitions out. These are from our JavaScript hooks.

Figure 8.6 Hooks triggered when element is removed from the DOM.

If you look at the source, you'll also notice the CSS being added and removed after every click. This is much like the CSS transition classes we saw previously.

8.4 *Transitioning components*

In the previous chapter we looked at dynamic components. These are components that we can swap out easily by use of the `is` attribute which points to a variable that's used to reflect the current component selected.

We can use transitions with components the way we did with the `v if` conditional directive that we used earlier. To make things easier, we'll modify the dynamic-components.html example from chapter 7. Grab a copy of listing 7.5 and make the changes that follow.

First surround the dynamic component, `<component :is="currentView"/>`, with the `<transition name="component-fade">` element. Before we go on, let's introduce transition modes.

By default, when transitioning components, you'll notice that one component will transition in while the other transitions out. This might not always be the desired outcome. We can add an attribute to our transition called `mode`. We can either have it set to `in-out` or `out-in`. If the element is set to `in-out`, the new element transitions in first; then when complete, the current element transitions out. But when it's set to `out-in` the current element transitions out first; then when complete, the new element transitions in. This `out-in` is what we need for our example so that way the previous component fades out before the new one appears. In this case, let's surround our dynamic component with `<transition name="component-fade" mode="out-in">`.

Next, we need to add in our transition classes, as shown in the following listing. Add the transitions class `component-fade-enter-active` and the `component-fade-leave-active`. We'll add an `opacity:0` to the `component-fade-enter` and the `component-fade-leave-to`. This is the completed code.

Listing 8.8   Transitioning dynamic components: chapter-08/component-transition.html

```
<!DOCTYPE html>
<html>
<head>
<script src="https://unpkg.com/vue"></script>
<style>
.component-fade-enter-active, .component-fade-leave-active {
  transition: opacity 2.0s ease;
}
.component-fade-enter, .component-fade-leave-to {
  opacity: 0;
}

</style>
</head>
<body>
  <div class="app">
    <button @click="cycle">Cycle</button>
    <h1>
      <transition name="component-fade" mode="out-in">
        <component :is="currentView"/>
      </transition>
    </h1>
  </div>
<script>
const BookComponent ={
  template: `
<div>
  Book Component
</div>
  `
}

const FormComponent = {
  template: `
<div>
  Form Component
</div>
  `
}

const HeaderComponent = {
  template: `
<div>
  Header Component
</div>
```

Shows the transition classes used to fade component

Shows the transition class used to set the opacity

Shows the transition component with the mode out-in

```
  }

new Vue({
  el: '.app',
  components: {'book-component': BookComponent,
               'form-component': FormComponent,
               'header-component': HeaderComponent},
  data() {
    return {
      currentView: BookComponent
    }

  },
  methods: {
        cycle() {
          if(this.currentView === HeaderComponent)
            this.currentView = BookComponent
          else
            this.currentView = this.currentView === BookComponent ?
FormComponent : HeaderComponent;
        }
    }

})
</script>
</body>
</html>
```

Open a browser with the current code and you'll see a Cycle button. Click the Cycle button and the previous component, Book Component, will fade out and the new component, Form Component, will fade in. Figure 8.7 shows a screenshot of the fade halfway through.

If you click the Cycle button again, the `Form` component will fade away to the `Header` component. It then starts over again at Book.

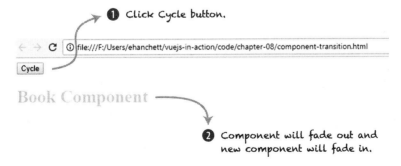

Figure 8.7 In-between transition of components

8.5   *Updating the pet store application*

We updated the pet store application in the last chapter when we switched it over to using Vue CLI with single-file components. Now that we have the power of transitions and animations, let's update the app to give it a little more flair.

Keep in mind that, depending on the web application you're creating, animations and transitions might be overkill. Unless you're creating a highly interactive app, you should probably stick to fewer animations and transitions. For this app, we'll add one animation and one transition. Let's look at the transition first.

8.5.1   *Adding a transition to the pet store application*

In our app, we want the page to fade in and out between routes. Let's add a simple fade-in and fade-out transition when navigating to the checkout page and back to the home page. As we did before, we'll use the Vue.js animation classes to accomplish this. Figure 8.8 shows what it will look like mid-transition from the home page to the check-out page.

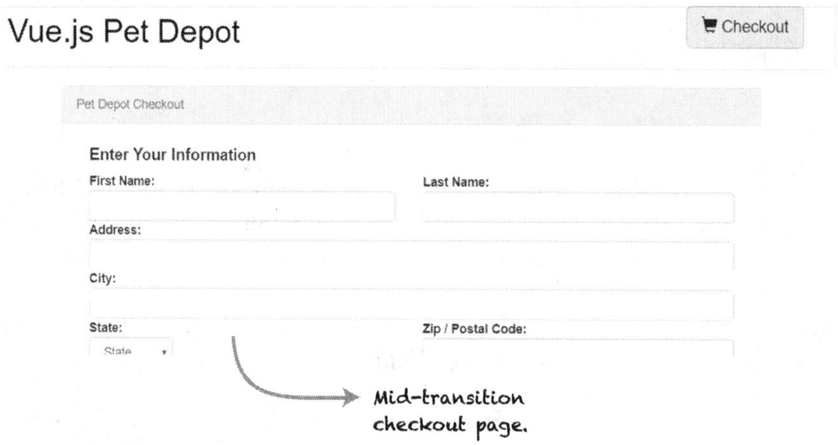

Figure 8.8   Page transitioning to the checkout page

Retrieve the pet store application we were working with in chapter 7 from the code included with this book. Go into the App.vue file inside the src folder. This file is where we set up our router from chapter 7. Similar to what we did with our previous examples, add a transition element and have it surround the router-view. Make sure to add the mode out-in as you see in listing 8.9.

Next, add the fade-enter-active and the fade-leave-active class to the style tag at the bottom. Set the transition to opacity with a .5s ease-out. Add the fade-enter and the fade-leave-to classes and set the opacity to 0.

Listing 8.9   Adding transition to pet store: chapter-08/petstore/src/App.vue

```
<template>
  <div id="app">
    <transition name="fade" mode="out-in">          ◁─┐  Transition component
      <router-view></router-view>                      │  with mode out-in
    </transition>                                       │  surrounds the router-view.
  </div>
</template>

<script>
export default {
  name: 'app'
}
</script>

<style>
#app {
}                                                   ┌  Vue.js transition classes
.fade-enter-active, .fade-leave-active {            ◁─┘  that set the transition.
  transition: opacity .5s ease-out;
}
.fade-enter, .fade-leave-to {        ◁─┐  Vue.js transition classes
  opacity: 0;                           │  that set the opacity.
}
</style>
```

After making these changes, save the file and run the npm run dev command. This will start the web server, and the web page should pop up in your browser. If not, navigate to localhost:8081 and check out the application. Click the checkout button and the home page and you'll see the page fade.

8.5.2   Adding an animation to the pet store application

When adding items to the cart, we added several v-if, v-else-if, and v-else directives. This lets the user know how much inventory is left that they can add to their cart. When the inventory runs out, an All Out message is displayed. Let's add an animation that shakes the text and briefly turns it red when the inventory is depleted for any item. To do this, we'll use the Vue.js animation CSS classes we learned about earlier. Figure 8.9 shows an example of how it will look with the All Out! animation moving left and right.

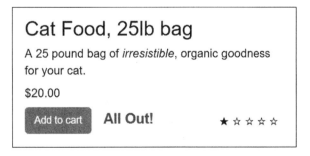

Figure 8.9   All Out! animation. The text moves left and right.

Open the Main.vue file and scroll all the way to the bottom. We're going to use one of the animation classes, `enter-active`, to create this animation. We don't need to worry about the animation when the element is removed from the DOM, so we'll skip adding the `leave-active` class.

Add an animation that shakes the text for around .72 seconds. We'll use a CSS `cubic-bezier` and a `transform`. In addition, we'll set up animation keyframes at every 10%. Copy this listing to the Main.vue file.

> **Listing 8.10   Add animation to pet store:**
> **chapter-08/petstore/src/components/Main.vue**

```
...
<style scoped>
.bounce-enter-active {                              Enter the active class that
  animation: shake 0.72s cubic-bezier(.37,.07,.19,.97) both;    starts the animation.
  transform: translate3d(0, 0, 0);
  backface-visibility: hidden;
}
                                                    Shows specific
@keyframes shake {                                  keyframes
  10%, 90% {
    color: red;
    transform: translate3d(-1px, 0, 0);
  }

  20%, 80% {
    transform: translate3d(2px, 0, 0);
  }

  30%, 50%, 70% {
    color: red;
    transform: translate3d(-4px, 0, 0);
  }

  40%, 60% {
    transform: translate3d(4px, 0, 0);
  }
}
</style>
...
```

After adding the CSS, we'll need to add the transition element for our animation. In the Main.vue file, look for the inventory messages. Each message will have the class of `inventory-message`. Add the `<transition>` element and surround the inventory-message. Make sure to add the `mode="out-in"` to the transition as you can see from listing 8.11.

In the previous examples, we transitioned or animated only one element. To animate more than one element, we need to add a key attribute to the `v-else-if` and `v-if` directives. Otherwise, Vue's compiler won't animate the content correctly.

THE KEY ATTRIBUTE   The key attribute is needed whenever you want to transition elements that have the same tag name. To make them distinct, you must add a unique key attribute. It's good practice to always add the key attribute when you're dealing with multiple items within a transition component.

Add a key attribute to the `v-else-if` and `v-if` directives. For the `v-else-if`, the key will be empty. This is intentional, so it won't animate. For the `v-if` directive we'll set the key to 0, as shown here.

> **Listing 8.11   Add animation to pet store transition element:**
> **chapter-08/petstore/src/components/Main.vue**

```
...
<transition name="bounce" mode="out-in">          The transition for bounce
  <span class="inventory-message"                 with a mode attribute
        v-if="product.availableInventory - cartCount(product.id) === 0"
        key ="0">
        All Out!                                  The key is added to
  </span>                                          v-if and set to zero.
  <span class="inventory-message"
        v-else-if="product.availableInventory - cartCount(product.id) < 5"
      key="">
    Only {{product.availableInventory - cartCount(product.id)}} left!
  </span>
  <span class="inventory-message"                 Another key is added
        v-else key="">Buy Now!                    so it won't animate.
  </span>
</transition>
...
```

Start the web server by running the `npm run dev` command and try out the app. Click the add to cart button until the inventory runs out. You'll see the All Out text move and shake for a few seconds and turn red.

Exercise

Use your knowledge from this chapter to answer this question.

What's the difference between an animation and a transition?

See the solution in appendix B.

Summary

- Transitions can move elements on your page.
- Animations can be scaled, and you can shrink text on the page programmatically.
- JavaScript animation hooks can be used to make complex animations.
- Transitions with dynamic components are useful for cycling through text.

Extending Vue

This chapter covers

- Learning about mixins
- Understanding custom directives
- Using the render function
- Implementing JSX

In the previous chapter we discussed transitions and animations. In this chapter we'll look at different ways we can reuse code in Vue.js. This is important because it allows us to extend the functionality of our Vue.js applications and make them more robust.

We'll begin by looking at *mixins*. Mixins are a way to share information between components; functionality is essentially "mixed" into the component. They're objects that have the same methods and properties that you'd see in any Vue.js component. Next, we'll look at *custom directives*. Custom directives allow us to register our own directives, which we can use to create whatever functionality we want. Then we'll look at the render *function*. With the render function we can go beyond using normal templates and create our own using JavaScript. Last, we'll look at using the render function with JSX, which is an XML-like syntax for JavaScript.

Don't worry, I haven't forgotten about the pet store application. In the next chapter we'll revisit it with Vuex.

9.1 Reusing functionality with mixins

Mixins are a great tool for many projects. They allow us to take small pieces of functionality and share them between one or many components. As you write your Vue.js applications, you'll notice that your components will start to look alike. One important aspect in software design is a concept known as DRY (don't repeat yourself). If you notice that you're repeating the same code in multiple components, it's time to refactor that code into a mixin.

Let's imagine you have an app that needs to collect a phone number or email address from your customer. We'll design our app to have two different components. Each component will contain a form with an input and a button. When the user clicks the button, it triggers an alert box that displays the text that was entered into the input box. It will look like figure 9.1 when we're done.

Figure 9.1   Mixin example with multiple components

This somewhat contrived example shows how we can extract logic as a mixin, in this case the logic that handles the button click and alert box. This keeps our code clean and avoids repeating code.

To get started with this example, create a file called mixins.html. To begin, we'll add our script tag for Vue.js and a link tag so we can add in Bootstrap for our styling. Then we'll add a basic HTML layout. The HTML will use Bootstrap's grid layout with one row and three columns. The first column will be set to col-md-3 with an offset of col-md-offset-2. This column will display our first component. The next column will have a column size of col-md-3. The third column will have a column size of col-md-3 and will show the last component.

Open your mixins.html file and enter the HTML code in the following listing. This is the first part of the code for this example. We'll add more code throughout this section. If you'd like to see the completed code for this example, look for the mixins.html file included with the code for this book.

Listing 9.1   Adding our mixin HTML/CSS: chapter-09/mixin-html.html

```html
<!DOCTYPE html>
    <script src="https://unpkg.com/vue"></script>
    <link rel="stylesheet"
href="https://maxcdn.bootstrapcdn.com/bootstrap/3.3.7/css
/bootstrap.min.css">                                      ⟵  Adds Bootstrap
<html>                                                        CSS code to file
<head>
</head>
<body>
  <div id="app">
    <div id="container">
      <h1 class="text-center">{{title}}</h1>
      <div class="row">
        <div class="col-md-3 col-md-offset-2">      ⟵
          <my-comp1 class="comp1"></my-comp1>
        </div>
        <div class="col-md-3">                       ⟵   Shows the Bootstrap grid
            <h2 class="text-center">Or</h2>                 system for columns
        </div>
        <div class="col-md-3">                       ⟵
          <my-comp2 class="comp2"></my-comp2>
        </div> <!--end col-md-2-->                   ⟵   Lists the second
      </div><!-- end row -->                              component
    </div> <!-- end container -->
  </div> <!-- end app -->
```

Lists the first component →

Now that we've added HTML, we'll work on the Vue.js code. Open the mixins.html file and add an opening and closing script tag. It's worth mentioning for this example that we aren't using single-file components with Vue-CLI. If we were to do so, this would work the same way. The only difference is that each component and mixin would be in its own file.

Add a new Vue instance in between the opening and closing script tag. Inside the Vue instance we'll add a data object that returns a title. Because we're using components, we'll also need to declare both components that we're using in this example. Add the code in this listing to the mixins.html file.

Listing 9.2   Adding the Vue.js instance: chapter-09/mixins-vue.html

```javascript
...
<script>
  new Vue({                          ⟵  Shows the root Vue.js
    el: '#app',                          instance declaration
    data() {                                                  Lists the data object
      return {                                                that returns the
        title: 'Mixin in example using two components'  ⟵    title property
      }
```

```
    },
    components:{
        myComp1: comp1,
        myComp2: comp2
    }

});
</script>
```

◁─── **Shows the declaration of components for myComp1 and myComp2**

We have a few other things left to do. We need to add both of our components and our mixin. Each component needs to display text, show an input, and show a button. The button needs to take whatever input was entered and display an alert box.

Each component is similar in a few ways. Both have a title, both have an input box, and both have a button. They also behave the same way after clicking a button. At first it might seem like a good idea to create one component but the visual look and feel of each component is different. For example, each button is styled differently and the input boxes themselves accept different values. For this example, we'll leave them as separate components.

With that said, we still have similar logic outside the template. We need to create a mixin that handles a method called `pressed` that displays an alert box. Open the mixin.html file and add a new `const` called `myButton` above the Vue.js instance. Make sure to add in the `pressed` function, an alert, and a data object that returns an item, as seen in this listing.

Listing 9.3   Adding the mixin: chapter-09/my-mixin.html

```
<script>
const myButton = {
  methods. {
    pressed(val) {
      alert(val);
    }
  },
  data() {
    return {
        item: ''
    }
  }
}
...
```

◁─── **Notes the myButton object mixin**

◁─── **Shows methods for the mixin**

◁─── **Notes the pressed function that shows alert box**

Now that we have the mixin in place, we can go ahead and add our components. After the `myButton` object, add two new components called `comp1` and `comp2`. Each one will contain an `h1` tag, a form, and a button.

In `comp1`, our input will use a `v-model` directive to bind the input to a property called `item`. In our button, we'll use the `v-on` directive shorthand @ symbol to bind the click event to the `pressed` method. Then we'll pass the item property into the method. The last thing we need to add to our `comp1` is to declare the mixin we created. We add the mixins array at the bottom, as you can see in listing 9.4.

For comp2, we'll add an h1 tag with a form, an input, and a button. For this component, we'll use the v-model directive to bind the item property. The button will use the v-on directive shorthand @ to bind the click event to the pressed method, as the same way we did in comp1. We'll pass the item property into the method. As with the other component, we'll need to define which mixins we want with this component by using the mixins property array at that bottom.

INFO   Mixins aren't shared between components. Each component receives its own copy of the mixin. Variables inside the mixin aren't shared.

I won't go into detail, but we've also added basic Bootstrap classes to the form elements to style them.

Listing 9.4   Adding in the components: chapter-09/comp1comp2.html

```
...
const comp1 = {                              ◁── Shows the component
    template: `<div>                              1 declaration
    <h1>Enter Email</h1>
    <form>
      <div class="form-group">
        <input v-model="item"                ◁── Inputs v-model directive
        type="email"                             binding item
        class="form-control"
        placeholder="Email Address"/>
      </div>
      <div class="form-group">
        <button class="btn btn-primary btn-lg"
     @click.prevent="pressed(item)">Press Button 1</button>   ◁──
      </div>                                          Shows the v-on directive
    </form>                                           with alias @ binds click
    </div>`,                                          event to pressed
    mixins: [myButton]        ◁── Notes the declaration
                                  of mixin for component
}
const comp2 = {
    template: `<div>
    <h1>Enter Number</h1>
      <form>
        <div class="form-group">          ◁── The v-model directive binds
          <input v-model="item"               the input to the item.
          class="form-control"
          placeholder="Phone Number"/>
        </div>
        <div class="form-group">
          <button class="btn btn-warning btn-lg"
     @click.prevent="pressed(item)">Press Button 2</button>   ◁──
        </div>                                         The v-on directive with
      </form>                                          alias @ binds the click
    </div>`,                                           event to pressed.
    mixins:[myButton]         ◁── Shows the mixin
                                  declaration at the bottom
}
...
```

Figure 9.2   The image from figure 9.1 after clicking Press Button 1

Open a browser and load the mixins.html file we're working on. You should see figure 9.1. Go ahead and enter an email into the Enter Email box. Click the button and you should see a pop up, as seen in figure 9.2.

This works the same if we enter values into the Phone Number box.

9.1.1   Global mixins

Until now, we've used named mixins that we've declared inside each of our components. Another type of mixin, a *global mixin,* doesn't require any type of declaration. Global mixins affect every Vue instance created in the app.

You'll need to be cautious when using global mixins. If you're using any special third-party tools, they'll also be affected. Global mixins are good to use when you're trying to add custom options that need to be added to every Vue.js component and instance. Let's say you need to add authentication to your app and you want the authenticated user to be available in every Vue component in the application. Instead of registering the mixin in every component, you can create a global mixin.

Let's look at our app from the last section. We'll go ahead and change it to a global mixin. First, take a copy of the mixins.html file from the previous example and copy it to mixins-global.html. We'll refactor our application in this file.

Look for the `const myButton` line inside the script tags. This is our mixin; to use global mixins, we need to change this from a `const` to a `Vue.mixin`. The `Vue.mixin` tells Vue.js that this is a global mixin and that it must be injected into every instance. Delete the `const` line and add the `Vue.mixin({` line to the top. Next, close the parenthesis at the bottom as you can see in the following listing.

> **Listing 9.5   Global mixin: chapter-09/global-mixin.html**

```
...
  Vue.mixin({
    methods: {
      pressed(val) {
```
← **Shows the declaration
of the global mixin**

```
            alert(val);
        }
    },
    data() {
        return {
            item: ''
        }
    }
});
...
```

| Notes the closing
←—┘ parenthesis

Now that we have the global mixin declared, we can remove the declarations for
myButton inside the components. Delete the mixins: [myButton] line from each
component. That should do it—now you're using global mixins! If you load the
browser with the newly created mixins-global.html file, it should behave and look the
exact same as you saw previously.

> **TROUBLESHOOTING**   If you run into any problems, it might be because you left
> the mixins declaration at the bottom of the component definitions. Make
> sure to delete any reference to myButton in your app or you'll get an error.

9.2   *Learning custom directives with examples*

In the last eight chapters, we've looked at all sorts of directives, including v-on,
v-model, and v-text. But what if we needed to create our own special directive?
That's where *custom directives* come in. Custom directives give us low-level DOM access
to plain elements. We can take any element on the page, add a directive, and give it
new functionality.

Keep in mind that custom directives are different than components and mixins.
All three, mixins, custom directives, and components, help promote code reuse but
there are differences. Components are great for taking a large piece of functionality
and separating it into smaller parts and making it available as one tag. Usually this
consists of more than one HTML element and includes a template. Mixins are great at
separating logic into smaller reusable chunks of code that can be shared in multiple
components and instances. Custom directives are geared toward adding low-level
DOM access to elements. Before using any of these three, take a minute to understand
which one will be best for the problem you're trying to solve.

Two types of directives exist, local and global. Global directives can be accessed
throughout the app at any place on any element. Typically, when you're creating
directives you want them to be global, so you can use them everywhere.

Local directives can be used only in the component that registered that directive.
This is nice to use when you have a specific custom directive that only needs to be
used in one component. For example, you might create a specific select drop-down
that works with only one component.

Before we look at each one, let's create a simple local custom directive that sets the
color and font size, and adds a Bootstrap class name to an element. It should look like
figure 9.3 when we're done.

Example of using a custom
directive with text.

← → C ⓘ file:///F:/Users/ehanchett/vuejs-in-action/code/chapter-09/directive-example.html ☆ ▼ ⋮

Hello World

Figure 9.3 Hello World text added using a custom directive.

Open a new file and name it directive-example.html. Inside the new file, add simple HTML. The HTML should include the script tag for Vue and the stylesheet for the Bootstrap CDN. Inside our app, we'll create a new directive called v-style-me, as you can see in this listing. This directive will attach to the p tag.

Listing 9.6   Vue.js local custom directive: chapter-09/directive-html.html

```
<!DOCTYPE html>
<html>
<head>
    <script src="https://unpkg.com/vue"></script>
    <link rel="stylesheet"
href=https://maxcdn.bootstrapcdn.com/bootstrap/3.3.7/css/bootstrap
 .min.css>
</head>
<body>
  <div id='app'>
      <p v-style-me>
          {{welcome}}
      </p>
  </div>
```

Shows the Bootstrap
added to the app

Lists the custom
directive for style-me

All custom directives start with a v-*. Now that we have our custom directive in place on our p tag, we can add the Vue logic to the app.

Create a Vue instance and a data function. This function will return a welcome message. Next, we'll need to add a directives object. This will register a local custom directive. Inside that directives object we can create our directives.

Create a directive called styleMe. Each directive has access to a number of arguments that it can use:

- *el*—The element the directive is bound to.
- *binding*—An object containing several properties, including name, value, oldValue, and expression. (See the custom-directive guide for the full list at http://mng.bz/4NNI.)
- *vnode*—The virtual node produced by Vue's compiler.
- *oldVnode*—The previous virtual node.

For our example we'll use only el, for the element. This is always the first argument in the list. Keep in mind that our styleMe element is in camelCase. Because it was declared in camelCase, it must be in kebab case (v-style-me) in the template.

All custom directives must specify a hook. Much like the lifecycle and animation hooks we looked at in earlier chapters, the custom directive also has many similar hooks. These hooks are called at various times of the custom directive's life cycle:

- *bind*—This hook is called only once, when the directive is bound to the element. This is a good place to do setup work.
- *inserted*—This is called when the bound element has been inserted into the parent node.
- *update*—This is called after the containing component VNode has updated.
- *componentUpdate*—This is called after the containing component's VNode and the children of the VNodes have updated.
- *unbind*—This is called when the directive is unbound from the element.

You may be wondering what a VNode is. In Vue.js the *VNode* is part of the virtual DOM that Vue creates when the application is started. VNode is short for virtual node and is used in the virtual tree that's created when Vue.js interacts with the DOM.

For our simple example, we'll use the bind hook. This is fired as soon as the directive is bound to the element. The bind hook is a good place to do setup work to style the element. Using JavaScript, we'll use the style and className methods of the element. First add the color blue, then the fontSize 42px, and finally the className text-center inside the bind hook.

Go ahead and update the directive-example.html file. Your code should match the following listing.

Listing 9.7   Local directive Vue instance: chapter-09/directive-vue.html

```html
<script>
  new Vue({
  el: '#app',
  data() {
    return {
      welcome: 'Hello World'          The data function returns
    }                                 the welcome property.
  },
    directives: {                     This is where directives
                                      are registered.
      styleMe(el, binding, vnode, oldVnode) {    Shows the name of the
        bind: {                                  local custom directive,
          el.style.color = "blue";     Notes the with arguments
          el.style.fontSize= "42px";   bind hook
          el.className="text-center";
        }
      }
    }
  });
</script>
```

```
</body>
</html>
```

Load up the browser and you should see the Hello World message. Now that we have this custom directive, we can use it on any element. Create a new `div` element and add the `v-style-me` directive. You'll notice that after you refresh the browser the text is centered, the font size is changed, and the color is blue.

9.2.1 *Global custom directives with modifiers, values, and args*

Now that we have a local directive, let's see what it looks like using a global directive. We'll convert our simple example, then we'll look at the binding argument. With the binding argument, we'll add a couple of new features to our custom directive. Let's give to the directive the ability to pass in the color of the text. In addition, we'll add a modifier so we can choose the size of our text, and we'll pass an arg for the class name. When it's all done it will look like figure 9.4.

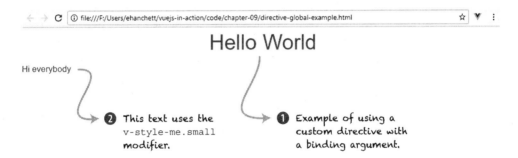

Figure 9.4   Using global directives with the binding argument

Copy the last example directive-example.html to directive-global-example.html. The first thing we need to do is to remove the directives object from the Vue.js instance. Go into our newly created directive-global-example.html file and remove the directives object below the data object.

Next, we'll need to create a new `Vue.directive`. This will tell Vue.js that we're creating a global directive. The first argument is the name of the directive. Go ahead and name it `style-me`. Then we'll assign the name of the hook. We'll use the bind hook the same way we did in the last example.

Inside the bind hook we'll have two arguments, `el` and `binding`. The first argument is the element itself. As we did in the previous example, we can use the `el` argument to manipulate the element the directive is attached to by changing its `fontSize`, `className`, and `color`. The second argument is called `binding`. This object has several properties; let's take a look at `binding.modifiers`, `binding.value`, and `binding.arg`.

The easiest binding property to work with is `binding.value`. When we add our new custom directive to an element, we can specify a value with it. For example, we could bind `'red'` to `binding.value`, as follows:

```
v-style-me="'red'"
```

We can also use object literals to pass in multiple values:

```
v-style-me="{ color: 'orange', text: 'Hi there' }"
```

We could then access each value using `binding.value.color` and `binding.value.text`. In listing 9.8, you can see that we set the element `el.style.color` to `binding.value`. If `binding.value` does not exist, it defaults to blue.

The `binding.modifiers` are accessed by adding a dot to the end of the custom directive:

```
v-style-me.small
v-style-me.large
```

When we access `binding.modifers.large`, it will return `true` or `false`, depending if the custom directive was declared when attached to the element. In listing 9.8, you can see that we check if `binding.modifiers.large` is `true`. If so, we set the font size to `42px`. Else if `binding.modifiers.small` is `true`, the font size is set to `17px`. If neither one of these modifiers is present, the font size isn't changed.

The last binding property we'll look at is `binding.arg`, declared in the custom directive with a colon and then the name. In this example, `text-center` is the argument:

```
v-style-me:text-center
```

With all that said, you can chain `modifiers`, `args`, and `values` together. We can combine all three. The `binding.arg` is `'red'`, the `binding.modifier` is set to `large`, and the `binding.value` is `text-center`.

```
v-style-me:text-center.large="'red'".
```

After adding the global custom directive make sure to go back into the HTML and add the second custom directive with text that displays `Hi` everybody. In this text, we'll use the binding modifier small on it, as shown in the following listing.

Listing 9.8   Completed Vue global directive: chapter-09/directive-global-example.html

```
<!DOCTYPE html>
    <script src="https://unpkg.com/vue"></script>
    <link rel="stylesheet"
href="https://maxcdn.bootstrapcdn.com/bootstrap/3.3.7/css/bootstrap
➥ .min.css">                                    ⟵┐
<html>                                             │  Shows the Bootstrap CSS
<head>                                             │  added to the app
```

```
</head>
<body>
  <div id='app'>
      <p v-style-me:text-center.large="'red'">
         {{welcome}}
      </p>
      <div v-style-me.small>Hi everybody</div>
  </div>
<script>
  Vue.directive('style-me', {
    bind(el, binding) {
        el.style.color = binding.value || "blue";

        if(binding.modifiers.large)
          el.style.fontSize= "13px";
        else if(binding.modifiers.small)
          el.style.fontSize="17px"

        el.className=binding.arg;
    }
  });

new Vue({
  el: '#app',
  data() {
    return {
      welcome: 'Hello World'
    }
  }
});
</script>
</body>
</html>
```

Notes the custom directive declaration with values, arg, and modifier

Lists the second custom directive with only a modifier

The global custom directive declaration uses the bind hook.

The element el.style.color is set to the binding.value or blue.

binding.modifiers are checked here to change the font size.

binding.arg is set to the class name on the element.

After loading up the browser, you should see the Hello World message. Notice how the second text, Hi Everybody, isn't centered and is smaller to the left of the screen. We got this because we used the v-style-me directive with only the small modifier. In that case, it changed the font size; however, it left the default color blue.

If you look closely at the source, you'll notice that a class of "undefined" was added to the second text div, because we assigned the binding.arg to el.className in the custom directive. However, because we didn't declare it, it's undefined by default. Beware this could happen: it would probably be a good idea to do a check on binding .arg before we set it to el.className. I'll leave that for you to do.

9.3   Render functions and JSX

Until now we've written all Vue.js applications using templates. This will work most of the time; however, there may be instances where you need to have the full power of JavaScript. For those cases, we can define our own render function instead of using a template. The render function will operate similarly to templates. It will output HTML, but you must write it in JavaScript.

JSX is an XML-like syntax that can be converted to JavaScript using a plugin. It's a way we can define our HTML inside JavaScript, like the render function. It's more commonly used with React, another frontend framework. We can use the full power of JSX with Vue.js, with the help of a Babel plugin.

Using JSX isn't the same as using the render function. To use JSX, you need to install a special plugin. But the render function works without any special setup inside your Vue.js instances.

In my experience, using the render function in Vue.js to create complex HTML is difficult. Common directives such as v-for, v-if, and v-model aren't available. You have alternatives for these directives, but you'll have to write extra JavaScript. But JSX is a strong suitable alternative. The JSX community is large and the syntax is much closer to templates, and you still get the benefit and power of JavaScript. The Babel plugin for Vue.js and JSX is well-supported and maintained, which is also nice. For those reasons, I'll only give a simple overview of the render function before we move on to JSX.

TIP If you'd like to learn about the render function in more detail, check out the official guides at https://vuejs.org/v2/guide/render-function.html.

9.3.1 *Render function example*

Let's create a simple example using render. Let's imagine we have a global Vue.js component that has a property named welcome. We want it to display the welcome message with an HTML header. We'll use a prop called header to pass in which header to use, h1, h2, h3, h4, or h5. In addition, we'll add a click event to the message so it shows an alert box. To make this good looking, we'll use Bootstrap's classes. Let's make sure our h1 tag also has a class of text-center on it. When it's all done it will look like figure 9.5.

Figure 9.5 An example of using the render function

Create a file called render-basic.html. In this file, we'll create our small app. Before we create our component, let's create the HTML. Inside the HTML, add your script for Vue and your link to the Bootstrap CDN.

Inside the body, include a div with ID of app and a new component called my-comp. The div is optional; we could assign the ID of app directly to the my-comp component. For the sake of clarity, we'll leave the `div` in as is. Inside that component, it will have a prop called `header` that will be assigned to 1. Inside the opening and closing brackets, we'll put in a name: Erik. Remember from a previous chapter anything in between the brackets of a component can be referenced with a slot. We can access slots using the `render` function, as we'll see next. Copy and paste the code from the following listing into the render-basic.html file.

Listing 9.9   Render basics html: chapter-09/render-html.html

```html
<!DOCTYPE html>
<html>
<head>
    <script src="https://unpkg.com/vue"></script>
    <link rel="stylesheet"
href="https://maxcdn.bootstrapcdn.com/bootstrap/3.3.7/css/bootstrap.min.css
">
</head>
<body>
    <div id="app">
        <my-comp header="1">Erik</my-comp>
    </div>
<script>
```

Vue.js script is added.

Bootstrap stylesheet is added.

Component is added with header prop.

Now that we have the HTML in place, we must add a root Vue.js instance before we can add a global component. At the bottom of the page inside the script tags, add new `Vue({el: '#app'})`.

After we add our root Vue.js instance, let's create our global component. Make sure to have the root Vue.js instance after the global component or you'll get an error. The first thing we'll need inside our component is a data function that returns welcome. We'll make it say, "Hello World." We also need to declare our prop header.

Instead of declaring a template property on the component, we'll declare a render function. Inside that function it will have one argument called `createElement`. (You may sometimes see this as h; it's the same thing.) Inside the `render` function, you must return `createElement` with the proper arguments.

When you return `createElement`, you're building a virtual DOM by describing the elements and child elements you'd like to define in your HTML. This is also known as a virtual node (VNode). You are essentially creating a tree of VNodes that represents the virtual DOM.

As you can see from listing 9.10, the `createElement` accepts three arguments. The first is a string, object, or function. This is usually where you put in the DOM element, such as a `div`. The second argument is an object. This represents the attributes you want included on the element. The third is an array or string. If it's a string, it represents the text that will be included inside the tag. But if it's an array, it usually represents the child VNodes. Each VNode is like adding another `createElement`. It has the same arguments. For this example, we'll use only a string.

Inside our `Vue.component` add the `render(createElement)` function. Inside the function, return `createElement`, as you see in listing 9.10. The first argument we want is the `header` tag. We need to use the prop passed in to form the header value. In this case we sent in 1, which we need to create an `h1`. We can concatenate the letter h with our prop `this.header`.

The next argument is the attribute object. Because we're using Bootstrap, we want to use the `text-center` class to align the text in the middle of the screen. To do that, we create an object and have the first property be `class`, with the value being `text-center`. In JavaScript, `class` is a defined keyword, so it must be in quotes. Our next attribute is our event. Event handlers are represented by the keyword `on` when using the render function. In this example, we use the click event and display an alert box that shows `clicked`.

The last argument is the array or string. This will define what we see inside our header tag. To make things more interesting, we'll combine the welcome message that we defined in the data function and the text inside the opening and closing brackets of the component, `Erik`. To get this text, we can use `this.$slots`
`.default[0].text`. This will get the text in the brackets as if it was the default text in a slot. We can now concatenate that with the welcome message. Copy this code into the render-basic.html. It should be all you need.

Listing 9.10   Adding the `render` function: chapter-09/render-js.html

```
Vue.component('my-comp',{        ⟵  Notes the global component
  render(createElement) {              called my-comp
    return createElement('h'+this.header,        ⟵  Returns the
      {'class':'text-center',     ⟵                    createElement
        on: {            The attribute object         argument
          click(e){     with the class and
            alert('Clicked');      click event defined
          }
        }
      },
      this.welcome + this.$slots.default[0].text  )  ⟵  Notes the string that will
    },                                                  show in the header element
    data() {
      return {
        welcome: 'Hello World '
      }
    },
    props: ['header']
  });
  new Vue({el: '#app'})        ⟵  Lists the root Vue.js instance
</script>                            that must be added
</body>
</html>
```

The render function is paired with the createElement argument.

Figure 9.6   The alert box created using the render function after clicking the message.

Load the render-basic.html file and look at the output, it should show the Hello World Erik message. Change the prop header to a different value. You should see the text get smaller as you increase the number. Click the message and you should see figure 9.6.

9.3.2   JSX example

With JSX, you can create HTML similarly to templates and still have the full power of JavaScript. To do this, we'll create an app using Vue-CLI. Our goal is to re-create the last example but use JSX instead. This example should accept a property, a class, and show an alert box when the message is clicked.

Before we start, make sure you have Vue-CLI installed: the instructions are in appendix A. Open a terminal window and create an app called jsx-example. You'll be asked to respond to a few prompts: enter no for all of them.

Listing 9.11   Terminal commands to create jsx project

```
$ vue init webpack jsx-example

? Project name jsx-example
? Project description A Vue.js project
? Author Erik Hanchett <erikhanchettblog@gmail.com>
? Vue build standalone
? Install vue-router? No
? Use ESLint to lint your code? No
? Setup unit tests No
? Setup e2e tests with Nightwatch? No

  vue-cli · Generated "jsx-example".

  To get started:

    cd jsx-example
    npm install
```

Next, change to the jsx-example directory and run npm install. This will install all the dependencies. Now we'll need to install the Babel plugin for JSX. If you have any problems with the installation of the plugin, please check the official GitHub page at https://github.com/vuejs/babel-plugin-transform-vue-jsx. The example I'm about to introduce to you only touches on the basics of JSX. I highly recommend reading the official documentation on the GitHub website on all the options available. Run npm install for all the recommended libraries, as shown here.

Listing 9.12   Terminal commands to install plugin

```
$ npm install\
  babel-plugin-syntax-jsx\
  babel-plugin-transform-vue-jsx\
  babel-helper-vue-jsx-merge-props\
  babel-preset-env\
  --save-dev
```

After you have the plugin installed, you'll need to update the .babelrc file. This is in the root folder. Inside it, you'll see many presets and plugins. Add "env" to the list of presets and "transform-vue-jsx" to the list of plugins, as in this listing.

Listing 9.13   Update .babelrc: chapter-09/jsx-example/.babelrc

```
{
  "presets": [
    ["env", {
      "modules": false
    }],
    "stage-2",                      Adds env to the
    "env"                           list of presets
  ],
  "plugins": ["transform-runtime", "transform-vue-jsx"],   Adds transform-vue-jsx
  "env": {                                                  to the list of plugins
    "test": {
      "presets": ["env", "stage-2"]    }
  }
}
```

Now that we've set up JSX, we can start coding. By default, Vue-CLI creates a Hello-World.vue file. We'll use that file, but we'll need to make several modifications. Go into the src/App.vue file and update the template. Remove the img node and add the HelloWorld component with two props. The first prop is our header, which will determine the header tag level. The second prop will be called name. In listing 9.10, we used slots instead of a named prop. In the following listing, we'll make a slight modification and pass the name in as a property instead. The result will be the same. Update your src/App.vue file so it matches this.

Listing 9.14   Update App.vue: chapter-09/jsx-example/src/App.vue

```
<template>
  <div id="app">
```

```
      <HelloWorld header="1" name="Erik"></HelloWorld>
    </div>
  </template>

<script>
import HelloWorld from './components/HelloWorld'

export default {
  name: 'app',
  components: {
    HelloWorld
  }
}
</script>

<style>
</style>
```

The Hello World component with two props, name and header

Because we're using Bootstrap, we need to include it somewhere. Find the index.html file in the root folder. Add the link to the Bootstrap CDN, as shown here.

Listing 9.15   Update the index.html file: chapter-09/jsx-example/index.html

```
<!DOCTYPE html>
<html>
  <head>
    <meta charset="utf-8">
    <meta name="viewport" content="width=device-width,initial-scale=1.0">
    <title>jsx-example</title>
    <link rel="stylesheet"
 href="https://maxcdn.bootstrapcdn.com/bootstrap/3.3.7/css/bootstrap
 .min.css">
  </head>
  <body>
    <div id="app"></div>
  </body>
</html>
```

Adds Bootstrap CDN

Open the src/components/HelloWorld.vue file. Delete the top template—because we'll be using JSX, we no longer need it. Inside the export default, let's set up the data object first. The data object will return welcome, as well as a message. The msg property will construct the HTML for the header and it will concatenate the message we want to show on screen using ES6 template literals.

Add a methods object as well. This will have a pressed method that will trigger an alert box that shows clicked. Last, add a props array at the bottom, for header and name.

The render function for JSX is similar to the render function we used in our first example. By convention, instead of using createElement, we use the letter h. Then we return the JSX we need.

As you can see in listing 9.16, the render function returns several tags. The first is a div tag that surrounds all the JSX. Then we have a div with a class that equals

text-center. We then add an on-click event handler that is assigned to `this`
`.pressed`. In normal Vue.js, data binding is done with text interpolation using the
Mustache syntax (double braces). In JSX, we use only a single brace.

The last thing we add is a special property called `domPropsInnerHTML`. This is a
special option added by the `babel-plugin-transform-vue` plugin. If you're familiar with React, it's similar to the `dangerouslySetInnerHTML` option. It takes
`this.msg` and interprets it as HTML. Be aware that taking user input and converting
it to HTML may lead to cross-site-scripting attacks, so be cautious whenever you use
`domPropsInnerHTML`. Copy the text from the following listing if you haven't already
and save it in your project.

> **Listing 9.16   Update HelloWorld.vue: chapter-09/jsx-example/HelloWorld.vue**

```
<script>
export default {
  name: 'HelloWorld',          A JSX render
  render(h) {                  function
    return (                              Notes a div tag
      <div>                               surrounding the JSX
        <div class="text-center"                            Notes a div tag with
        on-click={this.pressed}                             the class attribute
        domPropsInnerHTML={this.msg}></div>        The on click event handler
      </div>                                       that creates pop up box
    )
  },                          The domPropsInnerHTML
  data () {                   adds this.msg to div.
    return {
      welcome: 'Hello World ',                    The Hello World with
      msg: `<h${this.header}>Hello World ${this.name}     name added message
            </h${this.header}>`,
    }
  },
  methods: {
    pressed() {                      This is the method that
      alert('Clicked')               shows the alert box.
    }

  },
  props:['header', 'name']           Shows the two props
}                                    for header and name
</script>

<style scoped>
</style>
```

Save the file and start your server. Run `npm run dev` (or `npm run serve` if you're on
vue-cli 3.0) on the command line, and you can open the webpage at http://local-
host:8080. It should show the `Hello World Erik` message. Try to change several of
the values passed into the `HelloWorld` component inside App.vue. By changing the
header, you can change the level of header tag that's displayed.

Exercise

Use your knowledge from this chapter to answer this question:

What is a mixin and when should you use it?

See the solution in appendix B.

Summary

- You can share code snippets between multiple components using mixins.
- You can use custom directives to change the behavior of individual elements.
- You can use modifiers, values, and args to pass information into custom directives to create dynamic elements on the page.
- The render function gives you the full power of JavaScript inside your HTML.
- JSX can be used in your Vue.js application as an alternative to using the render function and still allow you to use the full power of JavaScript inside your HTML.

Part 3

Modeling data, consuming APIs, and testing

As your Vue.js applications grow larger and more complicated, you'll need to start thinking about a way to store data more efficiently in them. Luckily for us, Vuex offers an amazing solution that makes this process easy. We'll learn that in greater detail in chapter 10.

In chapter 11, dovetailing nicely from chapter 10, we'll look at communicating with a server. We'll discuss talking to a backend system and processing data. We'll then learn about server-side rendering, a new technology that will increase the speed of your application.

In chapter 12, we'll learn how to test. As a professional web developer, you'll need to know how to test your application. Testing helps eliminates bugs, and your applications will be more stable. We'll also take a peek at development operations, also known as DevOps. We'll learn how it can benefit our development lifecycle when deploying our application and making sure everything is working properly.

Vuex

In chapter 9, we looked at ways we could extend Vue.js and reuse part of its functionality without repeating code. In this chapter, we'll look at how we store data in our application and how that data is shared between components. One of the preferred ways of sharing data in an application is by using a library called *Vuex*. Vuex is a state-management library that helps create a centralized store that can be shared with all the components in the application.

We'll begin by looking at when we should use Vuex and when we shouldn't. Certain applications benefit more from Vuex than others. Next, we'll look at state and how we can centrally locate it. Afterward we'll explore getters, mutations, and actions. All three allow us to keep track of state in our application. Then we'll look at Vuex helpers, which will help us eliminate part of our boilerplate code. Last, we'll see what type of directory structure we can use to fully take advantage of Vuex in larger applications.

10.1   Vuex, what is it good for?

The Vuex state-management library mutates *state*. It stores state in a central location, which makes it easy for any component to interact with. State is the information or data that supports our application. This is important because we need to access that information in a reliable and understandable way.

If you've used other single-page frameworks, such as React, you may be already familiar with several of these concepts. React uses a similar state-management system called Redux. Both Redux and Vuex are inspired by a state-management system called Flux. Flux is an architecture that Facebook created to help build its client-side web applications. It promotes a unidirectional data flow from actions, to a dispatcher, to a store, to a view. This flow helps separate state from the rest of the application and it promotes synchronous updates. You can learn more about flux from the official documentation at https://facebook.github.io/flux/docs/overview.html.

Vuex uses these principles to help mutate state in a predictable, synchronous way. Developers don't have to worry about synchronous or asynchronous functions changing state in a way that we don't expect. Let's say we're interacting with an API on the backend that delivers a JSON payload to the application. But at the same time a third-party library is changing this information. We don't want a scenario where the third-party library mutates the data in an unpredictable way. Vuex helps protect us from this scenario by forcing all mutations to be synchronous.

You may be wondering why we need Vuex at all. After all, Vue.js gives us ways to pass information to components. As we learned from the components chapters, we can pass data using props and custom events. You could even come up with an event bus to pass information around and facilitate cross-component communication. You can see in figure 10.1 how this might look.

This works well for smaller applications with only a handful of components. In that scenario, we have to pass information to only a few components. What if our application were larger, with more complexity and levels? You can imagine that inside a larger application, keeping straight all the callbacks, passed props, and the event bus would be difficult.

This is where Vuex comes in. It introduces a more organized way to keep track of our state in one central store. Let's imagine a scenario where you might consider Vuex. In this scenario we're creating a blog, and inside that blog we have several components including post, comments, create, edit, and delete. We also have an admin interface where we can ban and add users.

Let's see how that would look with Vuex. As you can see in figure 10.2, the Edit Bio component is nested under the admin component. The Edit Bio component needs to have access to the user information, so it can update it. When using a central store

Simple example with a few components

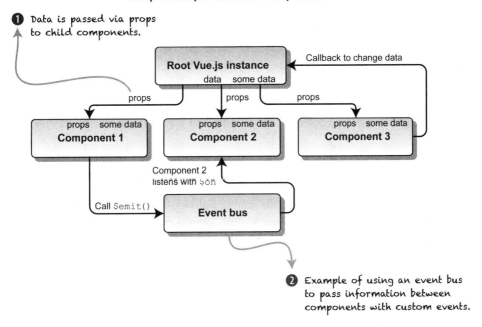

Figure 10.1   Simple example of using props and an event bus

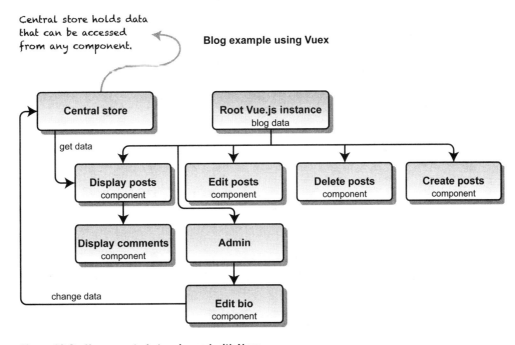

Figure 10.2   How a central store is used with Vuex

with Vuex, we can access the store, mutate the information, and commit it straight from the Edit Bio component. This is a significant improvement from having to pass the information down from the root vue.js instance to the admin component then finally to the `Edit Bio` component using props. Trying to keep the information straight from multiple places would be difficult.

With all that said, there's a price to pay with Vuex: adding Vuex will add more complexity and boilerplate code to your app. As I mentioned, you probably shouldn't use Vuex for simple apps with only a few components. Vuex thrives in larger applications where state can be more complicated.

10.2   *Vuex state and mutations*

Vuex uses a single object that contains the state for your complete application. This is also sometimes referred to as the *single source of truth*. As the name suggests, all the data is stored in exactly one place and isn't duplicated anywhere in the application.

> **TIP** It's worth mentioning that even though we're using Vuex, we don't have to put all our state in Vuex. Individual components can still have their own local state. In certain situations, this might be preferable. For example, in your component you might have a local variable that's only used in that component. That variable should stay local.

Let's create a simple example of using state with Vuex. For this example, we'll use a single file. Later, we'll see how we can add Vuex to a Vue-CLI application. Open a text editor and create a file called vuex-state.html. In this file we'll display a message that's stored in the central store and show a counter. When it's all done it will look like figure 10.3.

We'll first add a script tag CDN link to both Vue and Vuex. Next, we'll add in the HTML. For our HTML we'll use an H1, H2, H3 and a button tag. The h1 tag will dis-

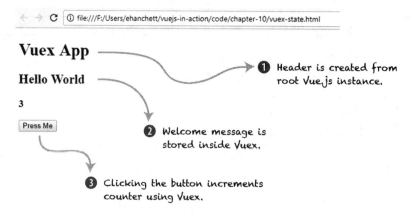

Figure 10.3   Creating a simple app using Vuex

play the `header`, which is a local variable defined in the Vue.js instance. The `welcome` and `counter` messages will be computed properties derived from our Vuex store. The button element will trigger an action called `increment`. Add the code in this listing to the top of the vuex-state.html file.

Listing 10.1 Adding HTML to our Vuex app: chapter-10/vuex-html.html

```
<!DOCTYPE html>
<html>
<head>
<script src="https://unpkg.com/vue"></script>          Shows a CDN script
                                                        tag for Vue
<script src="https://unpkg.com/vuex"></script>     Shows a CDN script
</head>                                             tag for Vuex
<body>
  <div id="app">
      <h1>{{header}}</h1>          Denotes the
                                   header variable
      <h2>{{welcome}}</h2>       Lists the welcome
      <h3>{{counter}}</h3>       computed property
      <button @click="increment">Press Me</button>   Shows the counter
  </div>                                              computed property
                         Notes the button with click
                         action set to increment
```

Now that we have our HTML in place, let's begin by adding in a Vuex store. The Vuex store will hold all our data for our example. This will include the `msg` and `count` properties.

To update the state, we'll use something called *mutations*. You can think of mutations as setters in other programming languages. *Setters* set values; mutations are what we use to update the state of the application. In Vuex, mutations must be synchronous. In our example, the counter will be triggered only when the button is pressed, so we don't have to worry about asynchronous code. (Later we'll look at actions that can help solve the problem when you're dealing with things that are asynchronous.)

Inside our mutations object we'll add an increment function that increments state. Take the code in this listing and add it to the bottom of the vuex-state.html file.

Listing 10.2 Add our Vuex state and mutations: chapter-10/vuex-state-mut.html

```
<script>
  const store = new Vuex.Store({
      state: {                          The Vuex.Store holds
        msg: 'Hello World',             state information.
        count: 0
      },
      mutations: {                      Shows the mutations
        increment(state) {              that increment the state
            state.count++;
        }
      }
  });
```

We have our HTML and Vuex store in place, and we can now add the logic that connects everything. We want to make sure that our template displays the msg and counter from the Vuex state and that we can update that count.

Create a Vue.js instance with a new data function. This will return the local header property that displays Vuex App. In the next section, we'll add a computed property which will have two functions, welcome and counter. The welcome property will return store.state.msg. The counter will return store.state.count.

Finally, we'll need to create a method called increment. To update the store and access the mutations we set up in Vuex, we can't call the mutation directly. We must use a special function called commit. This will tell Vuex to update the store and commit the change, so to speak. The store.commit('increment') does the commit to the mutation we created. Add the following code to the vuex-state.html file under the code you created in listing 10.2.

> **Listing 10.3   Adding our Vue.js instance: chapter-10/vuex-instance.html**

```
new Vue({
    el: '#app',
    data() {
        return {                        Shows the header property
            header: 'Vuex App'    ◁──┘  that displays the message
        }
    },
    computed: {
        welcome() {                     The computed property
            return store.state.msg  ◁──┘  returns the msg state.
        },
        counter() {                     The computed property
            return store.state.count;  ◁──┘  returns the counter state.
        }
    },
    methods: {
        increment() {                   The increment method triggers
            store.commit('increment')  ◁──┘  the Vuex increment mutation.
        }

    }
});
</script>
</body>
</html>
```

Now we have a fully functional app that uses Vuex! Click the button a few times, and you should see the counter increment by one after each button click.

Let's update this application so that each button click updates the count by 10. If you look closely at the mutations increment function, it has only one argument: state. However, we can pass another argument to it: we'll call it payload. This payload can be sent from the increment method we created in the root Vue.js instance.

Take the vuex-state.html file and copy it into a new file called vuex-state-pass.html. This file will hold our new application, which shows how to pass in a payload.

As you can see in listing 10.4, we need to update only the mutations object and the `increment` method. Add another argument called `payload` to the increment mutation. The `payload` will be added to the `state.count`. Inside the `increment` method, add `10` as another argument to the `store.commit`. Update the vuex-state.html as shown here.

```
...
mutations: {
  increment(state,payload) {         The increment mutation accepts a
      state.count += payload;        payload and adds it to the count.
  }
}
...
methods: {
  increment() {                      The increment method now
    store.commit('increment', 10)    passes 10 to the mutation.
  }
}
...
```

Save the vuex-state-pass.html file and reload your browser. After clicking the button, it should now increment by 10 instead of by 1. If it's not loading correctly, check your web browser's console. Make sure you didn't have any typos.

10.3   Getters and actions

In the previous example, we directly accessed the store from our computed properties. What if we had multiple components that needed to access these computed properties? What if we wanted to always display a welcome message in all caps? This is where getters can help us out.

Inside Vuex, we have something called *getters*. With getters, all components can access the state in the same way. Let's continue with our example from section 10.2. We're going to update it with getters instead of directly accessing the state in our computed properties. In addition, we want the getter for `msg` to convert the message to all uppercase letters.

Take the vuex-state-pass.html file from the previous example and copy it to vuex-state-getter-action.html. To make things simple, we'll leave the HTML the way it was before. When it's all done it should look like figure 10.4.

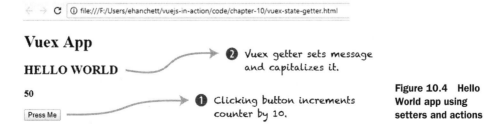

Figure 10.4   Hello World app using setters and actions

You can see that the Hello World message is now in capital letters. Clicking the Press Me button increments the counter as it did in the last example.

Inside your newly created vuex-state-getter-action.html file, look for the `Vuex.Store` below the `<script>` tag. Below the `mutations` object add a new object called getters. Inside getters we'll create `msg` and `count` as you can see in listing 10.5. Both `msg` and `count` take one argument, `state`.

In our `msg` getter, we'll return `state.msg.toUppercase()`. This will ensure that whenever we use the `msg` getter, it will return the value in all caps. For our `count` getter, it will return `state.count`. Update the vuex-state-getter-action.html with the new getters object under mutations.

> **Listing 10.5   Adding new getters: chapter-10/vuex-state-getter-action1.html**

```
...
mutations: {
  increment(state,payload) {
      state.count += payload;
  }
},
getters: {                              The new getters object
                                        defines getters for Vuex.
    msg(state) {
      return state.msg.toUpperCase();                 The msg getter returns
    },                                                msg in all caps.
    count(state) {
      return state.count;          Shows the
    }                              count getter
},
...
```

Actions are another integral part of Vuex. I previously mentioned that mutations are synchronous. But what if we're dealing with asynchronous code? How can we be sure that our asynchronous code will still affect state? That's where actions in Vuex comes in.

Let's imagine in our example that we are accessing a server, and we're waiting for a response. This is an example of an asynchronous action. Unfortunately, mutations must be synchronous, so we can't use that. Instead, we'll add the asynchronous operation using a Vuex action.

In this example we'll create a delay using a `setTimeout`. Open the vuex-state-getter-action.html file and add a new object called actions after the getter object we created. Inside that object, we'll have our `increment` action that takes a `context` and `payload`. The `context` is what we'll use to commit our changes. We'll wrap our `context.commit` inside a `setTimeout`. This is so we can simulate a delay from a server. We can also pass a payload to the `context.commit`. This will get passed to the mutation. Update the code based on this listing.

> **Listing 10.6   Adding actions: chapter-10/vuex-state-getter-action2.html**

```
...
},                          The actions object is used for asynchronous
actions: {                  and synchronous actions.
```

```
increment(context, payload) {
  setTimeout(function(){
    context.commit('increment', payload);
  },2000);
}
}
...
```

The increment function accepts a context and payload.

This triggers the increment mutation and passes the payload to it.

Now that we've updated our Vuex.Store, we can move on to the root Vue.js instance. Instead of accessing the store directly, we'll update the computed property to access the getters instead. We'll also update the increment method. We'll use the `store.dispatch('increment', 10)` to access the new Vuex action we created.

The first argument of `dispatch` is always the name of the action. The second argument is always the payload that will get passed into the action.

TIP The payload can be a simple variable or even an object.

Update the vuex-state-getter-action.html code with the new Vue.js instance from this listing.

Listing 10.7   Updating the Vue.js instance: chapter-10/vuex-state-getter-action3.html

```
...
new Vue({
    el: '#app',
    data() {
      return {
        header: 'Vuex App'
      }
    },
    computed: {
      welcome() {
        return store.getters.msg;
      },
      counter() {
        return store.getters.count;
      }
    },
    methods: {
      increment() {
        store.dispatch('increment', 10);
      }

    }
});
...
```

The computed property welcome returns the getters msg.

The computer property counter returns the getters count.

The method dispatches the increment action.

Load the app and click the button a few times. You'll notice a delay, but the counter will update by 10 after each press.

10.4   Adding Vuex to Vue-CLI with the pet store app

Let's return to the pet store application that we've been working on. If you remember the last time we worked on it, we added fancy animations and transitions. Now that we've learned the basics of Vuex, let's add it to the mix.

Let's move the product data into the store. If you recall from the previous chapters, we initialized the store in the created hook of the Main component in the pet store application. Instead, we'll have the create hook dispatch a new action that will initialize the store inside Vuex. We'll also add a new `products` computed property that retrieves our products using a Vuex getter that we'll set up. When all is done it will look and behave the same as it did before, as seen in the figure 10.5.

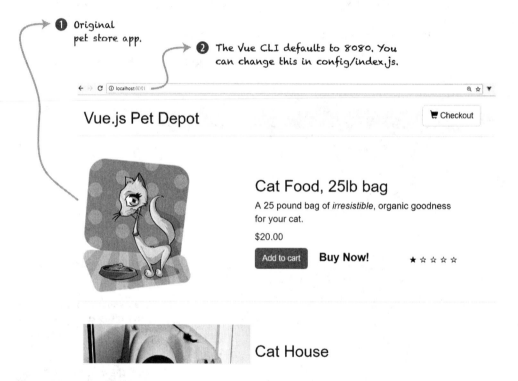

Figure 10.5   Showing the completed pet store application

10.4.1   Vuex installation in Vue-CLI

To begin, let's install Vuex! This is straightforward. If you haven't already, retrieve the latest version of the pet store application that we last worked on in chapter 8. Or you can download the completed code for this chapter from GitHub at https://github.com/ErikCH/VuejsInActionCode.

Open a terminal window and change directories into the root of the pet store application folder. Run the following command at the prompt to install the latest version of Vuex and save it into the package.json file in the pet store application:

```
$ npm install vuex
```

Next, we'll need to add the store to the main.js file in the src folder. We haven't created the store yet, but let's import it anyway. By convention, the store is usually located in the src/store/store.js file. This is up to you, and different developers come up with different conventions. For now, this will work for us. Later in the chapter, we'll discuss alternative folder structures with something called modules.

Inside the root Vue.js instance, we need to add the store, as shown in the following listing. Add the store to the root instance under router. By the way, because we're using ES6, we can use the shorthand store, instead of store: store.

> ### Listing 10.8 Updating the main.js file: chapter-10/petstore/src/main.js

```
// The Vue build version to load with the `import` command
// (runtime-only or standalone) has been set in webpack.base.conf with an
 alias.
import Vue from 'vue'
import App from './App'
import router from './router'
require('./assets/app.css')
import { store } from './store/store';        ⟵⎯⎤ Imports the store
                                                    │ into the main.js file

Vue.config.productionTip = false

/* eslint-disable no-new */
new Vue({
  el: '#app',
  router,
  store,                        ⟵⎯⎤ Adds it into the
  template: '<App/>',               │ Vue.js instance
  components: { App }
})
```

Now that we've added the store into the root instance, we can access it throughout the application. Create a file in src/store/store.js. This file will be our Vuex store and hold the information for the products in our pet store application. At the top of the file, add two import statements, one each for Vue and Vuex. Next, we'll add a Vue.use(Vuex). This will connect everything.

Inside the main.js file, we imported store from ./store/store. We need to export a store object inside the store.js file, so that the main.js file can import it. As you can see in listing 10.9, we export a const store of Vuex.Store.

We'll first add our state and mutations objects. The state object will hold an empty object called products. We'll load that using our initStore soon. Our mutations will be called SET_STORE. The mutation will take the passed-in products and assign it to state.products. Inside the newly create src/store/store.js file, add the code from this listing.

Listing 10.9   Creating the main.js file: chapter-10/store-part1.html

```
import Vue from 'vue';
import Vuex from 'vuex';

Vue.use(Vuex);

export const store = new Vuex.Store({
  state: {
    products: {}
  },
  mutations: {
    'SET_STORE'(state, products) {
      state.products = products;
    }
  },
  ...
```

Sets Vuex with Vue — points to `Vue.use(Vuex);`

Exports Vuex.Store so it can be later used in the main.js file — points to `export const store = new Vuex.Store({`

The state object shows products. — points to the state object

The mutations object shows our set store function. — points to the mutations object

---

We need to add the `action` and `getter` to the store. The `getter` will return products. The `action` is a little more complicated. What we want to do is move the created hook code that uses Axios to read the static/products.json file to the actions object in Vuex.

Remember that I mentioned that mutations had to be synchronous and that only actions inside Vuex would accept asynchronous code? To get around this, we'll put the Axios code inside a Vuex action.

Create the actions object inside the store.js file and add `initStore`. Inside this action, copy and paste the created lifecycle hook from the components/Main.vue file. Instead of assigning the `response.data.products` to the products object, we'll now use the commit function to trigger our mutation. We'll pass in the `response.data.products` as the payload to `SET_STORE`. After all is done, it should look like this.

Listing 10.10   Adding actions and getters to store.js: chapter-10/store-part2.html

```
...
actions: {
  initStore: ({commit}) => {
    axios.get('static/products.json')
    .then((response) =>{
      console.log(response.data.products);
      commit('SET_STORE', response.data.products )
    });
  }
},
getters: {
```

The actions object used for asynchronous code — points to `actions: {`

The initstore action commits the mutation. — points to `initStore: ({commit}) => {`

The products getter returns the store for products. — points to `getters: {`

```
      products: state => state.products
   }
});
```

We're getting close, and now all we need to do is update the Main.vue file so it uses the Vuex store instead of the local products object. Open the src/components/Main.vue file and look for the data function. Remove the line products: {}. We'll now access it from a computed property that returns the store.

Look for the computed properties after the methods inside Main.vue. You should see cartItemCount and sortedProducts. Add a new computed property called products and have it return the products getter.

Keep in mind that because we added the store to the root Vue.js instance in the main.js file, we don't have to do any special imports. Also, the store is always accessed by this.$store when using Vue-CLI. Make sure to remember the dollar sign or you'll get an error. Add the products computed property to the Main.vue file, as shown here.

> **Listing 10.11   Adding product's computed property: chapter-10/computed-petstore.html**

```
computed: {                                       ◁──┐  The computed property
  products() {                                         │  for the Main.vue file
    return this.$store.getters.products;   ◁──┐
                                               │
  },                                        The computed property for products
  ...                                       returns getters for products.
```

Locate the created hook that initialized the products object. Delete the contents of that object and instead have it call the initStore action we created earlier in the Vuex store. As we did with our previous example, use dispatch to trigger the action. Update the created hook inside the Main.vue file so it triggers the Vuex initStore action, as shown in this listing.

> **Listing 10.12   Updating created hook: chapter-10/created-petstore.html**

```
  ...
},
created: function() {                              │  Dispatches the code to
  this.$store.dispatch('initStore');   ◁──┘  initialize the Vuex store
}
  ...
```

That should be it. Run npm run dev from the console and you should see a window open with the pet store application. Try adding items to the cart and verify that all is working. If things aren't working, check the console for errors. It's easy to accidentally type Vuex.store instead of Vuex.Store inside the src/store/store.js file. Beware of these problems!

10.5   *Vuex helpers*

Vuex gives us a handful of helpers that can be used to reduce the amount of verbosity and repetition when adding getters, setters, mutations, and actions to our application. You can find a full list of all the Vuex helpers in the official guides at https://vuex.vuejs.org/en/core-concepts.html. Let's look at these helpers and see how they work.

The first helper you should know about is `mapGetters`. This helper is used to add all our getters to our computed properties, without having to type every one of them. To use `mapGetters` we'll need to import it into our component first. Let's look at our pet store application one more time and add in the `mapGetters` helper.

Open the src/components/Main.vue file and look for the script tag. Inside that tag you should see an import for the header component. Right after that import, add in the `mapGetters` from Vuex as seen here.

> **Listing 10.13   Adding `mapGetters`: chapter-10/map-getter.html**

```
...
...
<script>
import MyHeader from './Header.vue';
import {mapGetters} from 'vuex';          <———  Imports the
export default {                                 mapGetters
...                                              from Vuex
```

Next, we'll need to update our computed property. Look for the computed property for `products` that we added earlier. Delete it and add a new `mapGetters` object.

The `mapGetters` object is unique and to add it correctly, we need to use the ES6 `spread` operator which expands our expression in places where zero or more arguments are expected. You can find more information on the ES6 spread syntax from the MDN docs at http://mng.bz/b0J8.

The `mapGetters` will make sure that all our getters will be added as if they were computed properties. As you can imagine, this syntax is much simpler and cleaner than having to write a computed property for each getter. Each getter is listed in an array inside `mapGetters`. Add the `mapGetters` to the Main.vue file.

> **Listing 10.14   Adding `mapGetters` to computed properties:**
> **chapter-10/map-getter2.html**

```
...
},
computcd: {                    <———  Shows the
  ...mapGetters([                     mapGetters
      'products'                      helper array
  ]),                 <———  Shows the
  cartItemCount() {          list of getters
...
```

If you run npm run dev, you'll see that our pet store application runs normally. Using mapGetters in our application isn't too useful, but as it grows and we add more getters, this will save us time.

The other three helpers you should know about are mapState, mapMutations, and mapActions. All three behave the same way and are useful to help reduce the amount of boilerplate code you need to write.

Let's imagine you have several pieces of data in your store. In this instance, you don't need any getters and you'll be accessing the state directly from your component. In this case, you might use the mapState helper inside your computed properties.

Listing 10.15 mapState example: chapter-10/map-state.html

```
import {mapState} from 'vuex'          ◁─┐  Imports mapState
...                                       │  from Vuex
computed: {
  ...mapState([             ◁──┐  Uses the spread operator to
      'data1',                 │  define mapState and variables
      'data2',
      'data3'
  ])
}
...
```

As with mapState and mapGetters, let's say you also have several mutations you want access to in your component. You can use the mapMutations helper method to make this easy (shown in the following listing). The mut1 in the listing maps this.mut1() to 'this.$store.commit('mut1').

Listing 10.16 mapMutations example: chapter-10/map mut.html

```
import {mapMutations} from 'vuex'        ◁─┐  Imports mapMutations
...                                         │  from Vuex into component
methods: {
  ...mapMutations([          ◁──┐  The mapMutations helper
      'mut1',                    │  adds these methods.
      'mut2',
      'mut3'
  ])
}
...
```

Finally, we'll look at the mapActions helper. This helper maps actions to our app, so we don't have to create every method and have it dispatch each action. Using the same example, let's say this application also has some asynchronous operations. We can't use mutations, so we must use actions instead. We created these in Vuex and now we need to access them in our component method object. Adding mapActions to our methods will take care of this. The act1 maps this.act1() to this.$store .dispatch('act1'), as shown in listing 10.17.

Listing 10.17   `mapActions` example: chapter-10/map-actions.html

```
import {mapActions} from 'vuex'                    Imports the mapActions
...                                                from Vuex
methods: {
  ...mapActions([               The mapActions helper adds the
      'act1',                   act1, act2, and act3 methods.
      'act2',
      'act3'
  ])
}
...
```

These helpers will come in handy as your application grows, and it will cut down on the amount of code you need to write. Keep in mind that you'll need to plan the names in your store because they'll map out to the names in your components as you use these helpers.

10.6   *A quick look at modules*

In the earlier sections of this chapter, we created a store.js file in the src/store directory for the pet store application. This worked well for our relatively small application. However, what if our application were much larger? The store.js file would quickly become bloated and it would be difficult to keep track of everything in it.

The Vuex solution for this is *modules*. Modules allow us to divide our store into smaller pieces. Each module has its own state, mutations, actions, and getters, and you can even nest modules inside it.

Let's refactor our pet store application to use modules. First, we'll need to keep our store.js file; however, we need to create a new folder named modules inside our store folder. Inside that folder create a file called products.js. The folder structure should look like figure 10.6.

Inside the products.js file, we'll need to create four objects: state, getters, actions, and mutations. We'll need to copy and paste each of the values from our store.js to the products.js file.

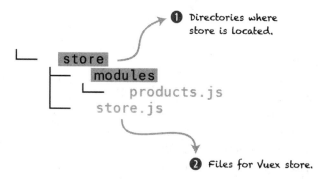

Figure 10.6   Folder structure for modules

Open the src/store/store.js file and start copying over the code. When you're done, your products.js file should look like the following listing.

Listing 10.18 Adding products modules: chapter-10/products-mod.js

```
const state = {                          Holds all the
    products: {}                         Vuex state
};

const getters = {                             Holds all the
    products: state => state.products         Vuex getters
};

const actions = {                             Holds all the
    initStore: ({commit}) => {                Vuex actions
      axios.get('static/products.json')
      .then((response) =>{
        console.log(response.data.products);
        commit('SET_STORE', response.data.products )
      });
    }
};

const mutations = {                           Holds all the
    'SET_STORE' (state, products) {           Vuex mutations
      state.products = products;
    }
};
```

After adding everything to the product.js file, we need to create an export. This will allow the file to be imported into the store.js file. At the bottom of the file, add an export default. This is an ES6 export command that allows you to import it from other files.

At the bottom of product.js, add the `default export`.

Listing 10.19 Adding the export: chapter-10/products-export.js

```
...
export default {                       Shows the ES6 export
    state,                             of everything
    getters,
    actions,
    mutations,
}
```

We'll need to update the store.js file. In this file we'll add a new module object, and in this object, we can list all the modules we added. Make sure to add an import to the modules/products file we created.

In our case, we have only one, so we'll go ahead and add it into the module object. Make sure to delete everything in the `Vuex.Store` so it matches the following listing.

```
Listing 10.20   New store.js file: chapter-10/store-update.js
```

```
import Vue from 'vue';
import Vuex from 'vuex';
import products from './modules/products';        ◁──┐ Imports the
                                                       │ products module
Vue.use(Vuex);


export const store = new Vuex.Store({
  modules: {                       ◁──┐ The modules object
    products                          │ lists all modules.
  }

});
```

Once we have the modules imported, we're ready to go. Refresh the application and it should behave as it always has.

Namespaces with Vuex

In certain larger applications, breaking up your store into modules might present a problem. As the program grows and more modules are added, the names of your actions, getters, mutations, and state might collide. You might, for example, name two getters with the same name in two different files accidentally. Because everything in Vuex shares the same global namespace, you'll get a duplicate getter key error in your console when this happens.

To alleviate this problem, you can use namespaces. By setting the `namespaced:` `true` at the top of your Vuex.store you can break up your modules per namespace. To learn more about namespaces and how to set this up in your file, please check out the Vuex official documentation at https://vuex.vuejs.org/en/modules.html.

Exercise

Use your knowledge from this chapter to answer this question:

What are several advantages of using Vuex over the normal data passing of a Vue.js application?

See the solution in appendix B.

Summary

- You can restructure your application to use centralized state management.
- You can access the data store inside the application from anywhere.
- You can avoid problems with your application store getting out of sync by using mutations and actions with Vuex.
- You can use Vuex helpers to reduce the amount of boilerplate code needed.
- In larger applications, you can use modules and namespaces to keep state more manageable.

Communicating
with a server

This chapter covers

- Using Nuxt.js for server-side rendering
- Retrieving third-party data with Axios
- Using VuexFire
- Adding authentication

We've discussed Vuex and how state management can benefit our larger Vue.js applications. Now we're going to look at communicating with a server. In this chapter, we'll look at server-side rendering (SSR) and how we can use it to help improve our app's responsiveness. We'll use Axios to retrieve data from a third-party API. Then we'll look at VuexFire. VuexFire is library that helps us communicate with Firebase, a backend service that helps with application development. Last, we'll see how to add simple authentication to our VuexFire app.

Before we move on, let me preface this chapter by saying there are many ways to communicate with a server in Vue.js. We could use an XMLHttpRequest or use any number of AJAX libraries out there. In the past, Vue officially recommended the Vue resource library as the official AJAX library. Evan You, the creator of Vue, retired the library in late 2016 from official recommendation status. As far as the Vue community goes, you can use whatever library you like.

With all that said, I determined that Axios, Nuxt.js, and VuexFire are several of the most popular libraries that could help us communicate with a server in one way or another. They're all different, however. Nuxt.js is a powerful framework for creating server-rendered apps, but Axios is a frontend HTTP client. VuexFire helps us communicate with Firebase. All three take different approaches to communication.

The purpose of this chapter is to give you working knowledge of all three of these libraries and frameworks. We'll create examples for each, but we won't go too deep. Each subject could warrant its own chapter—and in the case of Nuxt, its own book. Nevertheless, this will be a good primer for these topics, and I'll include links to each resource, so you can dive in deeper.

11.1 Server-side rendering

Vue.js is a single-page application framework that uses client-side rendering. The logic and routing of the application are written in JavaScript. When the browser connects to the server, the JavaScript is downloaded. The browser is then responsible for rendering the JavaScript and executing the Vue.js application. With larger applications, the time to download and render the application can be significant. You can see from figure 11.1 how this might look.

Server-side rendering (SSR) with Vue.js is different. In this case, Vue.js reaches out to the server, which then sends over the HTML so the browser can display the page immediately. The user sees the page load quickly. The server then sends the JavaScript, and it loads in the background. It's worth mentioning that even if the user sees the webpage, they may not interact with it until Vue is done executing (figure 11.2).

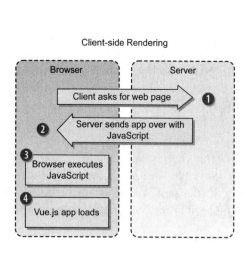

Figure 11.1   Client-side rendering

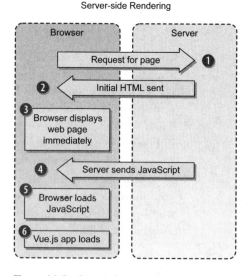

Figure 11.2   Server-side rendering

Typically, SSR is a more pleasant experience for the user because the initial load is fast. Most users don't have the patience to wait for slow apps to load.

SSR also has unique advantages for *search engine optimization* (SEO). SEO is a term that describes getting organic visibility (non-paid) on search-engine results. Although little is known of the precise methods Google and other search engines use when determining search-engine rankings, there's a worry that search-engine robots have problems when crawling client-side rendered pages. This could cause issues with rankings. SSR helps prevent these problems.

Vue.js doesn't come with SSR by itself, but there are great libraries that make it easy to add SSR to our app. The two most popular are vue-server-renderer and Nuxt.js. You can find more information on SSR from the official SSR guides at https:// ssr.vuejs.org/. Instead, we'll look at how we can create an SSR app using Nuxt.js.

11.2 Introducing Nuxt.js

Nuxt.js is a higher-level framework built on top of the Vue ecosystem that helps create SSR applications without having to worry about all the aspects of delivering a production-ready, server-rendered app.

Nuxt focuses on UI rendering, and much of the client/server layer is abstracted away. It can act as a standalone project or an addition to a Node.js-based project. In addition, it has a built-in static generator that can be used to create Vue.js websites.

When you create a project with Nuxt, you get Vue 2, the Vue router, Vuex, vue-server-renderer, and vue-meta. Under the hood it uses Webpack to help put everything together. It's an all-in-one package for getting up and running.

> **INFO** We can use Nuxt with an existing Node.js application but we won't look at that today. If you want more information on creating a Nuxt app with an existing Node.js project, check the official documentation at https://nuxtjs .org/guide/installation.

Nuxt provides a starter template to help us get started. This starter template can be downloaded from the official GitHub repository at http://mng.bz/w0YV. We can also create a project using the starter template with Vue-CLI. (If you haven't installed Vue-CLI, see appendix A for installation instructions.)

If you're using Nuxt, you'll need Node. Nuxt requires version 8 or later to work. Otherwise, you'll get async errors when you try to start the project.

> **INFO** The project listed in this chapter is working on Nuxt 1.0. But as of this writing, Nuxt 2.0 is in development and in beta. This example should work on both but if you encounter any problems, check the official GitHub repository for this book at https://github.com/ErikCH/VuejsInActionCode. This code will be maintained.

We'll use the Vue-CLI to create a project. At the command prompt, run the following command:

```
$ vue init nuxt-community/starter-template <project-name>
```

This will create a new Nuxt project using the starter template. Next, you'll need to change into the directory and install the dependencies with the following commands:

```
$ cd <project-name>
$ npm install
```

To launch the project, run the npm run dev command:

```
$ npm run dev
```

This will start a new project on localhost port 3000. If you open a web browser, you should see the welcome page (figure 11.3). If the welcome page isn't displayed, double-check to make sure you didn't skip the npm install step.

Nuxt.js server running on port 3000.

Figure 11.3   Nuxt.js starter template page

Let's look at how to use Nuxt.js in a real app.

11.2.1 *Creating a music search app*

Server-side rendered apps can be useful and powerful. Let's look at what Nuxt.js can do for us. Let's imagine you need to create an app that interacts with the iTunes API. The iTunes API has a list of millions of artists and albums. You want to search for any artist and display their discography.

> **NOTE**   You can find more information on the iTunes API in the official documentation at http://mng.bz/rm99.

In building our app, we'll use two different routes. The first route will display an input box for searching the iTunes API. This page will look like figure 11.4.

Figure 11.4 Search page for the iTunes API

The next route will display the artist's album information.

> **INFO** To make things look nicer, we'll use a material component framework called Vuetify. We'll talk more about that later.

To make things more interesting, we'll pass information from our search route into the results route by using a parameter. After entering an artist's name in the search box (Taylor Swift), the results page will be displayed (figure 11.5). You can see in the URL box at the top of the page that "Taylor%20Swift" has been passed in.

The search page will display all the albums associated with the artist. It will display the album name, artist name, and the cover art, and the card will link to the iTunes artist page. In this example we'll also look at middleware, which will allow us to write code before the route is rendered. We'll see how we can use the Axios library to communicate with the iTunes API. We'll wrap everything up by looking at Vuex again.

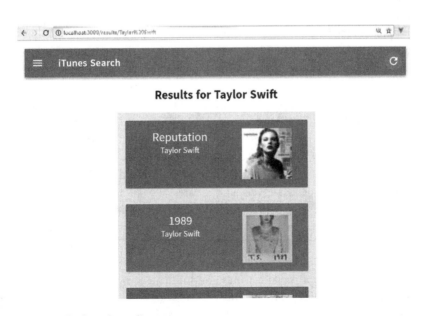

Figure 11.5 Search results page

11.2.2 *Creating a project and installing dependencies*

Let's begin creating our music API app by using the Vue-CLI starter template. We'll then install all our dependencies. Run the following command at the prompt:

```
$ vue init nuxt-community/starter-template itunes-search
```

After the application is created, install Vuetify and Axios as an npm package using the npm install command. In addition, Vuetify requires both the stylus and stylus-loader so we can set up our stylus CSS that Vuetify uses.

> **NOTE** Vuetify is a material component framework for Vue.js 2.0. It adds many easy-to-use and beautifully crafted components. It has similarities to other UI frameworks, such as Bootstrap. You can find more about Vuetify at the official website at https://vuetifyjs.com.

Run the following commands to install Vuetify, Axios, stylus, and stylus-loader:

```
$ cd itunes-search
$ npm install
$ npm install vuetify
$ npm install axios
$ npm install stylus --save-dev
$ npm install stylus-loader --save-dev
```

This will install all the dependencies we need to get started, but to get these dependencies to work correctly, we'll need a little more setup. We're going to set up Axios and Vuetify in our vendor file, register Vuetify inside our app, set up the Vuetify plugin, and finally set up our CSS and fonts.

The nuxt.config.js file is used to configure the Nuxt app, so navigate to the nuxt.config.js file in the root of the /itunes-search folder. Find the section that begins with extend (config, ctx). This section is used to automatically run ESLint on our code every time we save. (ESLint is a pluggable linting utility that checks our code for style and formatting, among other things.) We could edit the .eslintrc.js file and change the default linting, but for the sake of simplicity, we'll delete this section instead. This will turn off the automatic linting. Next add a new vendor option under build. We then need to add Axios and Vuetify to the vendor option, as seen in listing 11.1.

Let me explain how this works. Every time we import a module in Nuxt.js, the code is added to a page bundle that Webpack creates. This is a part of something called code splitting. Webpack splits our code into bundles, which then can be loaded on demand or in parallel. When we add the vendor option it makes sure that the code is only added once to the vendor bundle file. Otherwise each import would add to each page bundle and increase the size of the project. It's good practice to always add your modules to the vendor option so it won't get duplicated in your project. (Nuxt 2.0 no longer requires the vendor option. This can be removed.) Update the package.json file in the root /itunes-search folder with the new vendor options.

**Listing 11.1   Removing `ESLint` from nuxt.config.js:
                 chapter-11/itunes-search/nuxt.config.js**

```
...
  build: {
    vendor: ['axios', 'vuetify']
  }
...
```
◁— Adds Axios and Vuetify to vendor
bundle and removes linting.

Although we've added Axios and Vuetify as vendors, we're not done. Vuetify requires a little more setup. We'll need to add a plugins section to the nuxt.config.js file and add the plugin to the /plugins folder.

Plugins in Nuxt.js are a way of adding external modules to your application; they require a little more setup. Plugins run before the root Vue.js instance is instantiated. Unlike adding a vendor option, a corresponding file runs in the /plugins folder.

The official documentation for Vuetify recommends that we import Vuetify and tell Vue to use it as a plugin. We'll add this code to our plugin file. Add a new file in the plugins folder, and name it vuetify.js. Inside the file, register Vuetify with Vue, as shown here.

Listing 11.2   Adding the Vuetify plugin: chapter-11/itunes-search/plugins/vuetify.js

```
import Vue from 'vue'
import Vuetify from 'vuetify'

Vue.use(Vuetify)
```
◁— Adds Vuetify
to Vue app

Next, we'll need to add a reference to the plugin in the nuxt.config.js. Open the nuxt.config.js file in the root of the app folder and add the plugins.

Listing 11.3   Adding plugins reference: chapter-11/itunes-search/nuxt.config.js

```
...
  plugins: ['~plugins/vuetify.js'],
```
◁— Notes the reference
to the plugins file

The last thing we need to do to get Vuetify working is to add CSS. The official documentation recommends that you import the material design icons from Google and add a link to the Vuetify CSS file.

Remember earlier when we imported the stylus loader? Well now we can add a link to our own stylus file in the nuxt.config.js file. In the CSS block at the top, delete the main.css file, if it exists, and add a link to the app.styl file that we'll create in a moment. Also, add a stylesheet in the head section for the Google material design icons. The completed nuxt.config.js file should look like this.

Listing 11.4   Adding CSS and fonts: chapter-11/itunes-search/nuxt.config.js

```
module.exports = {
 /*
```

```
   ** Headers of the page
   */
   head: {
     title: 'iTunes Search App',
     meta: [
       { charset: 'utf-8' },
       { name: 'viewport', content: 'width=device-width, initial-scale=1' },
       { hid: 'description', name: 'description', content: 'iTunes search
       project' }
     ],
     link: [
       { rel: 'icon', type: 'image/x-icon', href: '/favicon.ico' },
       {rel: 'stylesheet', href: 'https://fonts.googleapis.com/
       css?family=Roboto:300,400,500,700|Material+Icons'}
     ]
   },
   plugins: ['~plugins/vuetify.js'],
   css: ['~assets/app.styl'],
   /*
   ** Customize the progress bar color
   */
   loading: { color: '#3B8070' },
   /*
   ** Build configuration
   */
   build: {
     vendor: ['axios', 'vuetify']
   }
}
```

◁— **Adds a link to material design icons**

◁— **Removes main.css and adds in a link to app.styl**

Now we need to create the assets/app.styl file, as shown in the following listing. This will import the Vuetify styles for the app.

Listing 11.5   Adding CSS stylus: chapter-11/itunes-search/assets/app.styl

```
// Import Vuetify styling
@require '~vuetify/src/stylus/main'
```

◁— **Imports the main CSS**

After this is done, run the npm run dev command and verify that you don't see any errors in the console. If you do, open the nuxt.config.js file and check for any missing commas or typos. Also, make sure you've installed all the dependencies, including stylus and stylus-loader. Those must be installed for Vuetify to work.

11.2.3   *Creating our building blocks and components*

Components are our building blocks of our application. It's where we can split our app into distinct parts that we can build back together. Before we build our routes, you may have noticed that there's a components folder. This folder is where we can put all our normal, plain components.

NOTE Nuxt.js gives us two different types of components. One is *supercharged* and the other is not. Supercharged components have access to special Nuxt-only configurations and are all located in the pages folder. These options let you access server-side data. The pages directory is also where we set up our routes and where our index component is located.

In this section, we'll discuss using the components in the components folder. We'll create two components for our iTunes search application: `Card`, which will hold the information for each artist album that we find, and `Toolbar`. The `Toolbar` component will create a simple toolbar that will be displayed at the top of each route. We'll use Vuetify to help create both components. I'll show you the HTML and CSS for these using Vuetify, but we won't go into much detail.

NOTE If you'd like to explore all the options of Vuetify, I recommend you read through the quickstart guide at https://vuetifyjs.com/vuetify/quick-start.

Create a file, Toolbar.vue, in the components folder. This file will hold our Toolbar template. Inside this template we'll use several of Vuetify's built-in components. We'll also add scoped CSS to remove the text decorations on the links. When we're done, the toolbar should look like figure 11.6.

The Toolbar.vue will be displayed at the top of every page.

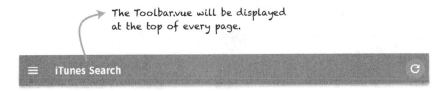

Figure 11.6 iTunes search ToolBar.vue

In Vue.js, we normally use the `route-link` component to navigate inside the application, but this component doesn't exist in Nuxt. To navigate between routes, we must use the `nuxt-link` component instead; it works exactly like the route-link. As you can see in listing 11.6, we'll use the `nuxt-link` component to create a link to the root of the application whenever someone clicks the iTunes Search text at the top. Add this code to the Toolbar.vue file.

Listing 11.6 Adding the `Toolbar` component: chapter-11/itunes-search/components/Toolbar.vue

```
<template>
  <v-toolbar dark color="blue">          ◁── Adds the v-toolbar
    <v-toolbar-side-icon></v-toolbar-side-icon>      Vuetify component
    <v-toolbar-title class="white--text">
```

```
      <nuxt-link class="title" to="/">iTunes Search</nuxt-link>
    </v-toolbar-title>
    <v-spacer></v-spacer>
    <v-btn to="/" icon>
      <v-icon>refresh</v-icon>
    </v-btn>
  </v-toolbar>
</template>
<script>
</script>
<style scoped>
.title {
  text-decoration: none !important;
}
.title:visited{
  color: white;
}
</style>
```

The nuxt-link component
navigates to "/".

Shows the scoped CSS
for this component

The next component we need to create is the Card component. It will be used in the results route, and will display each album from the artist. Once again, we'll use Vuetify to make this component look nice. When it's all done, it should look like figure 11.7.

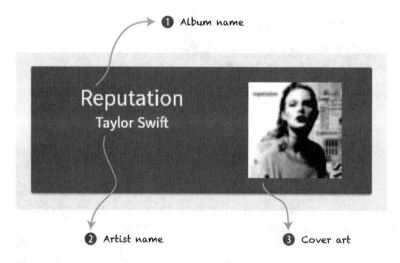

① Album name

② Artist name

③ Cover art

Figure 11.7 Card.vue component with example text

In addition to Vuetify, we'll also use props. The results route will be responsible for accessing the API and retrieving the album information. We'll then pass that information into the component using props. We'll pass in the title, image, artistName, url, and color.

The v-card component accepts an href and a color attribute. We can use a v-on directive to bind our props to them. The v-card-media component accepts an img attribute. Our image prop will bind to it. Finally, the artistName and title will be displayed using a class. This will center the title and artist name in the card. Copy the code from this listing and create a file in the components folder named Card.vue.

> **Listing 11.7 Adding the Card component:**
> **chapter-11/itunes-search/components/Card.vue**

```
<template>
  <div id="e3" style="max-width: 400px; margin: auto;"
  class="grey lighten-3">
      <v-container
      fluid
      style="min-height: 0;"
      grid-list-lg>
      <v-layout row wrap>
        <v-flex xs12>
          <v-card target="_blank"                          The Vuetify v-card component
:href="url"                                                accepts an href and color attribute.
:color="color"
class="white--text">
              <v-container fluid grid-list-lg>
                <v-layout row>
                  <v-flex xs7>
                    <div>
                      <div class="headline">{{title}}</div>
          A div with a      <div>{{artistName}}</div>              A div shows the
        class of headline  </div>                                  artist name
        displays the title. </v-flex>
                  <v-flex xs5>
                    <v-card-media
                    :src="image"                      The Vuetify v-card-media component
                    height="100px"                    that accepts an src image.
                    contain>
                    </v-card-media>
                  </v-flex>
                </v-layout>
              </v-container>
          </v-card>
        </v-flex>
      </v-layout>
    </v-container>
  </div>
</template>
<script>
export default {
    props: ['title', 'image', 'artistName',        A list of props being
'url', 'color'],                                   passed into the component.
}
</script>
```

These components—Toolbar and Card—will come in handy later when we put together our pages and default layout.

11.2.4 *Updating the default layout*

Now that we have our components in place, we need to update our default layout in the layouts folder. As the name suggests, the default layout is a component that wraps every page in the application. Inside each layout is a <nuxt/> component. This is the entry point for each page. The file default.vue implements the default layout. This can be overridden inside any page component. We'll look at the page structure in the next section. Pages are components that have special properties, and they help define the routing of the application.

For our simple app, we'll update the default.vue file and make several minor changes. We want to add the Toolbar.vue file to the top of every route, so we don't have to keep adding it to every page in our app. All we have to do is add it once to the default layout, and then it will appear on every page of our application. Update the default.vue file and add a new section element with a class named `container`. Import the `Toolbar` component in the <script> and add it to components. Then add the new <ToolBar/> component above the <nuxt/> component, in the following listing. Update the default.vue file in the /layouts folder so it matches this.

> **Listing 11.8 Updating the default layout: chapter-11/itunes-search/layouts/default.vue**

```
<template>
  <section class="container">            ◁⎯⎤ Shows the container for the
    <div>                                     section that surrounds div
      <ToolBar/>          ◁⎯⎤ Adds the Toolbar
      <nuxt/>                 component
    </div>                   to the template
  </section>
</template>

<script>
import ToolBar from '~/components/Toolbar.vue';     ◁⎯⎤ Imports the ToolBar
export default {                                         component
  components: {
    ToolBar
  }
}
</script>
<style>
...
```

Now that we have the layout in place, let's move on to Vuex.

11.2.5 *Adding a store using Vuex*

The album information from the iTunes API will reside in the Vuex store. In Nuxt.js, Vuex stores can be accessed anywhere in the application including in the middleware. The middleware allows us to write code before the route loads. We'll look at middleware in a later section.

Using Vuex, we'll create a simple store. It will have one property in the state, called `albums`, and it will have a mutation called `add`. The `add` will take the payload and assign it to the `state.albums` in the store/index.js file, as you can see in the following listing. Create a file in the store folder named index.js. Add this code to it.

> **Listing 11.9 Adding a Vuex store: chapter-11/itunes-search/store/index.js**

```
import Vuex from 'vuex'

const createStore = () => {
  return new Vuex.Store({
    state: {
      albums: []          ◁──┐ The albums property is the
    },                        │ only state in the Vuex store.
    mutations: {
      add (state, payload) {  ◁──┐ Adds mutation that adds
        state.albums = payload; │ the payload to albums
      }
    }
  })
}

export default createStore
```

Now that we have the store in place, we can have our middleware make a call to our API and save it in the store.

11.2.6 Using middleware

Middleware is a term used in Node.js and Express to refer to a function that has access to a request object and a response object. In Nuxt.js, middleware is similar. It's run on the server and client and can be set on any page in the application. It has access to both the request and response object and it's run before the route is rendered.

> **NOTE** Middleware and `asyncData`, which we'll learn more about later, are run on the server and the client. What this means is when a route loads for the first time the `asyncData` and middleware are run from the server. However, every subsequent time the route loads it's run on the client. In some instances, you may want to run code purely on the server and not the client. This is where the `serverMiddleware` property comes in handy. This property is configured in the nuxt.config.js and can be used to run application code on the server. For more information on `serverMiddleware` check out the official guides at https://nuxtjs.org/api/configuration-servermiddleware/.

Middleware is created in the /middleware directory. Each middleware file has a function that has access to an object called `context`. `Context` has many different keys, including `request`, `response`, `store`, `params`, and `environment`. You can find the full listing of `context` object keys in the official documentation at https://nuxtjs.org/api/context.

In our application, we want to send the name of the artist in a route parameter. This is accessible by using the `context.params` object. We can use that parameter to construct a request to the iTunes search API and retrieve a list of albums. We can then take that list and assign it to our albums property inside our Vuex store.

To make a request to the server, we need to use a library that simplifies the process. Many libraries exist, but I like Axios, the HTTP library that we can use from the browser or Node.js to make HTTP requests. It transforms our JSON data automatically and it supports promises. To learn more about Axios, check out the official GitHub page at https://github.com/axios/axios.

Create a file named search.js in the middleware folder. Add the code in listing 11.10. This code makes an HTTP GET request to the iTunes API and passes in the `params.id` as the search term in the request. When the promise returns, it calls the add mutation using the `store.commit` function. You may have noticed that we're using the ES6 destructuring for `{params, store}`. Instead of passing in the context, we can use destructuring to pull out the keys we need.

Listing 11.10 Setting up middleware: chapter-11/itunes-search/middleware/search.js

```
import axios from 'axios'

export default function ( {params, store} ) {        ⟵  Shows the default function that has
    return axios.get(`https://itunes.apple.com/           access to the store and params
        search?term=${params.id}&entity=album`)
            .then((response) => {                     ⟵  The response from
                store.commit('add', response.data.results)   the server request is
            });                                           added to the store.
}
```

We have everything in place now, so we can look at pages and the route.

11.2.7 *Generating routes using Nuxt.js*

Routing in Nuxt.js is a little different from what you see in a normal Vue.js application. You don't have a `VueRouter` that you have to set up for all the routes. Instead, routes are derived by the file tree created under the pages directory.

Each directory is a route in your application. Each .vue file in that directory corresponds to the route as well. Let's imagine you have a pages route and in that route you have a user route. To create these routes, your directory structure will look like figure 11.8.

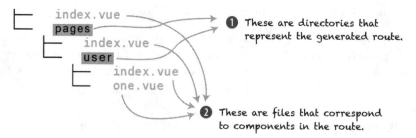

Figure 11.8 Directory structure to create routes

The directory structure in the pages folder will automatically generate the route shown in this listing.

Listing 11.11 Automatically generated route structure

```
router: {
  routes: [
    {
      name: 'index',
      path: '/',
      component: 'pages/index.vue'      ◁─┐ Notes the pages
    },                                     │ index route
    {
      name: 'user',
      path: '/user',
      component: 'pages/user/index.vue'
    },
    {
      name: 'user-one',
      path: '/user/one',
      component: 'pages/user/one.vue'
    }
  ]
}
```

This is a quick example of the type of routing you can do. You can find more information on routing from the official guides at https://nuxtjs.org/guide/routing.

For our app we'll have something much simpler. We'll only have two routes, and one of them will be dynamic. To define a dynamic route in Nuxt you must put an underscore before the name. As seen in figure 11.9 the root of the pages folder has an index.vue file. This is the root component and will be loaded when the application starts. You'll also see a README.md file. This file can be deleted; it's only there to remind you what should be inside the directory. The _id route is dynamic. The ID will match the artist name and will be passed into the route.

Inside the pages folder create a results directory. Then open the index.vue file. Delete everything and add the fairly simple code from listing 11.12. We have a template at the top with an `<h1>` tag and a `<form>` element. A v-on directive is attached to the submit event on the form. We'll also use the event modifier `prevent` to stop the form from submitting.

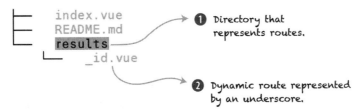

```
 ├──  index.vue
 ├──  README.md              ➊ Directory that
 └──  results                  represents routes.
     └──  _id.vue

                             ➋ Dynamic route represented
                               by an underscore.
```

Figure 11.9 Directory structure of iTunes search app

Inside the submit method, we'll use `this.$router.push`. This will route the application over to the results/ page. We'll pass the search results into the route as a parameter. Because we set up the `dynamic _id` route, the search results will show up as part of the URL. For example, if we search for Taylor Swift, the URL will be /results/taylor%20swift. Don't worry about the %20, this is added in automatically and represents a space character.

At the bottom of the page component, add a style tag, as shown in this listing. This will center the text and add a little padding.

Listing 11.12   Creating the index page: chapter-11/itunes-search/pages/index.vue

```
<template>
  <div>
    <h1>Search iTunes</h1>
    <br/>
    <form @submit.prevent="submit">          ⊲── Shows the form element with a
      <input placeholder="Enter Artist Name"      v-on directive that triggers the
  v-model="search"                                submit method on submit
  ref='search' autofocus     />
    </form>
  </div>
</template>
<script>
export default {
  data() {
    return {
      search: ''
    }
  },
  methods: {
    submit(event) {
      this.$router.push(`results/${this.search}`);   ⊲── Routes the app to
    }                                                      the results page
  }
}
</script>

<style>                    ⊲── Centers and adds
* {                           padding to the page.
  text-align: center;
}

h1 {
  padding: 20px;
}
</style>
```

The final piece to this app is the _id page that will display a card for each album in the result. It will also alternate the colors between blue and red on each card.

Earlier in this chapter, I mentioned that pages are supercharged components. In other words, they have certain Nuxt-only options available to them. These options include `fetch`, `scrollToTop`, `head`, `transition`, `layout`, and `validate`. We'll look at two other options called `asyncData` and `middleware`. If you want to learn more about Nuxt options, check out the official documentation at https://nuxtjs.org/guide/views.

The `middleware` option allows us to define the middleware we want to use in our page. This middleware will run each time the component is loaded. You can see in listing 11.13 that the _id.vue file is using the middleware search we created earlier.

The other option is called `asyncData`. This is helpful because it allows us to retrieve data and pre-render it on the server without using a store. As you saw in the middleware section, we had to use the Vuex store to save our data so it could be accessed by our components. When using `asyncData`, you don't have to do this. Let's look first at how to access the data using middleware. Then we'll refactor to use `asyncData`.

Create a file in the pages/results folder called _id.vue. Inside that new component, add a `v-if` directive for `albumData`. This will guarantee the album data is loaded before being displayed. Next, create a `v-for` directive that iterates through the `albumData`.

On each iteration, we'll show a card and pass into it the album data for `title`, `image`, `artistName`, `url`, and `color`. The color will be calculated by a method called `picker`. It will alternate between red and blue based on the index value.

At the top of the file, we'll access the `{{$route.params.id}}`. This is the parameter that's passed in from the search results.

As you can see in the next listing, we'll add a computed property called `album-Data`. This will retrieve the data from the store. The store is populated by the middleware search that's triggered as soon as the route loads, as shown here.

Listing 11.13　Creating our dynamic route:　chapter-11/itunes-search/pages/results/_id.vue

The message displays the route parameter passed in from the search.

The v-if directive that will only display if albumData is present.

The Card component that's passed-in album information.

The v-for directive that iterates through the albumData.

```
<template>
  <div>
    <h1>Results for {{$route.params.id}}</h1>
    <div v-if="albumData">
      <div v-for="(album, index) in albumData">
        <Card :title="album.collectionCensoredName"
              :image="album.artworkUrl60"
              :artistName="album.artistName"
              :url="album.artistViewUrl"
              :color="picker(index)"/>
      </div>
    </div>
  </div>
</template>
<script>
import axios from 'axios';
import Card from '~/components/Card.vue'
```

```
export default {
    components: {
      Card
    },
    methods: {
      picker(index) {
          return index % 2 == 0 ? 'red' : 'blue'
      }
    },
    computed: {
      albumData(){
        return this.$store.state.albums;
      }
    },
    middleware: 'search'
}
</script>
```

The picker method that returns red and blue alternately.

The computed property that returns the store property for albums.

Specifies which middleware to run for this route

Run the command npm run dev and open a web browser on localhost port 3000. If you already have it running, make sure to close and restart. You should see the iTunes search app open. If not, look in the console for the error. Sometimes it's as simple as a typo in the component name.

Let's do one more modification of our app. Like I said earlier, we have access to something called asyncData. This option is used to load data server side, on the initial load of the component. It's similar to using a middleware, because we'll have access to the context.

When using asyncData, be cautious. You will not have access to the component through this option because it's called before the component is initiated. However, it will merge the data you retrieve with the component so you don't have to use Vuex. You can find more information on asyncData from the official documentation at https://nuxtjs.org/guide/async-data.

Open the _id.vue file again and delete the albumData computed property. We won't use it. Instead create an asyncData option, shown in listing 11.14. Inside that option, we'll do an HTTP GET request using Axios. Similar to middleware, async-Data also has access to the context object. We'll use ES6 destructuring to retrieve the params, and then use them in the iTunes API call. In the response, we'll set the albumData object. This object will be available to us after the component is initialized, as shown in listing 11.14.

> **Listing 11.14 The asyncData example:**
> **chapter-11/itunes-search/pages/results/_id.vue**

The asyncData option has access to the params key.

```
...
    asyncData ({ params }) {
       return axios.get(`https://itunes.apple.com/
       search?term=${params.id}&entity=album`)
         .then((response) => {
```

The iTunes response appears after passing in the params.id to the axios.get command.

```
        return {albumData: response.data.results}
    });
},
...
```

> This will return a new albumData property
> that can be accessed in the component.

That should be it for `asyncData`. Save the file and run the `npm run dev` command again. You should see the page as it was before. As you can see, we have the same results, but we don't have to use the Vuex store.

11.3 Communicating with a server using Firebase and VuexFire

Firebase is a Google product that helps you create apps quickly for mobile and desktop. It offers several services, including analytics, databases, messaging, crash reporting, cloud storage, hosting, and authentication. Firebase scales automatically and is easy to get up and running. You can find more information about all the Firebase services at the official home page at https://firebase.google.com/.

For our example in this section, we'll use two of these services: authentication and the Realtime database. We're going to take our existing pet store application and modify it to include these services.

Let's imagine we were told that we needed to host our products for our pet store app in the cloud and add authentication. Recall from the previous chapter that our pet store application uses a flat file, products.json. We'll need to move the products.json contents to Firebase's Realtime database. We'll then modify our application so it pulls from Firebase instead of the flat file.

Another important aspect is to add simple authentication using one of Firebase's built-in cloud providers. We'll make a new button in our header to sign in and sign out, and we'll see how we can save our session data into our Vuex store. When all is done, our app will look like figure 11.10.

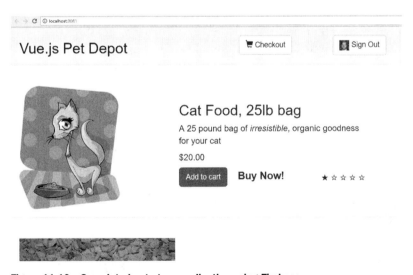

Figure 11.10   Completed pet store application using Firebase

11.3.1 Setting up Firebase

If you have a Google account, you can go to http://firebase.google.com and log in. If you don't have a Google account, head over to http://accounts.google.com and create one; it's free. (Firebase is free for a certain number of transactions a month; after that you'll have to pay.)

After logging in, you'll be presented with the Welcome to Firebase page. You'll then have an opportunity to create a project, as seen in figure 11.11.

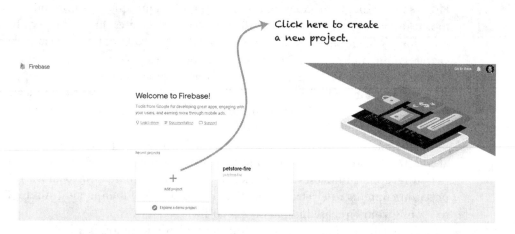

Figure 11.11   Creating a Firebase project

After clicking Add project, you'll need to type in a project name and country region. Click Create Project and you'll see the Firebase console. This is where we'll set up our database, authentication, and retrieve the keys we need to get started.

Click Database on the left side. You should see two options: Realtime Database and Cloud Firestore. We're going to use the Realtime Database. Click Get Started (figure 11.12).

At this point, we'll add the products.json file into the Firebase database. We could import the JSON file, but we'll add it manually so we can understand how everything works. Click the plus (+) symbol next to the name you gave the database. Add a Products child. Before clicking Add, click the plus symbol again. This will create another child. In the Name box, add a number. Click the plus symbol again and create seven children. These will be title, description, price, image, availableInventory, id, and rating. Fill in the information and repeat the process for another product. After you're done, it should look like figure 11.13.

Click Add and you'll see the two products in the database. Repeat this process and add a few more into it if you like.

Figure 11.12 Database selection

Figure 11.13 Firebase Realtime Database setup

This is where you will click to create a new sign-in method.

Figure 11.14   Setting up authentication

After this is done, we'll need to set up authentication. Click Authentication in the console on the left side. You'll see a window that has a button for SET UP SIGN-IN METHOD. Click that button, as you see in figure 11.14.

On the next page, choose Google. We'll be using this for our authentication in our app. We could as easily set up Facebook or Twitter, but for this example we'll assume that anyone who wants to log in to our app must also have a Google account. In the setup window, slide the Enable button and save your work, as shown in figure 11.15. That should be it; that will enable us to sign in with Google.

Finally, we need to grab configuration information. Head back to the project overview console page by clicking Project Overview on the left side. You'll see an Add Firebase to your web app button. Click this button and a window will open with your Firebase keys and initialization information. Record this information for later; we'll need it when setting up Firebase in our app.

11.3.2 Setting up our pet store app with Firebase

Now that we've set up Firebase, we need to update our pet store app to use it. The last time we used our pet store was in chapter 10, when we added in Vuex. Copy the pet store app from the previous chapter or download the code for the chapter. We'll use this code as a starting point.

For Firebase to work correctly with Vue, we'll need to use a library called VueFire. This will help us communicate with Firebase and set up the bindings we need. You can

Make sure to set this button slider to enable.

Figure 11.15   Enable Google sign-in.

find more information on VueFire on their official GitHub page at https://github .com/vuejs/vuefire.

Open your console and change directories to the location of your pet store app. Install VueFire and Firebase with the following commands:

```
$ cd petstore
$ npm install firebase vuefire –save
```

This will install and save all the dependencies we need.

Create a file named firebase.js in the src folder in the root of the pet store app. Remember when you copied the initialization information from the Firebase console? We'll need that now. At the top of the file, write import {initializeApp} from Firebase. After the import, create a const variable named app and paste in the initialization information you recorded earlier.

Create two exports, one called db and the other called productsRef. This will allow us to connect to the Firebase database and retrieve the product information we created earlier. If you'd like more information on the Firebase API, check the official API documentation at https://firebase.google.com/docs/reference/js/. Copy the code from listing 11.15 into the src/firebase.js file.

Listing 11.15   Setting up Firebase and initializing files: chapter-11/petstore/src/firebase.js

```
import { initializeApp } from 'firebase';          ◁─┐ Imports initializeApp
                                                        into the file
const app = initializeApp({           ◁─┐
    apiKey: "<API KEY>",                  Shows the keys for
    authDomain: "<AUTH DOMAIN>",          Firebase received from
    databaseURL: "<DATABASE URL>",        the Firebase console
    projectId: "<PROJECT ID>",
    storageBucket: "<STORAGE BUCKET>",
    messagingSenderId: "<SENDER ID>"
});
                                              ┐ Uses ES6 export
export const db = app.database();     ◁──┘   for the database

export const productsRef = db.ref('products');    ◁─┐ Uses ES6 export for
                                                      the products reference
```

We now need to set up our main.js file so it can see the VueFire library we installed earlier. We'll also need to make sure we import Firebase and the firebase.js we created earlier. The Vue.use(VueFire) line will set VueFire as a plugin for the app. This is required by the VueFire installation. Update the src/main.js file with this code.

Listing 11.16   Setting up main file: chapter-11/petstore/src/main.js

```
import Vue from 'vue'
import App from './App'
import router from './router'
require('./assets/app.css')                    Imports Firebase      Imports the
import { store } from './store/store';         into the app         firebase.js file.
import firebase from 'firebase';
import './firebase';                     ◁──────────────────────────◁
import VueFire from 'vuefire';
                                              ◁─┐ Imports
Vue.use(VueFire);                    ◁─┐          vuefire.
Vue.config.productionTip = false      │
                                       Sets up vuefire
/* eslint-disable no-new */            as a plugin.
new Vue({
  el: '#app',
  router,
  store,
  template: '<App/>',
  components: { App }
})
```

It's a good idea at this point to make sure we don't have any errors. Save all your files and run the npm run dev command in your console. This will start your server on localhost. Make sure you don't see any errors in the console. It's easy to forget an import, so make sure you didn't forget any inside the main.js file. Because we have everything set up, let's look at how to set up authentication in our app.

11.3.3 *Updating Vuex with authentication state*

Earlier I mentioned that we'll use authentication in our app. To save this information, we'll need to update the Vuex store. To make things easy, we'll create a state property called `session`. After a user is authenticated, Firebase returns a user object which holds session information. It's a good practice to save that information so it's available anywhere in the app.

Open the store/modules/products.js file, and add a new session property in state. The same way we did in the last chapter, we'll add in a `getter` and a `mutation`. We'll name the `mutation` SET_SESSION. Update the store/modules/products.js file so it matches this listing.

Listing 11.17 Updating Vuex: chapter-11/petstore/store/modules/products.js

```
const state = {
    products: {},
    session: false             ◁——  The session state property
};                                    defaults to false.

const getters = {
    products: state => state.products,
    session: state => state.session       ◁——  The getter for
};                                               the session

const actions = {
    initStore: ({commit}) => {
      axios.get('static/products.json')
      .then((response) =>{
        console.log(response.data.products);
        commit('SET_STORE', response.data.products )
      });
    }
};

const mutations = {
    'SET_STORE' (state, products) {
      state.products = products;
    },
    'SET_SESSION' (state, session) {     ◁——  The mutation called
      state.session = session;                SET_SESSION
    }                                          sets session data.
};

export default {
    state,
    getters,
    actions,
    mutations,
}
```

Now that we have a place to set the session data in Vuex, we can add the code to retrieve it from Firebase.

11.3.4 *Updating the header component with authentication*

Inside the header, we display the site name and Checkout button. Let's update the header so it shows a Sign In and Sign Out button.

When the header is complete, it will look like figure 11.16 after someone is signed in. Notice how in figure 11.16 a picture is shown next to the Sign Out text. This is retrieved from the user object from Firebase.

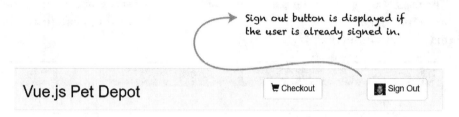

Figure 11.16   User is signed in.

After the user signs out, the button changes to Sign In, as figure 11.17 shows.

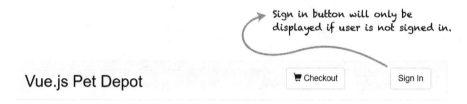

Figure 11.17   User is signed out.

Open the src/components/Header.vue file. In this file, we'll update the template with the new buttons. We'll also need to add two new methods for signing in and out. Under the `navbar-header`, add a new `div` section for the sign in (see listing 11.18). Below that, add another `div` section for sign out. Inside the sign out `div`, we'll also add an image that will be retrieved from the `mySession` property.

Surrounded by both `divs` will be a `v-if` directive. If the `mySession` property is `false` it will show the Sign In button. We'll use a `v-else` directive to show the Sign Out button if `mySession` is `true`. If the session is signed in, we'll see a Sign Out button; if the session is signed out, we'll see a Sign In button.

Because the code for the header component is so large, I've broken it into three listings (listing 11.18, 11.19, and 11.20). Make sure to take each of these listings and combine them. Take the combined code from the listing and overwrite the file for src/components/Header.vue, as shown next.

Listing 11.18   Updating header component: chapter-11/header-temp.html

```html
<template>
  <header>
    <div class="navbar navbar-default">
      <div class="navbar-header">
        <h1><router-link :to="{name: 'iMain'}">
{{ sitename }}
</router-link></h1>
      </div>
      <div class="nav navbar-nav navbar-right cart">
        <div v-if="!mySession">
          <button type="button"
class="btn btn-default btn-lg"
v-on:click="signIn">
            Sign In
          </button>
        </div>
        <div v-else>
          <button type="button"
class="btn btn-default btn-lg"
v-on:click="signOut">
            <img class="photo"
:src="mySession.photoURL" />
            Sign Out
          </button>
        </div>
      </div>
      <div class="nav navbar-nav navbar-right cart">
        <router-link
active-class="active"
tag="button"
class="btn btn-default btn-lg"
:to="{name: 'Form'}">
          <span class="glyphicon glyphicon-shopping-cart">
{{cartItemCount}}
          </span>
Checkout
        </router-link>
      </div>
    </div>
  </header>
</template>
```

> The mySession property will display the Sign In button if it's false.

> Shows the button with the v-on directive for sign in

> If the mySession property is true, the Sign Out button will be displayed.

> Displays an image from mySession

In the template, we created two methods, `signIn` and `signOut`. We also created a new property called `mySession`. Let's go ahead and create the script section of our component with these new methods and a computed property. Make sure to import `firebase from 'firebase'` at the top of the script (listing 11.19).

The first thing we need to do is add a lifecycle hook called `beforeCreate`. This hook fires before the component is created. In this hook, we want to set our Vuex store with the current session. Firebase conveniently has an observer that will do this called `onAuthStateChanged`. This observer is triggered whenever a user signs in or out. We can use this to update our store with the session information using

SET_STORE. For more information on onAuthStateChanged, check out the official documentation at http://mng.bz/4F31.

Now that we can track when a user signs in and out, we can create those methods. Create a method named signIn. Inside that method create a provider firebase.auth.GoogleAuthProvider(). Pass that provider into firebase.auth().signInWithPopup. This will create a popup asking the user to sign into their Google account. The signInWithPopup will create a promise. If the login is successful, we display "signed in" in the console. If it isn't successful, we see "error" in the console.

Remember, because we set up an observer for onAuthStateChanged inside the beforeCreate hook, we don't have to set up any other variable after a user logs in. The observer will update the store automatically after we sign in or sign out.

The signOut method works the same way. When the user signs out, a message "signed out" shows in the console. If there is an error, "error in sign out!" is displayed.

For our computed property mySession, we'll return the Vuex getter for session. If the session doesn't exist, it will be set to false. It's worth mentioning that we could have used mapGetters with Vuex. This would automatically map the getters session with the name session in our component. However, because we're dealing with one getter, I decided to return this.$store.getters.session instead.

Copy the code from the following listing and add it to the bottom of the new combined file that you'll be using for src/components/Header.vue.

> **Listing 11.19 Updating header component 2: chapter-11/header-script.js**

```
<script>
import firebase from 'firebase';
export default {
  name: 'Header',
  data () {
    return {
      sitename: "Vue.js Pet Depot"
    }
  },
  props: ['cartItemCount'],
  beforeCreate() {
      firebase.auth().onAuthStateChanged((user)=> {          ⟵  The onAuthStateChanged
        this.$store.commit('SET_SESSION', user || false)           observer is set inside
      });                                                           the beforeCreate hook.
  },
  methods: {
    showCheckout() {
      this.$router.push({name: 'Form'});
    },                                                         ⟵  The signIn method signs
    signIn() {                                                     the user in.
      let provider = new firebase.auth.GoogleAuthProvider();
      firebase.auth().signInWithPopup(provider).then(function(result) {
        console.log('signed in!');
      }).catch(function(error){
```

```
              console.log('error ' + error)
          });
      },
      signOut() {
        firebase.auth().signOut().then(function() {
          // Sign-out successful.
          console.log("signed out!")
        }).catch(function(error) {
          console.log("error in sign out!")
          // An error happened.
        });
      }
    },
    computed: {
      mySession() {
        return this.$store.getters.session;
      }
    }
  }
}
</script>
```

The signOut method signs the user out.

The mySession computed property gets the session information.

Finally, we'll need to add a new photo class to our CSS that will size the photo in our button. Take the code from the following listing and combine it with the previous listings to create the new Header.vue file in the src/components folder.

Listing 11.20   Updating header styles: chapter-11/header-style.html

```
<style scoped>
a {
  text-decoration: none;
  color: black;
}

.photo {

  width: 25px;
  height: 25px;
}

.router-link-exact-active {
  color: black;
}
</style>
```

The photo class that sets the width and height of image

After adding all the code for the new Header.vue file, make sure to run the npm run dev command and check for errors. It's easy to make a mistake on the onAuthState-Changed observer and not commit it to the Vuex store. Look out for that.

11.3.5   Updating Main.vue to use Firebase Realtime database

With all the authentication out of the way, let's start retrieving information from the database. By default, we left the database configuration in Firebase to read only. That will work for us.

First, update the `mapGetters` in the src/components/Main.vue file. You'll notice that we're retrieving the `products` getter. Remove that and add the `session` getter. We won't use this now, but it's nice to know we can use the session inside the main component.

To use the Realtime database with Firebase, all we need to do is import the `productsRef` from the firebase.js file. Then we'll need to create a Firebase object that maps `productsRef` to `products`. That should be it! All the other code in our Main.vue file can remain the same. Take the code in this listing and update the src/components/Main.vue file.

> **Listing 11.21   Updating Main.vue file: chapter-11/update-main.js**

```
...
import { productsRef } from '../firebase';        ◁──┐ Imports the productsRef
export default {                                       from firebase/.js file
  name: 'imain',
  firebase: {
      products: productsRef          ◁──┐ Maps productsRef
  },                                      to products
  ...
  computed: {
    ...mapGetters([
        'session'              ◁──┐ Updates mapGetters that only
    ])                             retrieves session not products
  ...
```

Save all the files and run `npm run dev`. Inside the browser, you'll notice a slight delay before the products show up. This indicates the products are being downloaded from Firebase. You could always go into Firebase and add a new product, and it should show up on your list of products.

One thing you may wonder is what we could do next. With the session property, we could set up different sections of the app that are accessible only if a user is logged in. We could do this with the `v-if` directive or through the router. With the router we can add a meta tag to a route. Then we could use the `router.before-Each` to navigate to certain routes if a user is logged in. This concept is called *navigation guards*. You can read up on the navigation guards section in the official documentation at https://router.vuejs.org/guide/advanced/navigation-guards.html. In the next chapter, we'll look at testing and how we can use it to make sure our app is doing what we expect.

Exercise

Use your knowledge from this chapter to answer the following question:

> What's one advantage of using `asycData` in your Nuxt apps versus using middleware?

See the solution in appendix B.

Summary

- You can use libraries like Axios to talk to web APIs.
- Fast-loading sites can be created with server-side rendered Nuxt.js apps.
- You can grab information from an online datastore using Firebase.
- Users can be authenticated inside your application.

12

Testing

This chapter covers

- Understanding why we test
- Implementing unit tests
- Testing components
- Testing Vuex

We've discussed many important topics in this book, but one often-neglected topic doesn't get enough attention: testing. Testing is an extremely important aspect in any software development project. It ensures that the app behaves the way we expect it to—without bugs. In this chapter, we'll discuss why you should create tests for your application. Then we'll look at the fundamentals of unit testing. Next, we'll look at component testing, both the output and the methods. Finally, we'll see how to get started testing with Vuex.

It's worth mentioning before we start that testing is a huge subject. In this chapter, I'll cover several of the most important aspects of testing with Vue.js. I strongly recommend you look over Edd Yerburgh's *Testing Vue.js Applications* (Manning, 2018). In his book, Edd delves into much more detail on creating and developing tests. He also covers server-side rendering testing, snapshot testing, and testing mixins and filters.

> **Snapshot testing**
>
> Snapshot tests are useful tools when you want to ensure that the UI doesn't change unexpectedly. In this chapter, I'll use mocha-webpack, which doesn't support snapshot testing as of this writing. However, if you want to learn more about snapshot testing, look over the official guides for more information on how to set up Jest with snapshot testing at http://mng.bz/1Rur.

12.1 Creating test cases

Typically, in the world of software development, there are two ways of testing code: manually and automated. Let's talk about coding manually first.

You probably started testing manually as soon as you started coding. For every line of code you've written, you've probably gone back and checked to make sure the output you expect is occurring. For example, in our pet store app we added a button that added a product to our cart. In the previous chapters we tested that manually by clicking the button and then checking the number of items in the cart.

In our pet store app, we also added a button that routes to the checkout page. Once again, we can click that button and make sure that it redirects properly. Manual testing works fine for smaller apps where there isn't much going on.

Now let's imagine a scenario where we're working with a team of developers. We have an app in production and many developers are working on the code. Developers are pushing code throughout the day to the version control system. As you can imagine, relying on every developer to thoroughly test their code manually and verify they haven't broken anything is impossible. Manual testing is a nightmare and bugs could certainly crop up.

In certain organizations, a quality assurance department is responsible for manually testing code after the development department releases it. This helps reduce the chances of a bug reaching production but it slows down the whole process. In addition, many quality assurance developers don't have the resources or time to run a complete *regression test* on the code.

> **DEFINITION** *Regression testing* is a type of software testing that verifies that the application still performs the same way after it was updated.

But automated testing can help solve several of the problems that manual testing runs into. In our imaginary scenario, we could create several automated tests that a developer could run before pushing their code to production. Automated tests run much quicker then manual testing and they're more likely to catch bugs immediately. With many automated test cases, a developer can run a full regression on a code base and not worry about having to manually test everything, which is time-consuming.

Although automated testing has many benefits, it has its disadvantages. The one disadvantage that you must consider is the upfront cost. Writing test cases takes time, and although you'll probably save time in the long run, you'll spend a longer time writing test cases when compared with writing the code. After everything is set up though, processes such as continuous integration, delivery, and deployment can save time, as we'll see in the next section.

12.2 *Continuous integration, delivery, and deployment*

Automated testing has the added benefit of enabling workflows such as continuous development. This workflow consists of continuous integration, delivery, and deployments. As the name suggests, these workflows are closely related. We'll briefly discuss each one.

Imagine we're creating a basic app that connects to a database and retrieves information for a book website. We have a team of developers working on the code base, but the team is running into a number of issues. Most developers are having merge conflicts when they push their code into their version control system every few weeks. In addition, every Friday one person is responsible for manually creating a *staging environment* for the latest code. (A staging environment runs production code for testing purposes.) This increasingly has taken more time to do because the code base has gotten larger and more complicated. Pushing to production is no better. Half the time the production code won't build correctly, and it takes hours to fix. The manager has decided to switch to continuous development to help fix these problems. The first step in that process is continuous integration.

12.2.1 *Continuous integration*

Continuous integration (CI) is the practice of merging code into a *master branch* several times a day.

> **DEFINITION** A *master branch* is where the production code usually resides. A *branch* is a version-control term that describes a duplication of a code base so modifications can happen in parallel in both branches.

The obvious benefit of CI is that it helps avoid merge conflicts. Merge conflicts happen when multiple developers try to merge or combine their code into a single branch. Merging code into a master branch several times a day helps avoid one developer's work-in-progress breaking another developer's code. Because the master branch is updated continuously, another developer working on the same project can easily pull the latest code down into their own development environment and be relatively sure it's up to date.

In our imaginary scenario, our manager decides to make the CI process smoother by implementing a service that helps run automated test cases before any developer can push their code. In version control systems like Git, developers can submit pull requests. Services such as Travis, CircleCI, and Jenkins can help check that the pull request passes all the test cases before the code can be merged. After the systems are in place, the team has seen fewer merge conflicts, but they still have problems with deployment.

12.2.2 Continuous delivery

Continuous delivery is a software-engineering approach that aims to build, test, and release software in a fast and frequent manner. The purpose is to create a fast and reliable deployment pipeline that's guided by a set of checks that must pass before the code is released. For example, before the software is released, all test cases must pass and the build must pass without any errors or warnings. These types of checks help provide more dependable, consistent releases.

Typically, CI isn't the responsibility of the development team. Usually a team of people known as DevOps or development operations is responsible for setting up and maintaining continuous delivery. It's good to understand the basics of this process and how it relates to testing.

With continuous delivery, merging or committing code to the master branch triggers a build of the website. This can save time because it removes the manual step of deploying the website to the staging environment. It has the added benefit that it will deploy only if all test cases pass, so it's less likely that the website will be broken.

With continuous delivery, our team no longer needs to have someone waste hours creating and deploying a staging environment. Continuous delivery will make sure that it occurs daily. With that said, what does continuous deployment have to do with continuous delivery?

12.2.3 Continuous deployment

Continuous deployment goes one step further than continuous delivery and deploys code directly to production on every single change. As with continuous delivery, developers can rest assured that all tests pass before the code is deployed to production.

As you can imagine, deploying to production after every change can be dangerous if the automated tests aren't robust enough to check all parts of the app. The worst-case scenario is that a broken website gets deployed to production. At that point, a rollback or emergency fix is needed. Now that we've seen the way we can integrate testing into a workflow, let's look into what type of tests are available and how we can use these test in Vue.js.

12.3 Types of tests

In the world of testing, we can create several types of tests. In this chapter we'll look at the most common, including unit and component testing.

Unit tests are tests against the smallest parts of our application. These are often functions in our apps, but not always. They can also be components. Let's begin by creating a basic unit test to see how it works.

Unit tests have unique advantages. For one, they're fast and run quickly. Because they only test a small piece of code, they can run fast. They can also act as documentation. They're instructions on how the code should behave. Unit tests are also reliable because they only test a small part of the code. They can be run thousands of times and produce the same output. Unlike other tests that might have to rely on APIs that frequently fail, unit tests should never have this problem. Imagine a scenario where you've created an application that converts the temperature from Fahrenheit to Celsius. In this app, we have one function that does the conversion. We could easily create a unit test to verify that the amount returned was correct. You can see that in this listing.

Listing 12.1   A basic unit test: chapter-12/unit.js

```
function convert(degree) {
  let value = parseFloat(degree);
  return (value-32)/ 1.8;
}

function testConvert() {
  if (convert(32) !== 0) {                    A basic unit test that checks
    throw new Error("Conversion failed");     the convert function.
  }
}

testConvert();
```

The second type of tests we're going to look at are *component tests*. These tests run against each component and verify how they should behave. They can be a little more complicated than unit tests because they test more of the application and they're more difficult to debug. But they verify that the component meets its requirements and achieves its goal.

12.4   *Setting up our environment*

Now that we have a good idea about the kinds of tests that are out there and why we should test, let's set up our environment. Our pet store app could use several tests, so let's add them.

In this section we'll modify our pet store application so we can use the latest testing libraries recommended by Vue.js. As of this writing, the Vue-CLI didn't have these libraries built in when we generated our project, so we'll need to do a little setup. This will require us to install several packages and configure a few files.

To begin our setup, we'll need to get a copy of our pet store app. If you've been following along, feel free to use the app you've created. If not, copy the pet store app from chapter 11 at https://github.com/ErikCH/VuejsInActionCode.

The vue-test-utils is the official unit-testing library for Vue.js. It makes testing Vue.js much easier and you should use it. We'll cover the basics of the library in this chapter; if you'd like more information, you can read how it works in the official guides at https://vue-test-utils.vuejs.org.

You may remember from chapter 7, that when we created the pet store app we said yes to Nightwatch and Karma. This will work but at the time of writing, the Vue-CLI doesn't support the vue-test-utils library out of the box. Because this library isn't installed by default, we need to install it.

We'll also need to make a choice regarding which test-runner we want to use within the vue-test-utils library. A test-runner will pick up the unit tests that we create and execute them. When we first installed our pet store app, Mocha and Karma were our only test-runner choices. Karma works with vue-test-utils but it isn't officially recommended. The vue-test-utils team recommends either Jest or mocha-webpack. Because we already have Mocha installed, we'll go ahead and install mocha-webpack. Jest is also an excellent choice, but it won't be covered in this book.

> **NOTE**   Keep in mind that if you choose Jest, all the tests in this book will still work, but you'll have a little different setup. You can find instructions on how to set up Jest at the official guides at http://mng.bz/3Dch.

Because we're going to use mocha-webpack as our test runner, we'll need to install a few other things. To run tests, we'll need a browser. We could run our tests in a real browser, such as Chrome or Firefox, but it's not recommended because running in a browser can be slow and it's not as flexible as using a headless browser. Instead we'll use modules called jsdom and jsdom-global. These modules will simulate a browser for us; they're *headless browsers* used to run our test cases.

> **DEFINITION**   A *headless browser* doesn't have a graphical user interface (GUI) and is used to facilitate automated control of a web page. The headless browser performs much the same as contemporary browsers, but interaction is typically accomplished through a CLI.

We'll need to pick an assertion library, and Chai and Expect are popular choices. Assertion libraries are used to verify things are correct instead of relying on things like `if` statements. The vue-test-utils team recommends using Expect with mocha-webpack, so we'll go ahead and install that. You can find more information on picking an assertion library at http://mng.bz/g1yp.

That last library we need to install is the webpack-node-externals. This will help us exclude certain npm dependencies from our test bundle.

Retrieve the latest version of the pet store app that's included with this book. Beware, if you download the latest version of the pet store app from chapter 11 you'll need to enter your Firebase configuration inside the firebase.js file in the src folder if you haven't done so already. If you forget this step the application will not load!

After you retrieve the latest version of the pet store app, install these dependencies by running the following commands:

```
$ cd petstore
$ npm install
$ npm install --save-dev @vue/test-utils mocha-webpack
$ npm install --save-dev jsdom jsdom-global
```

```
$ npm install --save-dev expect
$ npm install --save-dev webpack-node-externals
```

After the dependencies are installed, we'll add configuration. Edit the web-pack.base.conf.js file in the build folder of the pet store app. Copy and paste the code from the following listing at the bottom of the file to configure the webpack-node-externals and inline-cheap-module-source map. This is required by those modules for everything to work correctly.

> **Listing 12.2   Setting up source map and node externals: chapter-12/setup.js**

Sets up the test environment

```
if (process.env.NODE_ENV === 'test') {
  module.exports.externals = [require('webpack-node-externals')()]
  module.exports.devtool = 'inline-cheap-module-source-map'
}
```

Inside the test folder you'll notice the unit and e2e folders. We won't use these fold-ers, so feel free to delete them. Add a new file called setup.js inside the test folder. The setup.js file is where we'll set the global variables for jsdom-global and expect. This will make it so we don't have to import both modules into every single test case. Copy and paste the code from this listing into the test/setup.js file.

> **Listing 12.3   Setting up tests: chapter-12/petstore/setup.js**

Sets up jsdom-global

```
require('jsdom-global')()
global.expect = require('expect')
```
Sets expect inside app

Next, we need to update the test script in the package.json file. This script will run the mocha-webpack test runner and our tests. For the sake of simplicity, all tests will have a spec.js file extension. Edit the package.json file and replace the scripts test section with this line.

> **Listing 12.4   Updating package.json: chapter-12/testscript.js**

```
"test": "mocha-webpack --webpack-config
build/webpack.base.conf.js --require
 test/setup.js test/**/*.spec.js"
```
Notes the test script inside package.json file

That is all the configuration we need for our setup. Now we can start creating test cases!

12.5   *Creating our first test case with vue-test-utils*

For our first test using vue-test-utils, let's see if we can verify that our Form component works correctly after clicking the Order button. When you click the Order button on the form component, an alert box appears. We can test for an alert box, but it's not

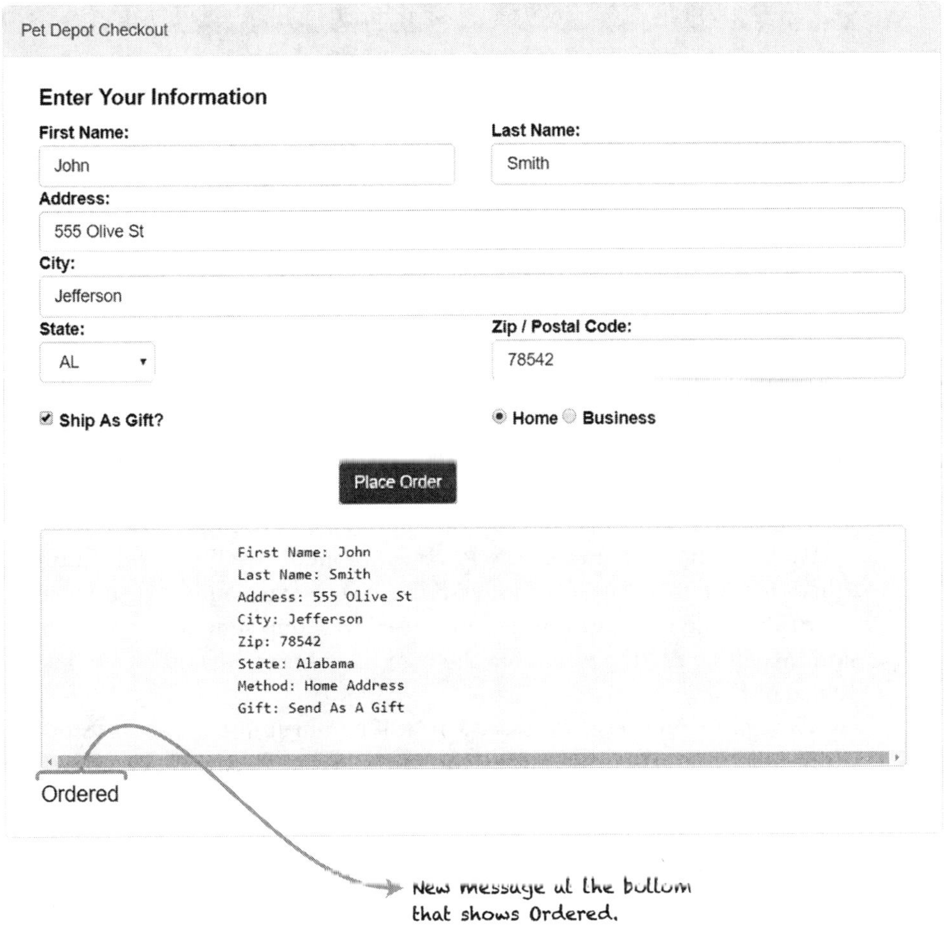

Figure 12.1   Pet depot checkout page that displays Ordered at the bottom

easy with our setup and will require us to change our jsdom-global configuration. For the purposes of this test, we'll create a property called madeOrder. This will be defaulted to false. After clicking the Order button, it will turn true.

The order form will be updated so it shows a message at the bottom that the order is complete (figure 12.1). When madeOrder is true, the text will appear. When it's false, the text will not show up. We add this so we can get a little more feedback when the order button is clicked, because we're no longer going to use the alert box.

To make this change, we need to update the src/components/Form.vue file Add a new property in the file called madeOrder in the data function. Edit the submit-Form method and delete the alert box, then add this.madeOrder = true. This will guarantee that the property is set to true when the app starts up. Update the src/components/Form.vue with the code in this listing.

> **Listing 12.5**   Update to the `Form` component: chapter-12/form-update.js

```
...
        dontSendGift: 'Do Not Send As A Gift'
      },
      madeOrder: false                    ◁——  Adds a new property
...                                              for madeOrder
  methods: {
    submitForm() {
      this.madeOrder = true;            ◁——  Sets madeOrder
    }                                           to true
  }
}
...
```

We're now ready to create our first test case. Let's verify that after the Place Order button is clicked, the `madeOrder` property is set to true. To test this, we'll use the vue-js-utils `shallow` function. The `shallow` function renders a Vue component and stubs out any child components it has. The other common function is `mount` which works the same as `shallow`, except it doesn't stub the child component.

We'll also need to import the `Form` component. We'll pass this into the `shallow` function later to create a wrapper around it. Next, you'll notice something called `describe`. The `describe` function is used to group similar tests together into a test suite. When we run the tests from the command line, we can see whether the test suite passed or failed.

The `it` function is a test case. This will be our unit test that tests our button and verifies that it updated the `madeOrder` property correctly. We can have multiple test cases in each test suite.

Because we're using the expect assertion library, we'll use it to make sure that the `madeOrder` property is set to `true`. In listing 12.6 we're using `wrapper.vm.made-Order` to access the property. The wrapper object returned from the `shallow` function has several properties including one called `vm`. We can use the `vm` property to access any Vue instance methods or properties, allowing us to run any method or get any property inside the Vue component. This is handy.

`wrapper` also has a `find` function that accepts a selector. The `find` function can use any valid CSS selector, such as tag names, IDs, or classes. We can then use the `trigger` function to trigger the event—in this case, a click event on the button. Take the following listing and create a new Form.spec.js file.

> **Listing 12.6**   Our first test case: chapter-12/petstore/test/Form.spec.js

```
import { shallow } from '@vue/test-utils'          ◁——  Imports shallow to
import Form from '../src/components/Form.vue'       ◁——  use in the test case

describe('Form.vue', () => {                         Imports the
                                                     form component
    it('Check if button press sets madeOrder to true', () => {
      const wrapper = shallow(Form)
      wrapper.find('button').trigger('click')       ◁——  Assigns the wrapper to shallow
                                                          version of component
```

Finds then triggers the button └——▷

```
        expect(wrapper.vm.madeOrder).toBe(true);    ◁──┐  Verifies madeOrder
    })                                                 │  is true

})
```

Let's run our test cases. Make sure you're in the pet store top-level directory and run the npm test command. This should run our test suite. If you see an error, make sure you installed all the dependencies that we discussed earlier and verify the package.json file has the test script inside it. Figure 12.2 displays what we'll see when all of our tests pass!

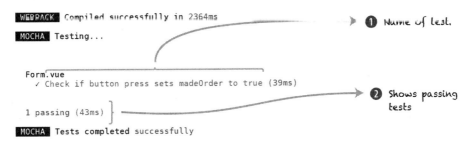

Figure 12.2   Checking our first test case, which is successful

Because everything passed, a successful message is displayed. Let's see what it looks like when it fails. Go back into the petstore/test/Form.spec.js file. Look for the expect statement and set the value to false instead of true. Run the command npm test again and it should fail. Notice from figure 12.3 that the expected value and the received value are displayed in the output.

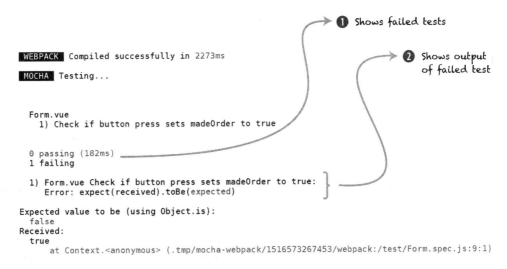

Figure 12.3   The test case fails

Now that we understand the basics of testing, let's look at testing components.

12.6   *Testing components*

Before we test our components, we need a general idea of our specifications. What should we expect the components to do? We'll use our pet store app as an example.

We have three components in our application: `Main`, `Header`, and `Form`. The `Header` component's job is to display the number of items in the shopping cart and to show either a Sign In or a Sign Out button. The `Form` component's responsibility is to show all our form inputs, and it gives us an option to order by clicking the Order button. `Main` is used to display all our products. It needs to render all the components from our Firebase store.

We won't test every component, but it's important to write down specifications for each component before creating any test cases. That way we'll know what to test.

12.6.1   *Testing props*

Many of our components will have props that are passed in to them. For example, in our pet store app, the `cartItemCount` is passed into our `Header` component and displayed in the top right corner. Let's create a test case that verifies that this prop is passed in.

Create a file in the petstore/test/ directory called Header.spec.js. This file will contain all our tests for the `Header` component. Before we can begin, we need to do a little setup.

If you look at the Header.vue file, you'll notice that we're using Firebase and Vuex. The `beforeCreate` hook calls a Firebase function and sets the value using a Vuex store command that commits the session. We won't test Vuex or Firebase in this example, but we'll need to import them, otherwise we'll get an error. Make sure to import both `../src/firebase` and `../src/store/store` as seen in listing 12.7.

At the top of the file, import `shallow` from the vue-test-utils library. In addition, import something called `createLocalVue`. We need this function so we can set up Vuex. Next, we'll create a `localVue` variable and assign it to `createLocalVue()`. This function returns a `localVue` class. You can think of it as a photocopier that produces a photocopy version of Vue. We can use this to help set up Vuex for our testing.

You can see from listing 12.7 that we use the `shallow` function again, but it looks a little different than the unit test we created earlier. The `shallow` function can accept an optional second argument. This object holds more information that the component needs. Inside it, we can set the props data using `propsData` as well as `localVue` and `store`.

To set the props, we must pass something in to it. The easiest way to do that is to add `cartItemCount`. We pass that variable into the `propsData`, and it will be set inside the `Header` component.

The last thing we do is check that the `wrapper.vm.cartItemCount` matches the `cartItemCount` variable. If they're the same, the test passes. Take the code in the next listing and copy it to the petstore/test/Header.spec.js file.

Listing 12.7 Testing a prop: chapter-12/header-prop-test.js

```
import { shallow, createLocalVue } from '@vue/test-utils';
import Header from '../src/components/Header.vue';          Imports Vuex
import Vuex from 'vuex';                                    into test case
import '../src/firebase';                                   Imports Firebase
import { store } from '../src/store/store';                 into test case

const localVue = createLocalVue();       Imports Vuex
localVue.use(Vuex)                       store into
                                         test case
describe('Header.vue', () => {

  it('Check prop was sent over correctly to Header', () => {    The new wrapper
    const cartItemCount = 10;                                   const has a
    const wrapper = shallow(Header, {                           second argument.
      store, localVue, propsData: { cartItemCount }
    })                                                          The props
    expect(wrapper.vm.cartItemCount).toBe(cartItemCount);       data is set to
  })                                                            cartItemCount.

});
```

Expect verifies that the cartItemCount
matches from the passed-in prop.

Now that we can check props, let's look at text.

12.6.2 Testing text

Sometimes you want to test if text is rendered somewhere in the component. It doesn't matter what element renders the text, only that an element renders it.

Keep in mind when writing tests that each test case should test only one thing. It might be easy to create multiple assertions inside a test case that checks text, but it's often better to take these types of tests and create multiple test cases out of them. We'll follow this rule of creating a single assertion in a test case.

Open the petstore/test/Header.spec.js file and add a new test case. In our last test case, we verified that the cartItemCount prop was being passed correctly into the Header component. Now we want to verify whether the text from the prop is displayed properly inside the component in the span tag.

To do this, we'll create another wrapper the way we did before. This time, we'll use the wrapper.find function to look up the span. We can then use the text() function to extract the text inside the span, which is our cartItemCount. We then use the toContain function to verify that the contents match. Copy the code from the following listing into the pet/test/Header.spec.js as another test after the last test.

Listing 12.8 Testing text: chapter-12/header-text-test.js

```
it('Check cartItemCount text is properly displayed', () => {
  const cartItemCount = 10;
  const wrapper = shallow(Header, {
    store, localVue, propsData: { cartItemCount }
  })
```

```
const p = wrapper.find('span');
expect(p.text()).toContain(cartItemCount)
})
```

The wrapper finds the span tag.

The assertion checks whether the text matches cartItemCount.

12.6.3 *Testing CSS classes*

When testing classes, we can use the method `classes`, which returns an array of classes attached to an element. Let's add a quick check to verify whether the class on one of our `div`s is correct.

Inside the petstore/test/Header.spec.js file, add a new test case. In this test case we'll create a new wrapper. This time we'll use a `findAll` which will return all the `div`s in the component. We can use the `at(0)` to retrieve the first `div`. From there we can use our `expect` statement on `p.classes()` to retrieve all the classes attached to the first `div`. The `toContain` will return `true` if any of the classes match.

If we look at the Header.vue file, we'll notice that both `navbar` and `navbar-default` are attached to the first `div`. Because we're looking for `navbar`, this test will pass.

Listing 12.9   Testing classes: chapter-12/header-classes-test.js

```
it('Check if navbar class is added to first div', () => {
  const cartItemCount = 10;
  const wrapper = shallow(Header, {
    store, localVue, propsData: { cartItemCount }
  })
  const p = wrapper.findAll('div').at(0);
  expect(p.classes()).toContain('navbar');
})
```

This looks for all the divs and returns the first one.

This checks the classes attached to see if navbar exists.

Before we get too much further, run `npm test` at the command prompt and verify that all the tests are passing (figure 12.4). If any are failing, double-check the `expect` statements and that you're importing everything correctly at the top of the file.

All tests are passing, so let's move on to Vuex.

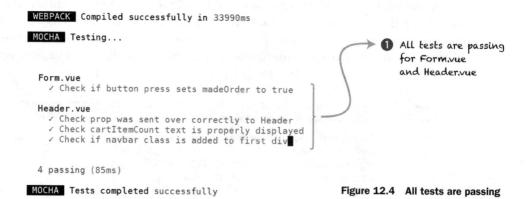

```
WEBPACK  Compiled successfully in 33990ms

MOCHA  Testing...


Form.vue
  ✓ Check if button press sets madeOrder to true

Header.vue
  ✓ Check prop was sent over correctly to Header
  ✓ Check cartItemCount text is properly displayed
  ✓ Check if navbar class is added to first div


4 passing (85ms)

MOCHA  Tests completed successfully
```

❶ All tests are passing for Form.vue and Header.vue

Figure 12.4   All tests are passing

12.6.4 *Testing with a mocked Vuex*

The Vuex store is a central location where we can hold data for the application. In our pet store app, we used it to set the session data and hold our product info. When using Vuex, it's a smart idea to test the store.

> **NOTE** Vuex testing is complicated and has many moving parts. Unfortunately, I won't cover them all here. To learn more about Vuex testing, start with the official Vuex testing guides at https://vue-test-utils.vuejs.org/guides/using-with-vuex.html.

For our test cases, we'll test our `Header` component and how it works when the session is set to `true` or `false`. We want to verify that if the session exists, the Sign Out button displays and if the session doesn't exist, the Sign Up button displays.

Earlier in this chapter, we imported the store directly into our test file. This was only a temporary workaround so we could create other test cases for the Header component. This won't work for testing Vuex. To test our Vuex store, we'll need to mock the store completely. This is much simpler than you think.

At the top of the petstore/test/Header.spec.js file, you'll see an import of the store. Delete this line. We'll create a *mock* of the store. A mock is an object that has the same structure as a complex object that you cannot use in your test (similar to our Vuex store), but with an implementation that you can control. Beneath the `describe` statement, add the new variables: `store`, `getters`, and `mutations`, as shown in listing 12.10. Then create a `beforeEach` function. The code inside the `beforeEach` runs before every test case. It's a good place to put setup code.

For the sake of simplicity, our store will be rudimentary. We'll have a `getter` for `session` that returns `false`, and a `mutation` that returns an empty object. We can use new `Vuex.Store` to create the store (make sure you use a capital `S` in Store). Copy the code in the following listing into the top of the petstore/test/Header.spec.js file.

Listing 12.10 Mocking Vuex: chapter-12/header-vuex-mock.js

```
describe('Header.vue', () => {          Shows the store, getters,
  let store;                            and mutations variables
  let getters;
  let mutations;                 Runs before
  beforeEach(() => {             each test                The session getter
    getters = {                                           is set to false.
      session: () => false
    }                                  The mutation SET_SESSION
    mutations = {                      returns an empty object.
      SET_SESSION: () => {}
    }                            A new store
    store = new Vuex.Store({     is created.
      getters,
      mutations
    })
})
```

Now that we've mocked our Vuex store, we can use it in our test cases. We can assume if the session is set to false, the Sign In button will be displayed. If this is a little confusing, go to the Header.vue file in the src folder, where you'll see a v-if directive that relies on a computed property called mySession. If mySession is false, the Sign In button is displayed. The v-else directive shows a Sign Out button if it's true. Copy the code from this listing into the petstore/test/Header.js file.

Listing 12.11   Testing Sign In: chapter-12/header-signin-test.js

```
it('Check if Sign in button text is correct for sign in', () => {
  const cartItemCount = 10;
  const wrapper = shallow(Header, {
    store, localVue, propsData: { cartItemCount }
  })

  expect(wrapper.findAll('button').at(0).text()).toBe("Sign In");

})
```

The assertion expect looks at the text of the button and verifies it's Sign In.

Conversely, we should also check that, if the session is signed in, that the Sign Out button displays. You can do this a few ways, but one of the easiest is to create a store with a new getter.session. When we create the wrapper, the new store will be added, and the Header component will act as if the session were set to true instead of false. Copy the code from the following listing and add it as another test case in the petstore/test/Header.spec.js file.

Listing 12.12   Testing Sign Out: chapter-12/header-signout-test.js

```
it('Check if Sign in text is correct for sign out', () => {
  const cartItemCount = 10;
  getters.session = () => true;
  store = new Vuex.Store({ getters, mutations})
  const wrapper = shallow(Header, {
    store, localVue, propsData: { cartItemCount }
  })
  expect(wrapper.findAll('button').at(0).text()).toBe("Sign Out");
})
```

Checks if button text is Sign Out

Run the test and they'll all pass. These are all the tests we're going to run for our pet store app. As an exercise, go into the Forms or Main component and add some test cases.

12.7   *Setting up the Chrome debugger*

When you're debugging tests, you often end up using the console.log to see what variables are doing during the execution of code. This works, but there is a better way. We can use the Chrome debugger to make our job much easier.

Inside your test cases, you can add a debugger statement. Add the debugger keyword anywhere in the test. This will stop the execution of code as soon as the debugger statement is parsed. This will work only if you use the node inspector with the

Chrome browser. The *node inspector* is a tool that is built into Node 8.4.0 or later and helps with debugging with the Chrome browser. To run tests with the node inspector, we'll need to run the following code. You can either run this from the command line or add it to your package.json file under scripts. Open your package.json file and add this line under the scripts section.

Listing 12.13 Adding inspect to the package.json file:
chapter-12/petstore/package.json

```
...
  "private": true,
  "scripts": {                              Runs the script command
...                                           to inspect the browser

    "inspect": "node --inspect --inspect-brk node_modules/mocha-
webpack/bin/mocha-webpack --webpack-config build/webpack.base.conf.js -
require test/setup.js    test/**/*.spec.js"                          ◁
...
```

To run this command type in `npm run inspect` in the console. This will begin the node inspector. Alternatively, you can run this command from the command line:

```
$ node --inspect --inspect-brk node_modules/mocha-webpack/bin/mocha-webpack
 --webpack-config build/webpack.base.conf.js --require test/setup.js
    test/**/*.spec.js
```

Either way, a new debugger on localhost 127.0.0.1 will start. You should see an output like this:

```
Debugger listening on ws://127.0.0.1:9229/71ba3e86-8c3c-410f-a480-
ae3098220b59
For help see https://nodejs.org/cn/docs/inspector
```

Open your Chrome browser and type the URL: chrome://inspect. This opens a Devices page (figure 12.5).

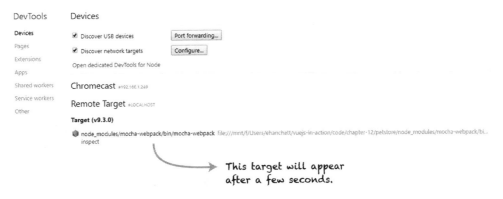

Figure 12.5 Chrome Devices page

After a few seconds, you should see a target at the bottom and a link that shows inspect. Click the Inspect button and a separate window opens. The Inspect window starts in the paused state. Click the arrow to start the debugger (figure 12.6).

Figure 12.6   Chrome Inspect window

After the debugger starts, it will stop at the place in our code where we added the debugger statement. From here, we can view the console, and look at variables, as you can see in figure 12.7. For example, if you click the wrapper, then __proto__, and then __proto__ again, you'll see all the wrapper methods.

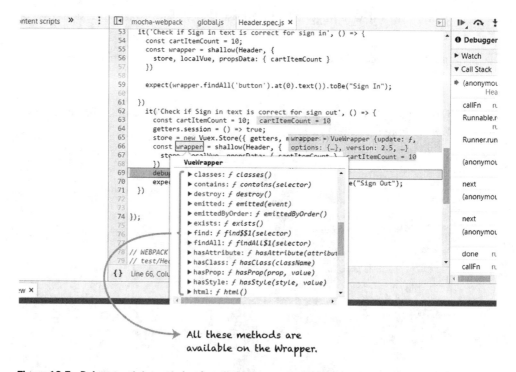

Figure 12.7   Debugger statement showing all the wrapper methods.

Use the Chrome inspector whenever you need to figure out a test, and you're not sure what variables do.

Exercise

Use your knowledge from this chapter to answer the following questions:

> Why is it important to test? What tool is made for Vue.js that can help with testing?

See the solution in appendix B.

Summary

- Unit test cases test small units of functionality.
- Writing tests allows you to test functions and verify they work as expected in the application.
- You can debug your test cases in real-time using the Chrome browser.

appendix A
Setting up your environment

Developing without the right tools is like exploring a cave without a flashlight: It will get done, but you'll be in the dark the whole time. That said, if you already have the tools that are covered in this section, or alternatives you feel comfortable with, skip to the next section.

A.1 Chrome Developer Tools

Far and away, our "best buddy" on this journey will be the Chrome Developer Tools. If you haven't done so, install the Chrome browser. You can find it at https:// www.google.com/chrome/. You can access the Developer Tools from the browser menu at View > Developer > Developer Tools or by right-clicking a page and choosing Inspect as seen in figure A.1.

The HTML used to mark up our web page or application is shown in this pane.

The pane on the right-hand side can be used to view many different aspects of the selected markup including the styles applied to it and the events bound to it.

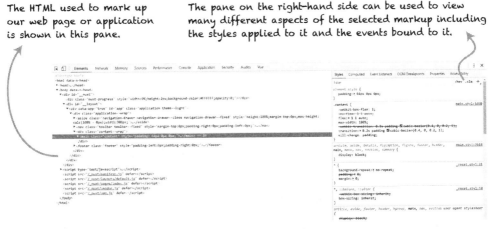

Figure A.1 The default view of Chrome's Developer Tools pane shows the HTML markup of a web page, and the CSS styles attached to a selected element.

265

When you inspect your code, you'll use the JavaScript console in Developer Tools most frequently. You can switch to it using the Console tab or open it directly from the menu at View > Developer > JavaScript Console.

You can even bring up a console while looking at any other tab in the Developer Tools by pressing the ESC key, as seen in figure A.2. This allows us to do things like look at the HTML while we manipulate it from JavaScript.

The JavaScript console lets us execute code, view representations of JavaScript objects, and interact with the DOM elements used by our application.

Figure A.2   The JavaScript console lets us inspect and interact with HTML markup as well as the JavaScript of our Vue application.

A.2   *vue-devtools for Chrome*

The core Vue team has developed a Chrome extension—vue-devtools—that's tailored to the task of inspecting Vue applications at runtime.

You can install the vue-devtools extension from the Chrome Web Store by visiting http://mng.bz/RpuC. The adventurous can build the extension from—and hack at—the code itself by cloning the GitHub repository located at https://github.com/vuejs/vue-devtools.

> **POST-INSTALLATION NOTE**   Chrome can be a little finicky right after an extension has been installed. If you open the Developer Tools pane and don't see a Vue tab after you install the extension, try opening a new tab or window before restarting Chrome.

After you've installed the extension, you need to enable it for use on local files, because we won't use a web server for the first few chapters. In Chrome, select Window > Extensions, then locate the Vue.js devtools entry. Tick the Allow access to file URLs check box and you're all set, as seen in figure A.3.

Figure A.3 Enabling vue-devtools to work with local files requires updating settings in the Extensions preference page.

After installing the extension, we can see data used by our application, isolate specific components from our application, and even time travel! It allows us to go back and replay activity that previously took place in our app, at least. Figure A.4 shows all the parts of the extension.

The Components tab lets you navigate an application's structure.

The Vuex tab is for inspecting the contents of a data store when using Vue's companion Vuex Library.

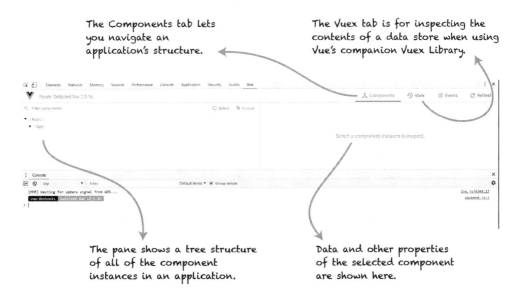

The pane shows a tree structure of all of the component instances in an application.

Data and other properties of the selected component are shown here.

Figure A.4 The vue-devtools extension lets us explore our Vue applications in real time.

A.3   Obtaining a chapter's companion code

The source code for this book is available to download from the publisher's website (www.manning.com/books/vue-js-in-action). Chapter code is available on GitHub at https://github.com/ErikCH/VuejsInActionCode. If you have any questions or find any mistakes, feel free to open an issue! This is also where you'll find all the pictures for each chapter.

A.4   Installing Node.js and npm

In the book we'll need Node.js and npm so we can use the Vue-CLI tool and have access to the hundreds of thousands of modules available. It's recommended that you download either the current or LTS (Long Term Support) version of Node. Either one will work fine.

Here are a few approaches that you can use to get Node, which includes npm:

- *Homebrew or MacPorts*—This is a popular choice for Mac OS users.
- *One-click installers*—Windows and Mac both have this option.
- *Install using the Linux package management system*—Yum, apt-get, or pacman can be used to install Node on a Linux environment.
- *Install using NVM*—NVM (Node Version Manager) is a script that helps manage Node.js versions. It's available for Windows and Mac. It's a great option.

A.4.1   Installing Node.js using one-click installers

By far, one of the easiest ways to download Node.js is using a one-click installer. Head over to http://nodejs.org/en/download. Choose your version of Windows or Mac, 32-bit or 64-bit, and download the .msi for windows or .pkg for Mac as seen in figure A.5.

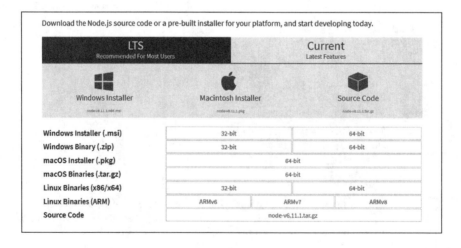

Figure A.5   The homepage to download Node

A.4.2 Install Node.js using NVM

NVM is another excellent choice. NVM is a script that helps manage multiple active versions of Node.js. You can install Node.js without even having to visit the website. The script separates each version of Node that you download. I recommend this to most beginners, although you need to understand how to use the command line. You can find NVM at https://github.com/creationix/nvm. A Windows version can be found at https://github.com/coreybutler/nvm-windows/releases.

To install NVM on a Mac, open the command prompt and run this command:

```
$ curl -o- https://raw.githubusercontent.com/creationix/nvm/v0.33.2/install.sh
➥ | bash
```

This will download the latest version of NVM.

To install NVM on a Windows system, click on the nvm-setup.zip file on the nvm-windows release webpage. Unzip the files and run the nvm-setup.exe file.

After installing NVM or NVM for Windows, run this command to download the latest version of Node.js.

```
$ nvm install node
```

That's it! Now you have Node and npm installed on your system!

A.4.3 Install Node.js via Linux package management system

All major Linux distributions offer Node.js packages in their repositories. For example, in Ubuntu you can use apt-get:

```
$ sudo apt-get install nodejs
```

In Fedora, you can use yum:

```
$ yum install nodejs
```

You need to check with your Linux distribution to find out more details on how to install packages on your system. Keep in mind that certain distributions may have outdated versions of Node.js available for download. In that case, you might be better off with NVM or downloading Node.js from the official website.

A.4.4 Install Node.js using MacPorts or Homebrew

Macports and Homebrew are package management systems for the Mac. To download Node.js, you need to first install Macports or Homebrew. You can find the latest information on how to install Homebrew at http://brew.sh and Macports at www.macports.org.

After you have one of these package managers installed on your Mac, you can run the following command to install Node.

For Homebrew:

```
$ brew install node
```

For MacPorts:

```
$ sudo port install nodejs
```

You should be good to go after this!

A.4.5 *Verifying that Node is installed*

To test the installation of Node.js run the -v command:

```
$ node -v
$ npm -v
```

These commands will display the current version of Node and NPM installed. As of this writing the latest LTS version is 6.11 and the latest current version is 8.2.1.

A.5 *Installing Vue-CLI*

Before installing Vue-CLI make sure you have at least Node.js >= 4.6, 6.x preferred, npm version 3+, and Git. In chapter 11, we use Nuxt.js. In that case, make sure to have Node.js >= 8.0. Vue-CLI will work fine either way. Follow the previous instructions to install Node. To install Git, follow the instructions on the official Git website at http://mng.bz/D7zz.

After installing all the prerequisites, open a terminal and run this command:

```
$ npm install -g vue-cli
```

Running commands in Vue-CLI is easy. Type in vue-cli init *template name* and then the project name like this:

```
$ vue init <template-name> <project-name>
$ vue init webpack my-project
```

That should be it.

Note, as of the writing of this book, Vue-CLI 2.9.2 is the latest version. The newest version of Vue-CLI 3.0 is still in beta. For information on how to install and work with Vue-CLI 3.0, follow the official guides at http://mng.bz/5t1C.

appendix B
Solutions to chapter exercises

Solutions to the exercise questions in chapters 2–12 are listed here.

Chapter 2

➤ **In section 2.4 we created a filter for the price. Can you think of any other filters that might be helpful?**

Filters in Vue.js are commonly used to do text filtering. One filter you may want to add is a way to capitalize the product title.

Chapter 3

➤ **Earlier in the chapter we looked at computed properties and methods. What are the differences?**

Computed properties are useful when you're trying to derive a value. The value will be automatically updated whenever any of its underlying values are updated. It's also cached to avoid repetitively calculating a value that doesn't need to be recalculated when it hasn't changed, as in a loop. Note that methods are functions bound to the Vue instance. They only evaluate when they're explicitly called. Unlike computed properties, methods accept parameters. Computed properties cannot. Methods are useful in the same situations where any JavaScript functions would be useful. An application isn't effective without supporting robust user interactions.

Chapter 4

➤ **How does two-way data binding work? When should you use it in your Vue.js application?**

In the simplest terms two-way data binding works when updates in the model update the view, and updates in the view update the model. Two-way data binding should be used throughout your application when dealing with forms and inputs.

Chapter 5

➤ **What's a `v-for` range and how does it compare to a normal `v-for`?**

A `v-for` directive is used to render a list of items based on an array. Usually it's in the format of `item in items`, where `item` is the source array and `item` is an alias for the element being iterated on. The `v-for` can also be used as a range in the format of `item in (number)`. In that case, it will repeat the template that many times.

Chapter 6

➤ **How do you pass information from a parent to a child component? What do you use to pass information from a child component back to a parent component?**

The typical way of passing information from a parent component to a child component is using props. Props must be explicitly set inside the child component. To pass information from a child component to a parent component you can use `$emit(eventName)`. It's worth mentioning that later we'll look at other ways of passing information between components, including using a data store.

Chapter 7

➤ **Name two ways you can navigate between different routes.**

To navigate between different routes, you can use two different approaches. Inside the template you can add a router-link element. Or inside the Vue instance you can use `this.$router.push`.

Chapter 8

➤ **What's the difference between an animation and a transition?**

Transitions move from one state to another, whereas animations have multiple states.

Chapter 9

➤ **What is a mixin and when should you use it?**

Mixins are a way to distribute reusable functionality for components. You should use mixins whenever you see that you're writing the same code over and over again between components. Repeating code goes against the DRY (don't repeat yourself) principal and should be refactored. Mixins will be "mixed" into the component's own options.

Chapter 10

➤ **What are several advantages of using Vuex over the normal data passing of a Vue.js application?**

Vuex uses a central store to capture the state of the application. This helps our Vue.js app mutate state in a predictable synchronous way. This helps prevent unintended consequences occurring when state in our application changes. One advantage this has is that it helps organize data in our application in one place. Larger Vue.js applications can be cumbersome. Passing information or relying on an event bus isn't ideal. Vuex helps abstract this problem away by providing one central store to hold all information.

Chapter 11

➤ **What's one advantage of using `asyncData` in your Nuxt apps versus using middleware?**

The `asyncData` object is loaded on page components before they're loaded. It has access to the context object and is loaded on the server side. One advantage it may have over using middleware is that its results will be merged with the data object on the page. This can be more advantageous than using middleware, where we might have to use a Vuex store to save data so it can be retrieved later inside the page component.

Chapter 12

➤ **Why is it important to test? What tool is made for Vue.js that can help with testing?**

Testing should be a fundamental part of any organization writing code. Automated testing is much quicker, and less error prone, than manually testing. It has a higher upfront cost, although it will save time in the long run. Vue.js offers many tools to help with testing. One of the most important is the vue-test-utils library. This will help do proper testing with our Vue.js applications.

index

O

oldVnode 181
onAuthStateChanged 243
one-click installers, installing Node.js with 268
one-way data binding 64
<option> tag 76
options object 18
order property 65
order.dontSendGift property 72
order.sendGift property 72
output filters 33–35
   adding filters to markup 34–35
   adding to markup 35
   testing values 34–35
   write filter functions 33–34

P

parameters, adding product routes with 146–148
parseInt method 55
<pre> tag 68
prefix property 46
pressed method 191
price property 29
product property 90
product routes, adding with parameters 146–148
product.json, importing products from 94–95
products
   displaying 29–32
      defining product data 29–30
      marking up product views 30–32
   importing from product.json 94–95
   looping 88–99
      adding star ratings with v-for range 88–89
      binding HTML classes to star ratings 90–92
      refactoring apps with v-for directives 95–99
   setting up 92–94
productsRef 237, 244
progressive framework 12
properties 23–24
props
   child props, modifying with .sync 120
   dynamic props 109–112
   literal props 108–109
   testing 256–257
   to pass data 108–114
   validation of 112–114

Q

query parameters 150
querySelector() method 78

R

radio buttons, value binding and 73–75
rating class 89
reactive programming
   applications in 7
   facilitating with Vue 12–13
Realtime Database 234
records, sorting 100–101
redirect option 154
redirection 154–156
refactoring apps with v-for directives 95–99
registration
   global 105
   local 106–107
regression testing 247
render(createElement) function 188
rendering
   functions 185–192
   JSX 185–192
   server-side 216–217
response.data.products 208
root Vue instances 17–19
router-link
   setting up with style 150–151
   setting up with tags 149–150
router-link component 149
router-link element 151
<router-link> tag 140
routes
   child edit routes, adding 152–154
   generating with Nuxt.js 228–233
   product routes, adding with parameters 146–148
   setting up 137–138
routing 122, 145–156

S

scoped slots 128–130
<script> tag 140
SEO (search engine optimization) 217
server-side rendering (SSR) 216–217
servers, communicating with 215–245
   Nuxt.js 217–233
   server-side rendering 216–217
   using Firebase 233–244
   using VuexFire 233–244
SET_SESSION mutation 239
SET_STORE mutation 207
setters 201
setTimeout 204
shallow function 254
showCheckout method 59
showProduct property 59, 83
signIn method 241